Mental Wellbeing in S

CW00735135

Teachers see the impact of pupils' mental wellbeing on the experience of school every day. But often there is not enough practical advice on what can be done to support pupils who might need help and especially for pupils from diverse backgrounds, who might face unique challenges. This important book is a practice-facing, evidence-based guide for teachers, support staff, education students, and schools, giving advice on the ways in which we can support the mental wellbeing of pupils from diverse backgrounds.

Bringing together advice and strategies for supporting pupil mental health and wellbeing, this book makes accessible key knowledge about mental health and examines how this might vary in different pupil populations by exploring the unique challenges for disadvantaged and minority pupils. Offering valuable insights into the diverse nature of pupils' mental health experiences, each chapter provides practical suggestions and approaches that teachers can use in the classroom, and schools can adopt into their pastoral care systems.

Including real-life case studies and key takeaways, *Mental Wellbeing in Schools* will be valuable reading for teachers in primary and secondary schools as well as school leaders.

Arif Mahmud is a Lecturer in Education Studies and a member of the Centre for Learning, Teaching and Human Development at the University of Roehampton. He researches on social, emotional, and mental health experiences of young people in national and international contexts with a focus of developing and evaluating intervention programmes.

Liam Satchell is a Senior Lecturer in Psychology at the University of Winchester and a member of the Childhood and Youth Psychology Research Group. He is an applied psychologist and methodologist with expertise in mental health and wellbeing, educational psychology, and applying research to everyday challenges.

Mental Wellbeing in Schools

What Teachers Need to Know to Support Pupils from Diverse Backgrounds

Edited by
Arif Mahmud and Liam Satchell

Routledge
Taylor & Francis Group

LONDON AND NEW YORK

Cover image: © Getty Images

First published 2022
by Routledge
4 Park Square, Milton Park, Abingdon, Oxon OX14 4RN

and by Routledge
605 Third Avenue, New York, NY 10158

Routledge is an imprint of the Taylor & Francis Group, an informa business

British Library Cataloguing-in-Publication Data
A catalogue record for this book is available from the British Library

Library of Congress Cataloging-in-Publication Data
A catalog record has been requested for this book

ISBN: 978-0-367-74964-4 (hbk)
ISBN: 978-0-367-74965-1 (pbk)
ISBN: 978-1-003-16052-6 (ebk)

DOI: 10.4324/9781003160526

Typeset in Melior
by codeMantra

Contents

Declaration

This text is a collaboration of authors from a range of diverse ideas and expertise. The chapters represent the views of the chapter authors. The editing process ensured consistency in format and structure, and the chapter authors' voices were preserved during this process.

Foreword

Important Questions in Practice

Pranav Patel

Educators in the UK may not feel well versed in supporting the mental health of children and young people in their care due to a lack of resources and training (Dewhirst *et al.*, 2014). The lack of experience is even more pertinent when viewed through the context of anti-oppression and the protected characteristics of pupils in our schools.

In the UK today, 50% of all mental health problems are identified at 14 years of age, and this increases by 25% by the age of 24. Currently, 10% of children and 25% of adults have diagnosable mental health problems. These percentages are increased by a range of social risk factors: poverty, unemployment, lower educational attainment, insecure and poor-quality shelter, and extreme stress (PHE, 2019). If we look at these factors, there are links between those 'othered' or minoritised people and those who present with mental health issues. Whether through the lens of any incommutable trait or belief, the very nature of othering is a socio-psychological phenomenon.

Humans feel safer in groups of people who look, behave, and believe in similar ways. The purpose of a social collective is to elevate the group's visions as true, denigrate others as false, and/or subjugate others. Without those functions, the idea would be meaningless and vain. This leads to the need to hate, and consequentially war and death (Von Mises, 1933). The concept of 'us and them' infiltrates every facet of the human experience for educators, from the way they accept knowledge (their epistemological viewpoint) to the propagation of the society's status quo both consciously and subconsciously in their daily acts.

As a man of colour, I will present this foreword primarily through the lens of race; this does not mean that I endorse a sociological hierarchy or an 'Oppression Olympics' model of sociological discourse or experience. Williams and colleagues (2019) highlight that "Racism is considered a fundamental cause of adverse health outcomes for racial/ethnic minorities and racial and ethnic inequities in health". This is so important for your pupils' heightened anxiety, and the consequent hypervigilance is a constantly fought battle. This may provide an essential contextual role in forming defences to attacks on mental and physical wellbeing. The cost of this constant heightened state impacts both physiologically and psychologically through issues with sleep, the immune system and other health concerns (Clark et al., 2006; Hicken et al., 2013; Williams and Mohammed, 2009 in Patel, 2022).

No matter the attribute involved, the mental health of pupils and learners is frequently framed through the legacy of their traumatic experiences and the perceptions and expectations of society and the schools in which they attend. For example, Felitti and colleagues (1998) screened 13,494 people for adverse trauma in childhood and compared the impact to measures of adult risk behaviour, health status, and disease. Adverse childhood experiences (ACEs) now form a good part of the educational canon – as it absolutely should.

However, the necessary evolution to include race in the ACEs model has sadly lacked over the past two decades. Racism is a type of trauma and leads to a similar outcome for its victims. Williams et al.'s (2019) literature review of 29 empirical research studies on racism's impact on health concluded that racism is a 'dynamic societal system' that impacts the lives of People of Colour through stereotypes, stigma and biases. Thus, these factors may harm pupils psychologically and biologically.

There is a movement towards a context-specific ACEs model. Bernard et al. (2020) provide an adapted ACEs model to incorporate historical trauma: the impact of colonisation, chattel slavery, war, mass genocide, and other race-based stresses. These events cause inter-generational damage, which is passed down through decades. Trauma may impact material risk factors such as mental and physical health and wellbeing, poverty, and the environment young people are raised in. Still, it will also affect the risk factors relating to the dispositional experience of People of Colour (factors related to pre-birth).

Before reading the work in this book, I would urge every educator to be humble enough to interrogate societies and then their own biases around their pupils. Challenge yourself and the norms, for example: Do school-aged members of Irish Traveller communities care about mental health? They do (Byrne, 2020). What do you think of the Black folx you serve? The girls of Chinese heritage or any other group? Who do you think is 'successful' and worthy? And how does this impact the mental health of those affected?

Archer presents 'success' through teachers' eyes as an 'impossible' position for minority ethnic pupils. She states that: "[O]nly White, middle-class students – but particularly boys – could enjoy an unproblematised association with 'traditional' academic success" (Archer, 2008, p23). This is coupled with the perception of virtues in idealised groups being perceived as vices in Minoritised groups. Merton (1948) cites sociologist Daniel Young in calling the process 'damned if you and damned if you don't'. Pupil success is often viewed through modelised (white) rose-tinted glasses, and thus, othered pupils are racialised, gendered, and/or classed, and as a consequence, idealised, othered, or demonised (Archer, 2008).

I would be remiss in writing this foreword without addressing the complexity of othering, racism, and mental health. Every pupil deserves to be supported, but teachers can be left in a quagmire of ignorance without the tools and the contextual knowledge, skills, and motivation to pull themselves out. I am grateful that this book seeks to provide some of those implements and perspectives of positionality to support practitioners in their classrooms.

References

Archer, L. 2008 The impossibility of minority ethnic educational 'success'? An examination of the discourses of teachers and pupils in British secondary schools, *European Educational Research Journal*, 7(1): 89–107. doi: 10.2304/eerj.2008.7.1.89.

Byrne, R. 2020 'Young Irish travellers' experiences and constructions of school belonging', Doctoral Thesis, University College London, London.

Dewhirst, S. *et al.* 2014 Are trainee teachers being adequately prepared to promote the health and well-being of school children? A survey of current practice, *Journal of Public Health*, 36(3): 467–475. doi: 10.1093/pubmed/fdt103.

Felitti, V.J., Anda, R.F., Nordenberg, D., Williamson, D.F., Spitz, A.M., Edwards, V., Koss, M.P., and Marks, J.S. 1998 Relationship of childhood abuse and household dysfunction to many of the leading causes of death in adults. The Adverse Childhood Experiences (ACE) Study, *American Journal of Preventive Medicine*, 14(4): 245–258. doi: 10.1016/S0749-3797(98)00017-8.

Merton, R. 1948 The self-fulfilling prophecy. *The Antioch Review*, 8(2): 193–210. doi:10.2307/4609267.

Patel, P. A. 2022 *The antiracist educator,* Corwin, London.

Public Health England. 2019. Wellbeing and mental health: Applying all our health. Retrieved 9 September 2021, from https://www.gov.uk/government/publications/wellbeing-in- mental-health-applying-all-our-health/wellbeing-in-mental-health-applying-all-our-health

Von Mises, L. 2003 *Epistemological problems of economics,* Ludwig von Mises Institute, Auburn, AL.

Williams, D., Lawrence, J., Davis, B., and Vu, C. 2019 Understanding how discrimination can affect health, *Health Services Research*, 54(Suppl 2). doi:10.1111/1475-6773.13222.

What Do Teachers Need to Know About Mental Wellbeing in Young People?

Liam Satchell

Synopsis

This chapter introduces readers to mental health and wellbeing terminology and complexities, relevant for understanding how to develop school and learning environments supportive of pupil's mental wellbeing. Specifically, three important ideas are emphasised to briefly summarise key sources of mental wellbeing, that is, young people should feel: (1) socially included and recognised by their family, peers, and society at large; (2) a sense of control and feel like they have agency in their own life; and (3) that they have the space and time to explore and understand their developing identity. There are significant barriers to these experiences and the following chapters provide a range of examples of how pupils from diverse backgrounds may be denied these core tenets of good mental wellbeing.

On mental wellbeing and this text

Mental wellbeing is important. Thanks to decades of awareness campaigning, such a statement is widely accepted and is readily incorporated into health policymaking in the UK. Defining what is 'good' mental wellbeing and mental health is difficult. Definitions of good mental wellbeing vary but often centre around a person living their most 'fulfilling life'. This definition is inherently personal, and different lifestyles will best support different people's mental wellbeing. Typically, having good mental wellbeing means having functional relationships with family, friends, work, and community. Barriers to good mental wellbeing can come from many internal and external sources, and a complete sense of a person's mental wellness comes from understanding a person in a place, their wants and needs, and how society can support or restrict them. The most extreme outcomes of poor mental wellbeing are what we might recognise as mental health conditions. These

DOI: 10.4324/9781003160526-1

are clinically identified diagnoses that are associated with the experience of distress or relate to disrupted experiences of everyday life.

Receiving a clinical diagnosis of a mental health condition allows for someone to receive help and support for the challenges they experience and, often, many resources are not available to someone until they have a formal diagnosis. However, this is not to say only those with diagnosed mental health conditions need support with their mental wellbeing. Mental health diagnostics is difficult and there are many debates about how we medicalise mental wellbeing. A holistic understanding of mental wellbeing is more than just diagnosed labels though, and people can experience significant challenges in their life without meeting specific clinical criteria. Changing our thinking to a spectrum of mental wellbeing, more than just the diagnostic categories, allows us to give support to anyone who needs it, perhaps preventing further difficulties. This is much like how we discuss diet, exercise, and healthy living as preventative measures for later potential clinical risks to physical health. Throughout this text, we will discuss 'mental wellbeing' as a broad term that includes diagnosed mental health conditions, but also more general psychological welfare. In this book, we are interested in how we might support the mental wellbeing of school pupils, and the unique concerns and opportunities for supporting pupils from diverse backgrounds.

This book is a collection of chapters written by experts on the specific needs of pupils from diverse backgrounds. We have written this book to be a reference material, with each chapter ready to be picked up and used when advice is needed. We have focused on integrating up-to-date academic research with concrete advice for teachers looking to support their pupils. Our aim is for the chapters to be of use to anyone who is a teacher, studying to be a teacher, or is interested in mental wellbeing in education. We recognise that every pupil is unique, and their educational journey and experience of mental wellbeing will be their own. However, it can be useful to have insights to experiences and cultures that we might not be personally familiar with, and as such, each of our chapters draws on a particular general experience that a group of pupils might share. We have focused our advice on the particular pupil groups who have 'protected characteristics' as detailed in the UK Equality Act of 2010. This includes support for pupils who might experience unique mental wellbeing challenges due to their disability, gender, race, ethnicity, religion or belief, sex, sexual orientation, and home life (e.g. looked after children). These groupings represent pupils who face similar challenges to their experience of learning and their mental wellbeing due to exposure to prejudice, social exclusion, lack of formal support, and a lack of research in their mental wellness. This book highlights what these specific challenges might be for different groups of pupils, in a teacher-focused text. It is our hope that our chapters provide a broad overview of the essential challenges perhaps experienced by these pupils, which could facilitate conversations about mental wellbeing with pupils, caregivers, schools, and policymakers.

In this introduction, we will become more familiar with 'mental wellbeing' as a challenge in schools. We will discuss the challenges with identifying causes of mental wellbeing difficulties and how to practically discuss mental health. Finally, we will focus on why this information is important for teachers.

Mental wellbeing in young people

In a routine National Health Service survey conducted in 2020, 16% of children aged 5–16 years self-reported that they were experiencing symptoms in line with a mental health condition (NHS Digital Lifestyle Team, 2020). Whilst this survey was conducted during the lockdown period of the COVID-19 pandemic, increasing rates of diagnosed mental health conditions in children is an established trend. For example, between 1995 and 2014, the prevalence of diagnosed long-standing mental health conditions in young people increased from 0.80% of the population to 4.80% (Pitchforth *et al.*, 2019). Statistics like this are concerning. They could be seen as suggesting that something has radically changed in our children and that they have become more vulnerable to significant mental distress. However, we should have caution with a conclusion like this on data which simply shows change over time. Time affects many things, including the awareness of, and political and financial support for, mental wellbeing interventions. When statistics show us that *diagnosis rates* are increasing, we could be looking at many different processes all occurring at once – not least that diagnosis prevalence could be reflecting increased access to mental health services for people who might have historically been underrepresented in psychiatric environments. Increased diagnoses are a sign of more people being recognised by medical professionals as having significant difficulties, but this might be to do with more people recognising the need for help. When we look at the data in more detail, you can find limited change in reported mental wellbeing at the same time as the changing diagnosis prevalence (Pitchforth *et al.*, 2019). In this case, children and adolescents' mental wellbeing does not change as much as it is the case that this translates to a diagnosis more frequently for young people in extreme distress. Historically, key barriers to accessing mental health resources for children has included issues with mental health awareness, such as perceived stigma and concerns (Owens *et al.*, 2002). With raising awareness about mental health and integration of mental wellbeing into the curriculum (Department for Education, 2021), some of these barriers may be less than they were before, leading to more young people receiving the diagnoses their symptoms reflect.

Elsewhere, there is stronger evidence for the argument that young people's mental health is deteriorating over time (such as Keyes *et al.*, 2019; Sellers *et al.*, 2019). Identifying the causes of this shift is difficult, and it is very likely that there are many complex factors in the change in culture and society over time. There is some evidence attributing a decline in mental wellbeing to increased perceived demands on young people (Schraml *et al.*, 2011) and more focus on the importance and competitive nature of education at a younger age, especially for girls (Högberg, Strandh & Hagquist, 2020; West & Sweeting, 2003). Identifying specific causes of mental health conditions is difficult, and the causes of poor mental wellbeing can vary from person to person and be dependent on a range of factors.[1] In the face of a potential rise in individuals meeting the diagnostic criteria for a significant mental health concern, early intervention through broad consideration of mental wellbeing is essential.

Broadly paraphrasing the most important social and cultural components in mental wellbeing, it is important for young people to feel:

1. Socially included and recognised by their family, peers, and society at large,

2. A sense of control and like they have agency in their own life,

3. Like they have the space and time to explore and understand their developing identity.

However, many societal processes can act as barriers to this experience. These barriers can come from many places, from being subject to overt prejudice and bullying from school peers or wider society to implicit and structural barriers, whereby biases, societal processes, and systems can restrict a young person's opportunities. Longitudinal research, following young people to adulthood, shows us the long-term consequences that adverse experiences can have at a young age, with experiences of bullying at school (Takizawa, Maughan & Arseneault, 2014), family disruption (Gilman *et al.*, 2003), childhood trauma (Horwitz *et al.*, 2001), and racism (Cave, Cooper, Zubrick & Shepherd, 2020) affecting adult mental health.

This book

We have dedicated this text to inform readers of the barriers specific groups of pupils might face. We highlight pupils who experience prejudice due to their ethnicity and religious beliefs (see Chapters 2–5, 12, and 13), developing gender identity and sexuality (see Chapters 8 and 9), societal gender expectations (see Chapters 6 and 7), family and homelife circumstances (see Chapters 10, 11, 15), or physical or mental impairments (see Chapter 14). Our list is not exhaustive, and here we hope to inspire more conversations and strategies for thinking about the personal experiences of mental wellbeing with pupils from diverse backgrounds.

Part of our aim of this book is to offer practical advice for helping pupils' wellbeing. It is known that teachers report that they do not feel like they receive adequate training for providing health and wellbeing guidance to their pupils (Dewhirst *et al.*, 2014) and, despite not receiving formalised training, many teachers are expected to support their pupils' mental wellbeing directly (Kidger *et al.*, 2009). On top of this, teachers may not be aware of the specific challenges that pupils from diverse backgrounds might experience. We encourage readers to use this text as a reference material, picking up each chapter when needed to try and better understand what they can do for pupils. Each chapter contains a review of the most up-to-date literature on the specific issues that group of pupils might face, advice for what teachers might practically do, and further specific reading when needed.

It is important to bear in mind that pupils have their own unique experiences, and their identity will consist of many overlapping spheres (intersectionality). Drawing on ideas expressed across this text (summarised in Chapter 16) will best help your practice and thinking about what teachers need to know about the mental wellbeing of pupils from diverse backgrounds.

Note

1 Including physical health factors like genetic risk factors (Larsson, 2021), diet (O'Neil *et al.*, 2014) and exercise (Biddle & Asare, 2011), which are important, but beyond the scope of this text.

References

Biddle, S. J. H. & Asare, M. (2011) Physical activity and mental health in children and adolescents: A review of reviews, *British Journal of Sports Medicine*, 45(11), pp. 886–895. doi: 10.1136/bjsports-2011-090185.

Cave, L., Cooper, M. N., Zubrick, S. R. & Shepherd, C. C. (2020) Racial discrimination and child and adolescent health in longitudinal studies: A systematic review, *Social Science & Medicine*, 250, p. 112864.

Department for Education. (2021) *Guidance physical health and mental wellbeing (Primary and secondary), GOV.UK*. Available at: https://www.gov.uk/government/publications/relationships-education-relationships-and-sex-education-rse-and-health-education/physical-health-and-mental-wellbeing-primary-and-secondary (Accessed: 28 April 2021).

Dewhirst, S. *et al.* (2014) Are trainee teachers being adequately prepared to promote the health and well-being of school children? A survey of current practice, *Journal of Public Health*, 36(3), pp. 467–475. doi: 10.1093/pubmed/fdt103.

Equality Act. (2010) Available at: https://www.legislation.gov.uk/ukpga/2010/15/contents

Gilman, S. E. *et al.* (2003) Family disruption in childhood and risk of adult depression, *American Journal of Psychiatry*, 160(5), pp. 939–946. doi: 10.1176/appi.ajp.160.5.939.

Högberg, B., Strandh, M. & Hagquist, C. (2020) Gender and secular trends in adolescent mental health over 24 years – The role of school-related stress, *Social Science & Medicine*, 250, p. 112890. doi: 10.1016/j.socscimed.2020.112890.

Horwitz, A. V. *et al.* (2001) The impact of childhood abuse and neglect on adult mental health: A prospective study, *Journal of Health and Social Behavior*, 42(2), p. 184. doi: 10.2307/3090177.

Keyes, K. M. *et al.* (2019) Recent increases in depressive symptoms among US adolescents: Trends from 1991 to 2018, *Social Psychiatry and Psychiatric Epidemiology*, 54(8), pp. 987–996. doi: 10.1007/s00127-019-01697-8.

Kidger, J. *et al.* (2009) Supporting adolescent emotional health in schools: A mixed methods study of student and staff views in England, *BMC Public Health*, 9(1), p. 403. doi: 10.1186/1471-2458-9-403.

Larsson, H. (2021) Quantitative and molecular genetics of child and adolescent mental health disorders: Recent advances, knowledge gaps and directions for future research, *JCPP Advances*, 1(1). doi: 10.1111/jcv2.12014.

NHS Digital Lifestyle Team. (2020) *Mental health of children and young people in England, 2020: Wave 1 follow up to the 2017 survey.* Survey. National Health Service Digital. Available at: https://digital.nhs.uk/data-and-information/publications/statistical/mental-health-of-children-and-young-people-in-england/2020-wave-1-follow-up.

O'Neil, A. *et al.* (2014) Relationship between diet and mental health in children and adolescents: A systematic review, *American Journal of Public Health*, 104(10), pp. e31–e42. doi: 10.2105/AJPH.2014.302110.

Owens, P. L. *et al.* (2002) Barriers to children's mental health services, *Journal of the American Academy of Child & Adolescent Psychiatry*, 41(6), pp. 731–738. doi: 10.1097/00004583–200206000-00013.

Pitchforth, J. *et al.* (2019) Mental health and well-being trends among children and young people in the UK, 1995–2014: Analysis of repeated cross-sectional national health surveys, *Psychological Medicine*, 49(08), pp. 1275–1285. doi: 10.1017/S0033291718001757.

Schraml, K. *et al.* (2011) Stress symptoms among adolescents: The role of subjective psychosocial conditions, lifestyle, and self-esteem, *Journal of Adolescence*, 34(5), pp. 987–996. doi: 10.1016/j.adolescence.2010.11.010.

Sellers, R. *et al.* (2019) Cross-cohort change in adolescent outcomes for children with mental health problems, *Journal of Child Psychology and Psychiatry*, 60(7), pp. 813–821. doi: 10.1111/jcpp.13029.

Takizawa, R., Maughan, B. & Arseneault, L. (2014) Adult health outcomes of childhood bullying victimization: Evidence from a five-decade longitudinal British birth cohort, *American Journal of Psychiatry*, 171(7), pp. 777–784. doi: 10.1176/appi.ajp.2014.13101401.

West, P. & Sweeting, H. (2003) Fifteen, female and stressed: Changing patterns of psychological distress over time: Increased psychological distress among females over time, *Journal of Child Psychology and Psychiatry*, 44(3), pp. 399–411. doi: 10.1111/1469–7610.00130.

2 Black Pupils, Mental Wellbeing, and Resilience

Jason Arday and Laura Morton

Synopsis

Mental health and wellbeing are closely related to educational outcomes. This chapter examines the mental health of Black pupils, considering the inescapable role of racism and how it manifests in the classroom. It explores the negative dominant stereotypes that encircle Black children and how these can impact identity, self-esteem, self-belief, and a range of other wellbeing factors. To this end, this chapter seeks to positively reframe these discourses by focusing on the many strengths present within the Black community, the most salient of which, when on the topic of mental health, is resilience. By exploring the specific attributes that lend themselves to resilience, including cultural and social capital, this chapter attempts to provide strengths-based guidance for teachers and schools to promote racial equality and support and develop mental health and wellbeing in Black pupils. In doing so, it also attempts to centre the lived experience of Black children and their families, as well as the role and value of the wider community.

Background

No matter which generation we hail from, including even the newborns who will one day enter our classrooms, we have been born into a country that privileges white people. Black children experience racism from the womb (Collins et al., 2004) and are disadvantaged by racial inequality both directly (Equality and Human Rights Commission, 2020) and via intersecting variables such as socioeconomic class (e.g. Office for National Statistics, 2020). Alongside statistics that point to lower attendance, absenteeism, and higher rates of exclusion among Black children (e.g. Timpson, 2019), there are those that also tell us 95% of young Black people have experienced racism in school, 49% see racism as the greatest barrier to attainment in school, and 50% feel teacher perceptions of them inhibit educational

DOI: 10.4324/9781003160526-2

success (YMCA, 2020). If we are going to talk about poor educational outcomes among Black children, we must never stray far from the topic of racism.

Unsurprisingly racism is associated with poor mental health in Black children, which itself is linked to lower attainment and attendance in school (Lereya et al., 2019). The link between racism and mental health, including depression, anxiety, and self-esteem, is well-established in the literature (e.g. Pachter & Coll, 2009; Trent et al., 2019). A systematic review of studies into the impact of racism on well-being in children (Priest et al., 2013) shows a positive relationship between racial discrimination and negative mental health outcomes, such as anxiety, depression, and psychological distress, and a negative relationship between racial discrimination and positive mental health outcomes, such as self-esteem, self-worth, psychological adaptation, and adjustment. In essence, racism does not just target mental health vulnerabilities; it erodes the protective factors that could otherwise buffer against or minimise their impact. Childhood is the stage of development where what other people think matters most, and it can be a painful experience when littered with micro-aggressions and incidents of rejection, harassment, or bullying on account of race. Think back to the trials and tribulations of your own teenage years. What led to the moments of angst? What boosted your self-esteem? How did racism impact you? If you do not feel the last question applies to you, then you have a privilege not afforded to Black pupils in your classroom.

While the review by Priest and colleagues (2013) provides strong evidence of racism as a key determinant of child mental health, it is not without its constraints. First, Priest et al.'s focus is on research from the US and so we must exercise caution when extrapolating to the UK context. Second, for many of the included studies, racial discrimination was not always well defined or conceptualised; in some cases, race was 'lumped in' with religious, age-based, and other forms of discrimination. This is a limitation often present when conducting research into any minority groups, the greatest casualties of which are undoubtedly Black, Asian, and Minority Ethnic ("BAME") people. As the authors acknowledge, many studies homogenise ethnic minorities, treating people within one categorisation as the same, making it a challenge to understand and interrogate differences between groups. The mental health needs and experiences of British Pakistani females, for example, are distinct from those of Black British males, perhaps united most by being racialised as a "minority" or "other". It is essential that more research is carried out in the UK that is sensitive to intra-ethnic differences (Goodman et al., 2008), including amid Black people.[1] Nevertheless, in a society that places value on whiteness, this shared facet holds particular importance to adolescent mental health when considering how internalised racism can manifest among teens of colour.

Internalised racism

Racism is said to occur at three different levels, one of which is "internalised" (Berman & Paradies, 2010). Internalised racism is where racist attitudes, beliefs, and ideologies are incorporated into the worldview of those who are oppressed, and has been linked to anxiety symptoms and distress in a recent US study on Black college students (Sosoo et al., 2020). Whilst the other two levels, "interpersonal" and "systemic" racism, are also effective in upholding white supremacy, internalised racism is particularly insidious; as with many features of whiteness, it functions in the absence of white people. One way in which this manifests is colourism, which has been referred to as a "global adolescent health concern" and has significant implications for child mental health (Craddock et al., 2018).

Colourism typically privileges those with lighter skin tones (Hunter, 2016) who are seen as closer in proximity to whiteness. In a world where current beauty ideals herald lighter skin tones, "beauty capital" is granted to those with lighter complexions. Colourism reflects anti-blackness and intersects with racism, gender, and patriarchal patterns of desire (Phoenix, 2014), with females in particular facing societal pressures to aspire to unrealistic and prejudicial standards of beauty (Hunter, 2002). It has been associated with body dissatisfaction, eating disorders, anxiety, and depression (Bucchianeri & Neumark-Sztainer, 2014; Craddock et al., 2018) and is also reflected in the global uptake of skin-lightening practices (Peltzer et al., 2016), as depicted in the North American documentary *Dark Girls*:

> I can remember being in the bathtub asking my mum to put bleach in the water so that my skin would be lighter and so that I could escape the feelings I had about not being as beautiful, as acceptable, as loveable.
>
> (Duke and Berry, 2011)

There is evidence that colourism can affect educational outcomes, including preferential treatment by both teachers and peers (Adams et al., 2016; Hunter, 2002, 2016). Given its relationship to mental health and wellbeing, it is imperative teachers seek to sensitively and compassionately disrupt current narratives that may emerge in the classroom or playgrounds. While many of the current research findings arise from the US, this highlights a lack of UK research (Phoenix, 2014) rather than exonerating British schools from the issue. In my own research interviews with Black British girls, I was told: "I know I'm not attractive because I'm dark" and "I'm not desirable". These same girls spoke of the pressures they felt in school, the unfavourable comparisons that were made against lighter-skinned girls, and the bullying and disrespectful comments that were directed to them by others, including from Black boys. Internalised racism often presents itself as intra-racial discrimination (also conceptualised as "horizontal hostility", see White & Langer, 1999), and it is essential that this is recognised *as a function of whiteness*, not a separate form of racism. As Madriaga (2018) notes, the anti-blackness that casts Black children and young people as "uneducable" and "unworthy of education" (Dumas, 2016, p. 16) is simply a reproduction of the influence of whiteness in education. This anti-blackness underpins not only the way Black children perceive themselves in terms of appearance, but how they are seen in terms of age and development.

Adultification bias

Research shows that from as young as ten years old Black boys are misperceived as older than their white peers who are in contrast estimated to be younger than their chronological age (Goff, 2014). Black girls, too, are seen as more mature (Morris, 2016) and compared to white girls of the same age are perceived as being more independent and knowing more about adult topics and sex, whilst needing less nurturing, protection, comfort, and support (Epstein et al., 2017). These basic human needs are crucial to healthy child development, including self-worth, esteem, identity, and other tenets of positive mental health. Having the opposite effect, adultification bias leads to the denial of these needs, projecting the harmful stereotypes that encircle Black women onto Black girls from as young as five years old (Epstein et al., 2017, p. 5). These are stereotypes such as the following categories:

- **Sapphire:** emasculating, loud, aggressive, angry, stubborn, and unfeminine;

- **Jezebel:** hyper-sexualised, seductive, and exploitative of men's weaknesses;

- **Mammy:** self-sacrificing, nurturing, loving, and asexual.

The effect of such objectification of Black girls is significant, not least through internalised racism, patriarchy, and negative expectations. It also reduces and alters professionals' senses of their safeguarding responsibilities; for example, if Black girls are not seen as girls but as hypersexual beings, this can become an unconscious bias so that adults fail to correctly identify child sexual abuse or exploitation (Davis, 2019). This of course also impacts Black males, whose masculinity is often conflated and associated with aggression, hyper-sexuality, and violence (e.g. Hooks, 2004). Within the education system, the perception of Black boys and girls as less innocent, and therefore more culpable, contributes to harsher punishments and disproportionate school exclusions (Epstein et al., 2017), which is linked to negative mental health outcomes such as anxiety and depression (Timpson, 2019). Research has already indicated that Black boys are more likely to be viewed as guilty than their white counterparts (Goff, 2014). As Epstein and colleagues note, "adultification is a form of dehumanisation, robbing Black children of the very essence of what makes childhood distinct from all other developmental periods: innocence" (2017, p. 6).

Such biases can also translate to fewer mentorship opportunities or pastoral care and mental health intervention in schools. Meanwhile white children, who are perceived as more fragile, vulnerable, and innocent (Epstein et al., 2017), continue to be advantaged through the support, comfort, protection, and nurture that all children need for emotional development and good mental health.

General mental health

While there is a clear link between mental health and racism, UK-based research into the general mental health of Black children and young people is relatively scarce (e.g. Lavis, 2014) and is an area requiring further study. In one of the relatively few surveys into child mental health, which included over 9,000 children living in England aged 5–19 (NHS Digital, 2018), Black children were three times less likely than white children to report a mental health disorder and less than one in a hundred Black children were diagnosed with behavioural disorders, compared to six in a hundred of their white counterparts. While the report did not interrogate possible reasons for lesser diagnoses, which may include distrust and therefore potential underuse of statutory mental health services by Black families (e.g. YMCA, 2020), against the backdrop of research on racism and mental health, these findings may be considered surprising. Nevertheless, this survey reinforced the findings of an earlier systematic review (Goodman et al., 2008), which indicated that Black African children had overall better mental health than white British children and fewer emotional problems. Black Caribbean and Mixed Race children were similar to that of white British, although when it came to less common mental health disorders such as psychosis or psychotic-like experiences, Black children were at higher risk of receiving a diagnosis in several of the studies. Again, pointing to the need for research that interrogates ethnic differences, the review highlighted variance in the mental health of children between ethnic groups, including within categorisations of Black children. Importantly, it also called for future research to pay more attention to issues of explanation. This is a really important point when reflecting on evidence because while data and statistics hold importance, they tend to lend themselves better to framing problems (the "what") than they do to driving solutions (the "how"). If we are to better understand how to move forward, we need to make sure we ask the right follow-up questions.

When considering explanatory factors, perhaps a helpful question might be: Why, when Black children experience such disadvantage compared to their white counterparts, are these figures as they are? Should we not expect the mental health of Black children to be worse? The latter question in itself is problematic as it conceals an underlying assumption; those children who thrive are often seen as doing so *in spite* of being Black (e.g. "usually white teachers don't expect you to achieve"; Fuller, 2002, p. 156), which reinforces negative representations of Blackness. But in a world where Black people have to "work twice as hard to get half as far"[2] (DeSante, 2013), if anything this suggests these achievements are *because* of it. So what attributes do Black children possess that protect their mental health even in the face of such adversity? Wright and colleagues (2016) say that researching and theorising on problematic experiences actually diverts attention from the creative and dynamic ways Black males negotiate barriers and achieve personal and educational success. Perhaps what is most helpful to advancing discussions around Black mental health in schools, therefore, is to focus on the factors that have sustained Black people through many centuries of oppression. As Joy DeGruy writes: "that we are here at all can be seen as testament to our willpower, spiritual strength and resilience" (2005, p. 59).

Resilience

The importance of resilience[3] has become increasingly more recognised and embedded within the UK education system (e.g. The All Party Parliamentary Group on Social Mobility, 2014). The World Health Organization confirms that mental health is a fundamental element of child and adolescent resilience, which can help buffer against risk factors and promote protective factors (Friedli, 2019). This makes it of particular relevance among children experiencing disadvantage, and for Black children, particularly those who straddle the intersection, is essential to navigating a racist, unjust world. Black children are highly resilient (Bernard, 2012), evidenced by studies showing that even in severe poverty, they achieve social and academic success in spite of low socioeconomic status, minimal expectations, and negative representation (see APA Task Force on Resilience and Strength in Black Children and Adolescents, 2008). This tells us that resilience in Black children is not only key to their mental health and wellbeing, but is an existing strength that should be recognised and further developed.

Sadly, depictions of Black children within the education sphere are not often positive, which detracts from the positive capital contributing to their resilience (Wright et al., 2016). Among Mixed Race children, teachers have been shown to make negative assumptions about their identities and emotions (Edwards et al., 2008), when in fact research shows that what might appear as a disadvantage on the outside may not be the case (Ungar et al., 2007). These assumptions have been shown to erode their resilience (Lewis, 2016), which increases the risk of mental health problems. Thinking about the role of the teacher or school in these studies, what this also tells us is that resilience is not just an individual attribute, but a collective one. Resmaa Menakem provides an excellent example of collective resilience in practice:

> Suppose you're running a marathon. Halfway through, exhausted, you trip and fall. Your legs ache and you're bleeding from both knees. You pull yourself to your feet and decide it's time to quit the race. Then five of your friends and family members show up beside you. "You can do it!" they shout. "You finished last year; you can finish this time. Go for it!" Next thing you know, you're off and running again. Clearly this required resilience. But the resilience wasn't just inside of you. It was also from the words and actions of people who care for you, and from your relationship with them.
>
> (2017, p. 50)

We are communal beings, and a central tenet of Black resilience is in what Yosso (2005) describes as *community cultural wealth*. Having access to supportive relationships, observing cultural traditions, and experiencing cohesion with others and feeling a part of something larger than oneself are all key factors of resilience (Ungar et al., 2007). Relationships are prized among the Black community, and teachers who build strong relationships with Black pupils based on mutual trust and respect tend to yield more positive outcomes (DeGruy, 2005). This is consistent with more general policy guidance on child mental health (Public Health England, 2015), which implicates the role of equality, social inclusion, support, trust, culture, and participation in child mental wellbeing. Given the significance of community, teachers should strive to build resilient classrooms that seek to honour and celebrate each of the Black children in them.

What can teachers do?

Now more than ever, children and adolescents depend on the resilience of inter-dependent systems such as family, school, and community. This is especially the case since the COVID-19 pandemic (Dvorsky et al., 2020) with the intermittent closure of schools and where inequalities, particularly among ethnic minorities, have been further exposed (The Doreen Lawrence Review, 2020). The following strategies draw on factors associated with wellbeing and resilience in Black children, encompassing a strengths-based approach.

Bringing others in and along

Taking steps to build *community cultural wealth* (Yosso, 2005) can instil a strong sense of belonging and connection from Black males to the people and systems that support them (Wright et al., 2016), which can improve mental wellbeing and behaviour (DeGruy, 2005). Teachers and schools can support Black children to develop specific capital that contributes to this wealth:

Aspirational capital. This is about having the desire to be ambitious even in the face of barriers, which when combined with parental aspiration can act as a key protective factor (Merolla, 2013). To develop aspirational capital, schools can:

- Involve parents at every opportunity;

- Communicate unconditional positive expectations for Black children;

- Develop a "culture of possibility".

Navigational and resistant capital. This is about helping children to see through the ways in which institutions disadvantage them and to resist negative stereotyping, which supports positive identity shift. This can include positive racial socialisation (i.e. how children come to see themselves and others) education and additional emotional support (Wright et al., 2016). Developing navigational and resistant capital could involve:

- Bring in other wellbeing and support services, such as mentoring;

- Be affirming and inspirational with advice and tutoring services;

- Create opportunities for positive racial socialisation (see *centring the voice of the Black child*).

Social and familial capital. This is about who can be turned to in times of need and is a strong contributor to wellbeing. It includes cultural resilience and emotional support, the capital from which has been shown to convert to educational, personal, and social prestige in Black males (Mirza, 2009). Social and familial capital can be built with teachers taking steps to:

- Involve parents at every opportunity;

- Recognise that "family" may encompass a variety of members and important roles (Tran, 2014);

- Recognise the value of the community (e.g. Black churches, organisations, and services);

- Consider application of Restorative Justice principles in promoting peace among peers and staff.

Linguistic capital. This is about recognising how communication skills, including additional languages, support connection to a variety of communities. Schools can support this when they:

- Support and celebrate, not prohibit, the use of other language and dialects between children;

- Ensure all aspects of support are accessible to non-English-speaking parents and families.

Research suggests that different types of capital can interact with each other to have a positive compounding effect (Wright et al., 2016). Together, and separately, they contribute to several resilience factors, in particular, around experiencing a sense of cohesion with others and access to supportive relationships (Ungar et al., 2007). Taking the steps above also serves to challenge our own assumptions and expectations and helps decentre and dismantle the effects of whiteness, offering Black children and families a powerful form of allyship and community within and beyond the school gates. For those children educated at home during the COVID-19 pandemic, these steps became even more critical as reliance on parents and wider family increases.

Centring the voice of the Black child

When it comes to racism, the metaphorical courtroom places the burden of proof on people of colour and in a world that values objectivity and reason (DiAngelo, 2018). This means that empirical evidence often weighs in over lived experience. While policy and research can offer useful insights, there is nothing more powerful than the voice of the child. Centring the voice of each Black child and their family is essential to understanding who is in your classroom and how best to promote their wellbeing (Bernard, 2020). Ways in which this can be done by teachers and schools start with actions that lend themselves to personalisation of care:

- Recognise the different wellbeing needs within and between Black and Mixed Race children. The resilience framework from Ungar and colleagues (2007) can be applied to individuals in centring their lived experience and support teachers to understand this further;

- Recognise that there may be potential gender differences in how racism is enacted and how it impacts mental health, such as how colourism affects Black girls or the "failure" narrative affects Black boys. Challenge these narratives at every opportunity, in yourself and others;

- Be aware of conflating a child's resilience or maturity with your own adultification biases (e.g. the "mammy" stereotype outlined above). Regardless of their strengths or coping strategies, all children need support, comfort, protection, and nurturing. This should be prioritised over discipline;

- Create opportunities for each child to share and participate in their culture, traditions, and values with dignity and respect, being mindful not to single Black children out in a way that may be experienced as anxiety-evoking, fetishising, or voyeuristic.

It is important to challenge negative dominant discourses and stereotypes around Black children, and indeed adults, and teachers should flood their classrooms with positive examples and stories of Blackness. Joy DeGruy summarises the healing power of storytelling:

> Telling our stories can be redemptive. Telling our stories can free us. Telling our stories can help lift others up. I believe an integral part of racial socialisation is learning the histories of those in our family and community. Story telling is an important part of our education; it strengthens us and helps us build resilience. It helps us put things in the proper perspective.
>
> (2005, p. 72)

As well as the decolonising effect on the learning environment, positive racial socialisation can also support decolonisation of the Black mind, which is essential to developing a positive identity, dismantling internalised racism, and strengthening existing resilience factors. Together with those outlined above, these steps all act as preventative, protective strategies that can optimise the mental health of Black pupils.

Knowing when to seek specialist services

Invariably, there will be Black children for whom preventative strategies are not sufficient and, in these instances, specialist support may be required. The first step is the identification of this need, which is why it is so important to get to know each child in the ways described above. With strong knowledge and a personal understanding of each child, this can then act as a baseline against which teachers and learning assistants observe individual changes in mental health or resilience. It is important to bear in mind the research on adultification bias and how this can impact perceptions of need, particularly among Black girls (Epstein et al., 2017). When there is concern regarding mental health and there is a need for additional services, it is important to be respectful and sensitive. The general evidence suggests Black people are less likely to seek support from mainstream or statutory services, which has been associated with distrust (e.g. YMCA, 2020) and stigmatisation (Arday, 2021). Ways of minimising distress, maintaining the dignity of, and maximising positive outcomes for the child might include:

- Prioritising the relationship, which should be built on mutual trust and respect (DeGruy, 2005). This supports greater likelihood of the child opening up and being receptive to help;

- Recognising that there may be alternatives to statutory services that better meet the needs of Black children. Consider and explore these, involving the family and support services wherever possible;

- Ensuring that interventions are individualised and culturally responsive.

On a final note, it is important for teachers and learning assistants to maintain their own mental health and wellbeing, without which it can be harder to address one's own biases, challenge others, and be appropriately vigilant to the needs of each child. Self-reflection and care can counteract the apathy that often comes with being tired, burned out, or disillusioned. It is of course, a vital ingredient to resilience.

Takeaway points

- Black mental health is a complex topic, underscored by internalised, interpersonal, and systemic racism.

- Alongside a tendency of research to focus on theorising and conceptualising (Wright et al., 2016), there are many gaps in the literature on the mental health of Black children.

- Teaching staff should feel heartened at the simplicity of the evidence-informed strategies described above, which focus on the existing strengths of the Black community.

- They illustrate the "ordinariness" of resilience, which emerges from commonplace adaptive systems such as self-belief, close relationships with caring adults, committed families, and effective schools and communities (Masten, 2014a).

■ It is the role of teachers, learning assistants, and the wider school to nurture these systems by developing cultural community wealth in each Black child by supporting them to increase their social and cultural capital and centring the voice of each child and their family and taking steps to understand and validate their lived experience.

■ Schools and practitioners should engage in positive racial socialisation as well as challenging and disrupting:

● Internalised racism, recognising it as a function of whiteness;

● Micro-aggressions, harassment, and bullying behaviours by others;

● Negative narratives, stereotypes, and expectations of Black children.

■ It is imperative to build relationships with Black pupils that foster openness and trust and develop connections with culturally relevant community and support services, and it is possible for these strategies to be adopted at any level, whether it be by teachers, learning assistants, and other school staff, or across schools or networks.

■ Racial equality is most effectively achieved when mainstreamed through a whole-systems approach. In the context of mental health and educational outcomes among Black children, this is no different; narratives, stereotypes, and expectations are accepted through repetition and so it is essential that negative discourses about Black pupils are systematically replaced with positive ones.

■ Wherever possible, the emotional labour of this work should be undertaken by those with race-related privilege so that the burden of race and racism becomes more than that of Black children, parents, families, and staff. This supports racial equity whilst promoting and protecting Black mental health and wellbeing.

■ These actions need to occur at school level for full effect, otherwise what the classrooms give, the school halls, fields, corridors, and canteens take away. As Ann Masten (2014b) says: "Resilience emerges from multiple processes. It's not one trait; it's not one thing. There are many different systems that contribute. And those are what I call 'ordinary magic.'"

Notes

1 Black people are often defined as Black African, Black British, Black Caribbean, Mixed White and Black African, and Mixed White and Black Caribbean (e.g. YMCA, 2020). It feels salient to note that while Black mixed-race people tend to be racialised as Black, their lived experiences, privileges, and positionality are not homogeneous (Campion, 2019). Of course, this is the case for any group positioned within the collective Black identity.

2 This phrase is also reflected in the lyrics of the autoethnographic song *Black*, by Dave Omoregie and Smith (2019), which we recommend listening to.
3 Interestingly the word resilience stems from the Latin verb *resilire*, which means to rebound. It refers to the capacity to adapt successfully to disturbances that threaten how we function and develop (Masten, 2014a).

Further reading

Lewis, K. (2016) Helping mixed heritage children develop 'character and resilience' in schools. *Improving Schools,* 19(3), 197–211. Available at: https://doi.org/10.1177/1365480216650311

Masten, A. S. (2014a) *Ordinary Magic.* New York, NY: The Guildford Press.

Saad, L. (2020) *Me and White Supremacy: How to Recognise Your Privilege, Combat Racism and Change.* UK: Hachette.

Ungar, M., Brown, M., Liebenberg, L., Othman, R., Kwong, W. M., Armstrong, M. & Gilgun, J. (2007) Unique pathways to resilience across cultures. *Adolescence,* 42(166), 287–310.

References

Adams, E. A., Kurtz-Costes, B. E. & Hoffman, A. J. (2016) Skin tone bias among African-Americans: Antecedents and consequences across the life span. *Developmental Review,* 40, 93–116.

Arday, J. (2021) No one can see me cry. *Higher Education.* Available at: https://doi.org/10.1007/s10734-020-00636-w

Berman, G. & Paradies, Y. (2010) Racism, disadvantage and multiculturalism: Towards effective anti-racist praxis. *Ethnic & Racial Studies,* 33(2), 1–19.

Bernard, C. (2020) *PSDP resources and tools: Understanding the lived experiences of black and ethnic minority children and families.* London, UK: Department for Education. Available at: https://practice-supervisors.rip.org.uk/wp-content/uploads/2020/01/KB-Understanding-the-lived-experiences-of-black-Asian-and-minority-ethnic-children-and-families.pdf

Bernard, D. M. (2012) Learning mathematics while Black. *Educational Foundations,* 26(1–2), 47–66.

Bucchianeri, M. & Neumark-Sztainer, D. (2014) Body dissatisfaction: An overlooked public health concern. *Journal of Public Mental Health,* 13(2), 64–69.

Campion, K. (2019) "You think you're Black?" Exploring Black mixed-race experiences of Black rejection. *Ethnic and Racial Studies,* 42(16), 196–213.

Collins, J. W., David, R. J., Handler, A., Wall, S. & Andes, S. (2004) Very low birthweight in African American infants: The role of maternal exposure to interpersonal racial discrimination. *American Journal of Public Health,* 94(12), 2132–2138. https://doi.org/10.2105/ajph.94.12.2132

Craddock, N., Dlova, N. & Diedrichs, P. C. (2018) Colourism: A global adolescent health concern. *Current Opinion,* 30(4), 472–477.

Davis, J. (2019) *Safeguarding Black girls from child sexual abuse: Messages from research.* Community Care Inform Children. Available at: https://www.ccinform.co.uk/research/child-sexual-abuse-and-safeguarding-black-girls-messages-from-research/

DeGruy, J. (2005) *Post-traumatic slave syndrome.* Milwaukie, OR: Uptone Press.

DeSante, C. D. (2013) Working twice as hard to get half as far: Race, work ethic, and America's deserving poor. *American Journal of Political Science,* 57(2), 342–356.

DiAngelo, R. (2018) *White fragility.* Boston, MA: Beacon Press.

Duke, B. & Berry, D. C. (Directors & Producers). (2011) *Dark girls.* [Motion picture]. Los Angeles, CA: Urban Winter Entertainment, Inc.

Dumas, M. J. (2016) Against the dark: Antiblackness in education policy and discourse. *Theory into Practice*, 55(1), 11–19. Available at: https://doi.org/10.1080/00405841.2016. 1116852

Dvorsky, M. R., Breaux, R. & Becker, S. P. (2020) Finding ordinary magic in extraordinary times: Child and adolescent resilience during the Covid-19 pandemic. *European Child & Adolescent Psychiatry.* Available at: https://doi.org/10.1007/s00787-020-01583-8

Edwards, R., Caballero, C. & Puthussery, S. (2008) *Parenting 'mixed' children: Difference and belonging in mixed race and faith families.* York: Joseph Rowntree Foundation. Available at: www.jrf.org.uk

Equality and Human Rights Commission. (15 October 2020) *Race report statistics.* Available at: https://www.equalityhumanrights.com/en/race-report-statistics

Epstein, R., Blake, J. J. & González, T. (2017) *Girlhood interrupted: The erasure of Black girls' childhood.* Centre on Poverty and Inequality, Georgetown Law. Available at: http://www. endadultificationbias.org/

Friedli, F. (2009) *Mental health, resilience and inequalities.* Copenhagen, Denmark: World Health Organisation.

Fuller, V. (2002) *Perceptions of achieving black pupils: Factors contributing to success.* Doctoral thesis, Institute of Education, University of London. Available at: https://discovery. ucl.ac.uk/id/eprint/10020426/

Goff, P. A., Jackson, M. C., Di Leone, B. A. L., Culotta, C. M. & DiTomasso, N. A. (2014) The essence of innocence: Consequences of dehumanising Black children. *Personality & Social Psychology*, 106(4), 526–545.

Goodman, A., Patel., V. & Leon, D. A. (2008) Child mental health differences amongst ethnic groups in Britain: A systematic review. *BMC Public Health,* 8(1), 258. Available at: http:// www.biomedcentral.com/1471-2458/8/258

hooks, b. (2004) *We real cool: Black men and masculinity.* New York, NY: Routledge.

Hunter, M. L. (2002) If you're light you're alright' light skin colour as social capital for women of colour. *Gender & Society*, 16(2), 175–193.

Hunter, M. (2016) Colourism in the classroom: How skin tone stratifies African American and Latina/o students. *Theory into Practice*, 55, 54–61.

Lavis, P. (2014) *The importance of promoting mental health in children and young people from Black and Minority ethnic communities: A race equality foundation briefing paper.* London, UK: Race Equality Foundation. Available at: http://raceequalityfoundation.org. uk/wp-content/uploads/2018/02/Health-Briefing-332.pdf

Lereya, S. T., Patel, M., Garcez Aurelio dos Santos, J. P. & Deighton, J. (2019) Mental health difficulties, attainment and attendance: A cross-sectional study. *European Child & Adolescent Psychiatry*, 28, 1147–1152. https://doi.org/10.1007/s00787-018091273-6

Lewis, K. (2016) Helping mixed heritage children develop 'character and resilience' in schools. *Improving Schools,* 19(3), 197–211. Available at: https://doi.org/10.1177/1365480216650311

Madriaga, M. (2018) Antiblackness in English higher education. *International Journal of Inclusive Education,* 24(11), 1143–1157. Available at: http://shura.shu.ac.uk/22297/

Masten, A. S. (2014a) *Ordinary magic.* New York, NY: The Guildford Press.

Masten, A. S. (2014b, September 17) *Ann Masten: Children's natural resilience is nurtured through 'ordinary magic'* (Interview by Andy Steiner for Minnpost). Available at: https://www.minnpost.com/mental-health-addiction/2014/09/ann-masten-children-s-natural-resilience-nurtured-through-ordinary-m/

Menakem, R. (2017) *My grandmother's hands: Racialised trauma and the pathway to mending our hearts and bodies.* Las Vegas, NV: Central Recovery Press.

Merolla, D. (2013) The net black advantage in education transitions: An education careers approach. *American Educational Research Journal*, 50(5), 895–924. Available at: https://doi.org/10.3102/0002831213486511

Mirza, H. S. (2009) *Race, gender and educational desire: Why black women succeed and fail.* London: Routledge.

Morris, M. W. (2016) *Pushout: The criminalisation of Black girls in schools.* New York: The New Press.

NHS Digital. (2018) *Mental health of children and young people in England, 2017: Summary of key findings.* Available at: https://files.digital.nhs.uk/A6/EA7D58/MHCYP%20 2017%20Summary.pdf

Office for National Statistics. (2020) *Child poverty and educational outcomes by ethnicity.* Available at: https://www.ons.gov.uk/economy/nationalaccounts/uksectoraccounts/compendium/economicreview/february2020/childpovertyandeducationoutcomesby-ethnicity

Omoregie, D. O & Smith, F. T. (2019) Black. [Recorded by D. Omoregie (Dave)]. On *Psychodrama* [YouTube file]. London, England: Neighbourhood.

Pachter, L. M. & Coll, C. G. (2009) Racism and child health: A review of the literature and future directions. *Journal of Developmental & Behavioural Practice,* 30(3), 255–263.

Peltzer, K., Pengpid, S. & James, C. (2016) The globalisation of whitening: Prevalence of skin lighteners (or bleachers) use and its social correlates among university students in 26 countries. *International Journal of Dermatology*, 55, 1.

Phoenix, A. (2014) Colourism and the politics of beauty. *Feminist Review,* 108, 97–105.

Priest, N., Paradies, Y., Trenerry, B., Truong, M., Karlsen, S. & Kelly, Y. (2013) A systematic review of studies examining the relationship between reported racism and health and wellbeing for children and young people. *Social Science & Medicine*, 95, 115–127.

Public Health England. (2015) *Measuring mental wellbeing in children and young people.* London, UK: Author. Available at: https://assets.publishing.service.gov.uk/government/uploads/system/uploads/attachment_data/file/768983/Measuring_mental_wellbeing_in_children_and_young_people.pdf

Sosoo, E. E., Bernard, D. L. & Neblett, Jr., E. W. (2020) The influence of internalised racism on the relationship between discrimination and anxiety. *Cultural Diversity and Ethnic Minority in Psychology*, *26*(4), 570–580.

The All Party Parliamentary Group on Social Mobility. (2014) *Character and resilience manifesto.* London: The all part group on Social Mobility. Available at: http://www.educationengland.org.uk/documents/pdfs/2014-appg-social-mobility.pdf

The Doreen Lawrence Review. (2020) *An avoidable crisis. The disproportionate impact of Covid-19 on Black, Asian and Minority Ethnic communities: A review by Baroness Doreen Lawrence.* Available at: www.lawrencereview.co.uk

Timpson, E. (2019) *Timpson review of school exclusion.* London, UK: Department for Education. Available at: https://assets.publishing.service.gov.uk/government/uploads/system/uploads/attachment_data/file/807862/Timpson_review.pdf

Tran, Y. (2014) Addressing reciprocity between families and schools: Why these bridges are instrumental for students' academic success. *Improving Schools*, 17, 18–29.

Trent, M., Dooley, D. G. & Douge, J. (2019) The impact of racism on child and adolescent health. *Paediatrics*, 144(2), e20191765. Available at: https://doi.org/10.1542/peds.2019-1765

Ungar, M., Brown, M., Liebenberg, L., Othman, R., Kwong, W. M., Armstrong, M. & Gilgun, J. (2007) Unique pathways to resilience across cultures. *Adolescence*, 42(166), 287–310.

White, J. B. & Langer, E. J. (1999) Horizontal hostility: Relations between similar minority groups. *Journal of Social Issues,* 55(3), 537–559.

Wright, C., Maylor, U. & Becker, S. (2016) Young black males: Resilience and the use of capital to transform school "failure". *Critical Studies in Education*, 57(1), 21–34. Available at: https://doi.org/10.1080/17508487.2016.1117005

YMCA. (2020) *Young and Black: The young Black experience of institutional racism in the UK.* London, UK: YMCA England & Wales. Available at: https://www.ymca.org.uk/research/young-and-black

Yosso, T. (2005) Whose culture has capital? A critical race theory discussion of community cultural wealth. *Race Ethnicity and Education*, 8(1), 69–91. Available at: https://doi.org.10.1080/1361332052000341006

Appendix 1

Mental health in Black children: A resilience framework

The first two columns of the table below reflect the framework developed by Ungar and colleagues (2007). In the third column, you can think about specific questions or prompts to ask your pupils that explore their lived experiences; in essence, their "story".

A seven factor resilience framework (adapted from Ungar et al., 2007)

Factor	Explanation	What questions can you ask?
Access to material resources	Availability of financial, educational, medical, and employment assistance, and/or opportunities, as well as access to food, clothing, and shelter	
Relationships	Relationships with significant others, peers, and adults within one's family and community	
Identity	Personal and collective sense of purpose, self-appraisal of strengths and weaknesses, aspirations, beliefs, and values, including spiritual and religious identification	

(Continued)

Factor	Explanation	What questions can you ask?
Power and control	Experiences of caring for one's self and others; the ability to affect change in one's social and physical environment in order to access health resources	
Cultural adherence	Adherence to one's local and/or global cultural practices, values, and beliefs	
Social justice	Experiences related to finding a meaningful role in community and social equality	
Cohesion	Balancing one's personal interests with a sense of responsibility to the greater good; feeling a part of something larger than one's self socially and spiritually	

3

British Bangladeshi Pupils' Mental Wellbeing in Schools

Nilufar Ahmed, Arif Mahmud, and Fuad Ali

Synopsis

Adolescence is a vulnerable period during which mental health problems are likely to develop (Blakemore, 2019). Although previous research demonstrates ethnic variations in the incidence and prevalence of mental ill-health (Roberts et al., 1998), there is uncertainty about which specific lifestyle and behavioural correlates of ethnicity confer health risks or advantages. Discrimination, place of birth, gender roles, religious practice, and migration stressors may all be relevant. This particular chapter focuses on the mental health of British Bangladeshi pupils who continue to experience multiple challenges within a localised and historical backdrop of alienation, resistance, mental health stigma, racial exclusion, disaffection, and a working-class reality. This chapter will conclude by recommending teachers, and institutions explore and embrace Bangladeshi pupil identities and their trajectories, cultures, and everyday issues within the curricula and pedagogy in order to positively recognise and enhance pupil's psychological and cognitive development. This will, in turn, provide a framework for both teachers and pupils to nurture a wider plurality and enhance their confidence and wellbeing (Hoque, 2017).

Background

British Bangladeshis in the UK

The Bangladeshi population in the UK is a sizeable minority with over 450,000 people recorded in the 2011 census. Most UK Bangladeshis live in urban areas, with more than half living in London alone. The People's Republic of Bangladesh was established in 1971 as the eastern wing of Pakistan following a 23-year period immediately after Independence from colonial British rule. It comprises territory that has previously been known to the colonial British state as Bengal, then East Bengal, and Assam. Although the movement of people and goods stretches back hundreds of years, significant migration to the UK began during the 1970s. This movement reached its height in the 1980s as wives and families of men who had migrated earlier reunited in the UK (Ahmed, 2005). A process of chain migration and a work voucher system led to early arrivals settling in areas that housed existing communities and jobs. Early male migrants found factory work in London's East End or other industrial areas in the Midlands and the North of England. With increased de-industrialisation in the North of England and Midlands in the post-1980s, many families relocated to East London, where they hoped they would be able to find work in the still active factories (Gardner, 2009), further consolidating the population in London. In the mid-1990s, it was estimated that over 95% of Bangladeshis in the UK hailed from Sylhet (Gardner, 1995), where the regional Sylheti variety of language has a literary and printing tradition adjacent to the specific form of Bengali developed in colonial Calcutta and nationalised into the educational system of the modern nation state of Bangladesh (Ahmed, 2016; Ghosh, 2006; Mazhar, 2008). The flattening of a diverse linguistic reality to a controlling nationalist imperative is not unique to Sylheti within Bangladesh, or Bengali(s) in Britain or the erstwhile East Pakistan. However, it benefits educational providers in the UK to deny fluidity and plurality of linguistic forms within the Bangladeshi-heritage population.

The long-term experience of minority ethnic populations is not static. There are challenges that arise with an evolving sense of identity that cuts across and between one's ancestral and current place of residence. This experience is largely understudied, and we do not know as much as we would like about the evolving experience of identities for immigrants. However, we do know that such events can bring about mental health and wellbeing issues for new immigrants that can cascade through subsequent generations (Lee, 2007; Ying & Han, 2007; Kulis et al., 2007). This interacts with previous legacies of economic and educational exclusion in earlier (pre-migration) generations to shape the building of educational horizons, survival strategies, trajectories, and learning practices.

The Bangladeshi community has been recognised as one of the most disadvantaged in the UK, with high unemployment rates among adults and high levels of poverty (Main & Bradshaw, 2016). Bangladeshi pupils generally perform better than many disadvantaged groups academically and go onto Higher Education in greater proportions than the general population (Shain, 2021). However, this success is not translated into the workplace as they continue to face poorer outcomes in the labour market (Stevenson et al., 2017), which can contribute to mental health issues. Pupil confidence and wellbeing may be at risk if it becomes the perception that hard work and good grades are not enough to secure success. As such, these later life impacts are vital for understanding and supporting pupil's mental wellbeing.

It is well established that discrimination can have significant negative effects on psychological wellbeing (Adams et al., 2006) across generations and cultural groups (Arbona & Jimenez, 2014; Cheng et al., 2015; Han & Lee, 2011; Miranda et al., 2013;

Polanco-Roman & Miranda, 2013). Previous research has highlighted that experience of deeper and more frequent racial micro-aggressions have a detrimental effect on mental health and are significantly correlated with depressive symptoms and negative emotional states (Nadal et al., 2014). Willen (2007) emphasised that ethnic minority populations' perception of prejudice (of being discriminated against or racially abused) was connected to their increased body vigilance and anxiety when in public spaces. Low self-esteem has also been linked to perceived prejudice (Umaña-Taylor & Updegraff, 2007). Experiences of both empowerment and humiliation in schools vary hugely, but this is perhaps the most obvious area where a difference can be made; supporting pupils, encouraging self-belief, and equipping them to combat discrimination and flourish through hardships will develop resilience, but this needs to be met with schools and staff being antiracist in their outlook and behaviours.

Wellbeing and support inequalities

For educational institutions to have an impact in reducing inequalities and improving mental health of young Bangladeshi pupils, it is important that the wider context that frames their lived experiences is incorporated into their educational lives. Adolescence is a precipitous time for mental health as young people navigate their independent identities (Blakemore, 2019). In a systematic review on ethnic differences in children's mental health, Goodman and colleagues (2008) concluded there was evidence of an unmet need in service provision for Bangladeshi children (Beck & Naz, 2019; Cooper et al., 2013; National Institute of Mental Health, 2013). As with many communities, mental illness in the Bangladeshi community carries high levels of stigma and confusion, which often goes unreported (Memon et al., 2016). This may prevent pupils and parents from knowing about, let alone seeking and receiving, adequate support services. It is important to understand that it is not the community which is 'problematic' in seeking support, but rather that services available may not be accommodating their needs. A role schools might play is to address this by taking the time to develop trusting relationships with parents. Doing so could encourage greater dialogue about different concerns. The disconnect and mistrust in society and discriminatory health services are evidenced in systematic qualitative studies reviewed by Bhui and colleagues (2003) who reported that even when Bangladeshis shared their symptoms with their primary care provider, they would not be referred to support services or specialists. Bangladeshi women have also been blamed for somatising their mental health issues (Khan, 2018). Thus, it is unsurprising that Bangladeshi service users have expressed distrust in clinicians who may misinterpret their religion or religious beliefs as being connected to their mental illness (Islam et al., 2015). Bowl (2007) reported poor awareness of cultural norms and expectations has an impact on perceived mental wellness, for instance, a participant explained that their decision to pray at a certain time was misinterpreted as a sign of mental illness by a clinician.

In educational settings, discrimination can also have an impact on young Bangladeshi pupils' wellbeing. In his study, Hoque (2017) reported that participants felt their school rejected and dismissed their Bangladeshi identity. He believed that deliberately eradicating a community's first language was a type of "symbolic violence" (p. 88) committed against minority groups. While the Bangladeshi participants in his study understood that their first language presented a link to their "culture and identity", the Bangladeshi third generation started to internalise that their first language would not be useful for financial growth or cultural capital (p. 189). Hoque addressed how pressurising young people to abandon their first language and other facets of their cultural identity puts them at risk of not belonging to either British culture or their own group, further complicating their identity formation. This weaponising of first languages was seen after the UK riots in 2005, when a lack of English fluency among the first generation was constructed as a causal factor for potential violence among subsequent generations (Ahmed, 2008). The common opinion is that British Bangladeshi young people face frequent prejudice and marginalisation from mainstream society. This has a negative effect on their sense of identity and belonging, placing their mental health and wellbeing at risk.

There is limited data on Bangladeshi pupils' experiences of mental health as too often samples in studies exploring ethnicity and mental health are so small that all South Asians are analysed together, or Pakistani and Bangladeshi samples are aggregated. This loses nuance by merging groups with different identities, and masks group-level differences, tensions, and 'starting' points (Furnham & Adam-Saib, 2001). Where studies have focused on Bangladeshi adolescents, they often recruit from areas such as London and Luton with large Bangladeshi populations. Some schools where participants are recruited from have a majority (from 50% to 90%) of Bangladeshi pupils (e.g. Houghton et al., 2020; Rothon et al., 2009). Studies such as these have shown that a strong sense of cultural identity is associated with better mental health for Bangladeshi adolescents (Bhui et al., 2008). Areas like the London Borough of Tower Hamlets, which are home to many citizens of Bangladeshi ancestry, are likely to foster a high sense of cultural identity as the size of the community can offer protection for continuities and hybrid cultural practices (Ahmed, 2016). Houghton et al. (2020), in their research in East London, reported second-generation Bangladeshis were no more likely to adopt western clothing than first generation. In East London, traditional clothing is widely worn by different generations in public spaces. This may not be the case in other areas of the UK where the protective factor of a large community is absent, and people may feel uncertain about dressing in ways to attract attention to their 'otherness'. According to Bhui et al. (2008), young Bangladeshi females in East London who chose and favoured their conventional clothes were less likely to have mental health problems than those who wore 'integrated' clothing. This brings focus to the importance of cultural inclusion as potentially a factor in building resilience and social support. However, previous literature has also shown that 'integration' may be a valuable protective factor. In a study of adolescents aged between 11 and 14, Brøndbo and colleagues (2011) discovered that young Bangladeshis whose social groups contained both people from their own community and those from the host community had less wellbeing issues. This, perhaps, speaks to the importance of broad and diverse social support groups supplementing one's sense of cultural identity. We can understand the above evidence as suggesting that identity is important to mental health and having a community of diverse friends can offer a broader base for support.

Urban-rural differences

Findings from urban areas (with often multi-ethnic cultural groups) cannot be easily applied to other areas as, in terms of educational outcomes, large communities offer a sense of belonging and emotional infrastructure to each other, which can create a more positive experience. Strand and colleagues (2010) found that large numbers of Bangladeshi pupils in a school (more than 50%) correlated with more positive educational attainment. Additionally, a large minority group presence in the student body creates more incentive to support the attainment of those pupils by the school (through fostering positive identity and providing support where needed) for the overall performance of the school. Larger minority communities can offer greater social capital (Putnam, 1993) for pupils to draw on in the form of informal tutors and role models to emulate. To centre Tower Hamlets again, given the size and the established nature of the community, young pupils exploring future careers will be more easily able to identify role models across a range of occupations. The clarity around reasonable long-term goals is important for pupils' understanding of the reason and outcomes of their learning, thus making school less of a place of stress. When considering the mental wellbeing of our pupils, it can often be important to think about the significance of positive role models and the support and clarity of life plans.

There continues to be a lack of research into the educational experiences of minority pupils outside of areas with large concentrations of minority communities (Biggart et al., 2013). Connolly (2002) has called these areas the 'White hinterlands'; the regions of the UK and Ireland which have a very small minority of ethnic populations. Given the multitude of additional factors which support children and their families in concentrated communities, it is not appropriate to assume that the experiences of minority ethnic children highlighted through existing studies of schools undertaken in urban, multi-ethnic areas can be applied wholly to those children living in other areas. Instead, we encourage a place-based approach to understanding the needs of pupils, which situates their cultural and religious identity within a local context of services and networks.

Inter- and intra-generational intersections

Bangladeshi families experience a range of intersecting exclusions in the education system. The relatively recent arrival of a large Bangladeshi population in the UK, from mainly rural areas of Bangladesh means that these second- and later-generation school pupils are generally less likely to have parents with post-secondary school-level education. Moreover, education carries enormous prestige for Bangladeshi parents who view their difficult experiences in the labour market arising from a lack of education (or lack of qualifications recognised by the UK). Education is revered as an opportunity for a more comfortable life, and Bangladeshi parents are keen to support their children's studies (Crozier, 2009; Hassan, 2020). Lower attainment in Bangladeshi pupils before KS4 can be attributed to a large extent to poverty and deprivation (Strand et al., 2010). Highlighting the intersection of poverty, gender, and educational attainment across communities, Goodman and Gregg (2010) report that "Parental aspirations and attitudes to education vary strongly by socio-economic position (SEP) with 81% of the richest mothers saying they hope their 9-year-old will go to university, compared with only 37% of the poorest mothers" (p. 6). However, this finding does not appear to apply equally to the Bangladeshi community where a lower socioeconomic position does not correlate with poorer educational attainment, and mothers often have high aspirations for their children to attend university (Ahmed, 2016).

High parental and pupil aspiration among the Bangladeshi community is reflected in attainment. But this aspiration is not always obvious to teachers. Crozier and Davies (2007) discuss how parents have been constructed as being 'hard to reach' because they engage differently with schools compared to White British parents. They report that while Bangladeshi parents may not attend parent evenings together, or school plays, they are always responsive when schools contact them. Bangladeshi parents said they did not attend social events regularly because they were not culturally meaningful, and subsequently Crozier and Davies (2007) argue that it is more often schools that do not engage with Bangladeshi parents appropriately rather than parents not engaging with schools. Additionally, pupils may be protecting their parents from judgement by concealing school engagement opportunities. Crozier and Davies report how in their study, one pupil said his parents were unaware of teachers' evenings as he was worried that they may feel discriminated against or insulted by the school because of their faith, culture, and specifically, the way they dressed. These narratives may impact the engagement of parents with schools if they feel they will be judged for their difference and put pressure on young people as they take on a responsibility for protecting the wellbeing of their parents. As mentioned earlier in this chapter, having parents engaged with the school environment is important for community recognition of mental health challenges that pupils might face. Increasing access to school systems and observations of teachers to parents can be an important part of looking out for pupil wellbeing.

The landscape for British Bangladeshis is changing. In previous generations, parents spoke little or no English and had limited understanding of the school system and its expectations of parental involvement (Rahman & Azim, 2015). As the Bangladeshi community settles into the third and fourth generation in the UK, many defining features of early migrants are no longer applicable for example, fewer immediate family links and, consequently, visits to Bangladesh. However, other aspects remain or have become more visible markers of difference; the Bangladeshi community continues to proudly retain its cultural heritage as much as the early arrivals, whereas up until the start of the century, Muslims were relatively invisible and all Asians were viewed as a homogeneous group, and the War on Terror dramatically shifted the Western narrative towards Muslims. So to understand Bangladeshi pupils, it is imperative their religious identity is also foregrounded.

Hyphenated identities

As Bangladeshis in the UK are overwhelmingly Muslim, historic and contemporary Islamophobia (APPG, 2018) is an important factor in the negative experience of mental health and wellbeing of adolescents (Jasperse et al., 2012; Maynard & Harding, 2010), self-esteem (Every & Perry, 2014), and increased vigilance (Rippy & Newman, 2006). Perhaps most pertinent to this discussion, Muslim youth in the UK have experienced and have been discriminated against by the government's Prevent policy in schools (Goodfellow, 2018) and the wider securitisation agenda around them. Consider the citizenship stripping of Shamima Begum who was groomed at the age of 15 (BBC, 2021); a four-year-old boy being referred to Prevent after talking about the popular video game, Fortnite (Guardian, 2021); and another four-year-old boy being questioned by counter-terrorism police for drawing a picture of a man cutting a cucumber and mispronouncing it as a "cooker bomb" (Independent, 2016), to name a few. According to Williams (2017), Bangladeshi girls face "triple jeopardy" as a result of being female, belonging to a minority ethnic group, and being Muslim, which exposes them to several levels of discrimination, including violent attacks and hate crimes. This rise in public violence and harassment generates fear, causing many to withdraw, especially young girls. Impacts may include a weakened, deformed sense of identity, as well as fear and depression (Adams et al., 2006). For areas across the UK where there is not a sizeable Bangladeshi and/or Muslim community that can offer protection in numbers, this heightened sense of fear can have a greater and more long-lasting impact on mental wellbeing.

However diversely and dynamically practiced and approached, factors associated with Islam may be protective against mental ill-health (Dabbagh et al., 2012). Religious commitments are socially and institutionally engaging, with many young pupils receiving Islamic education through their local mosque (in areas that have a mosque), or through home tutoring schemes alongside their regular schooling. As with other kinds of communities, there is an educational ecology at play and a practical research opportunity. A study conducted by Kibria (2008) found young people are more likely to engage with Islamic identities than Bangladeshi or British identities. He explored the lengths that parents went to in order to reproduce a Bangladeshi identity in the UK, and the push back from younger generations drawn more towards Islamic identities (which have their own relationships with post-Imperial British Nationalism and postcolonial Bengali Nationalisms). This perpetual cultural and familial movement can have an effect on generational relationships and may also be claimed to have an impact on both generations' wellbeing.

Many Bangladeshi pupils attend additional cultural and religious classes outside of the traditional schooling curriculum (Walters, 2011). Supplementary schools offer Bengali language classes and in some parts of the UK there is an option for pupils to take a GCSE in Bengali. Depending on the size of the community and its resources, these classes may be delivered through informal one-to-one arrangements, semi-formal hiring of space, or more formal schools with lessons that are modelled on Western pedagogical approaches. This extra-curricular learning by many Bangladeshi pupils is an important part of their identity formation and connects their cultural and religious heritage past, present, and future. As these classes are held after school and at weekends, they can have an impact on pupils' ability to attend and engage in after-school events. Institutional awareness of Bangladeshi pupils' wider educational lives is beneficial when planning extracurricular events as well as something to recognise and draw upon in teaching practice to validate this important part of pupils' identity.

What can teachers do?

Working successfully with Bangladeshi pupils

What the research has shown is that schools and teachers are crucial in shaping educational outcomes for Bangladeshi pupils. As with all pupils, where they feel supported and listened to, there is greater engagement and positive attainment. Lander (2011) reports over 60% of Newly Qualified Teachers felt unprepared to teach pupils from minority backgrounds. The narrow monoculture identity nurtured by the historic British education system (Dorling & Tomlinson, 2019) and the perception of minority groups as homogeneous entities can contribute to this feeling of distance. There are multiple points of entry and opportunity that can help education professionals develop areas that can be improved and built upon by individual schools and teachers. The section below pulls together the data discussed above to suggest ways in which teachers can work positively with Bangladeshi pupils.

Working with families and creating dialogical spaces

The family is an important source of social capital that the school can work with (Rothon et al., 2012). We know the value Bangladeshi parents place on education and working to involve parents more closely as part of the school can help to create a stronger sense of belonging for pupils. Au (1993) discusses how minority pupils often experience cultural discontinuity when they move from their homes to their classrooms, and involving parents more can reduce this source of tension. Parental aspirations are a key driver for pupil aspirations (Strand et al., 2010). Working with parents to develop a positive attitude to schooling for parents and pupils alike can not only promote a positive self-concept beneficial for wellbeing, but, in turn, can foster ongoing productive relationships between Bangladeshi families and teachers. Building relationships with parents and the community is key in establishing the school as a dialogical space for parents to come and discuss their concerns about their children's wellbeing and, in turn, for the school to discuss concerns with parents about children's schooling and/or wellbeing issues. Many Bangladeshi parents may not have any experience of wellbeing and support services and may find themselves unsure of where to go for help. Schools are often the spaces in which wellbeing and emotional health issues first present or are first noticed due to the changes in the behaviour and engagement of pupils. By building relationships and safe dialogical spaces, trust can be developed between parents and schools to work together to support the pupil and to bring in support services early to meet needs as they arise. Schools will be better informed of formal mental health services and structures than most parents (regardless of ethnicity). If a positive relationship is already established, parents can feel safe to raise any concerns they have about such services and talk them through with staff. This will likely increase uptake of mental health services at an earlier stage of need.

Representation

A minority of Bangladeshi parents hold formal positions within schools. Encouraging and supporting parents to be part of committees to plan events, or to join the Board of Governors, offer ways in which pupils can see their own culture being positively promoted in schools and reduce 'cultural discontinuity'. As discussed, Bangladeshi parents are not unwilling to engage with the school. Their distance is often a mark of respect for the teacher's domain and parents are willing to engage more if requested and the engagement is seen as appropriate, i.e. pertaining directly to education or having cultural resonance to their own culture. Including pupil's ancestral history, geography, language, and culture into the learning space either formally through the taught curriculum or informally through community events, can help create the protective element to wellbeing that is found in a school environment with significant Bangladeshi constituency.

Place

Experiences differ according to context. Research conducted in urban areas with large Bangladeshi communities cannot be generalised to other parts of the country. The maturation of this community, and the value given to education means education professionals and leaders are emerging from it, albeit often located in areas with large Bangladeshi populations. In such places, having a cultural presence encourages parents to have greater engagement with the school as they can express their feelings and questions without feeling intimidated and othered in the way Crozier and Davies (2007) describe in their research. Their work fundamentally points to a lack of communication and understanding, and this is something that teachers can work on by involving parents more through direct invitation to collaboratively work on ways in which parents want to be more involved, in addition to the general open evening invitation.

Celebrate and recognise

Celebrate and share experiences of religious and cultural holidays (e.g. Bengali new year, Eid, and Puja) to support the growth of collective cultural experience and humanity. Reflect cultural, economic, and political heritage in the curriculum. Where English is not a first language, celebrate the mother tongue as part of the strategy to encourage multilingualism. Invest in multilingual books to encourage language learning and children will take these home and read with their parents, which, in turn, will boost parents willingness to engage with the school through seeing a valuing of their culture and language.

Recognise the efforts and value of pupils by supporting any external supplementary religious and language classes they do with affirmations of recognition of their commitment to learning, excellence, and community. This will encourage pupils to discuss these threads of their lives openly and not feel as though they should be hidden or cannot be discussed. Identify exemplars from the Bangladeshi community, e.g. *Great British Bake Off* winner Nadiya Hussain, politician Rupa Huq, choreographer Akram Khan, and Professor Mushtaq Khan, to highlight key Bangladeshi figures in British society.

Takeaway points

- British Bangladeshi youth are faced with multiple difficulties and assimilation stressors. They are vulnerable to multiple layers of discrimination based on race, cultural practices, and religious beliefs.

- Discrimination appears to present itself in many ways (e.g., educational inequities, employment inequalities, access to services, and hate crimes). Experiences of discrimination throughout a family can have a serious impact on the mental health of pupils.

- When Bangladeshis seek psychological help, they are often met with poor treatment.

- Education is highly valued by Bangladeshi parents and pupils and schools offer a valuable opportunity to support wellbeing.

- Most of the research on Bangladeshis in the UK is conducted in urban areas with highly concentrated Bangladeshi populations. This means the data has limited generalisability across the group.

- Cultural, linguistic, and religious identity and practices remain strong across the third and fourth generations in the UK.

Further reading

Bowl, R. (2007). The need for change in UK mental health services: South Asian service users' views. *Ethnicity and Health*, 12(1), 1–19.

Crozier, G. & Davies, J. (2007). Hard to reach parents or hard to reach schools? A discussion of home—school relations, with particular reference to Bangladeshi and Pakistani parents. *British Educational Research Journal*, 33(3), 295–313.

Hoque, A. (2017). Third-generation British-Bangladeshis from east London: Complex identities and a culturally responsive pedagogy. *British Journal of Sociology of Education*, 39(2), 182–196.

Kibria, N. (2008). The 'new Islam' and Bangladeshi youth in Britain and the US. *Ethnic and Racial Studies*, 31(2), 243-266.

Rahman, M. & Azim, F. (2015). Bangladeshi migrant parents' involvement in their children's schooling: Identifying the barriers. *International Journal of Education and Applied Sciences Research*, 2, 36–47.

References

Adams, G., Fryberg, S. A., Garcia, D. M. & Delgado-Torres, E. U. (2006). The psychology of engagement with indigenous identities: A cultural perspective. *Cultural Diversity and Ethnic Minority Psychology*, 12(3), 493.

Ahmed, N. (2005). Women in between: The case of Bangladeshi women living in London. In M. Thapan (Ed.) *Transnational migration and the politics of identity*, Sage, pp. 99–129.

Ahmed, N. (2008). Language, gender and citizenship: Obstacles in the path to learning English for Bangladeshi women in London's east end. *Sociological Research Online*, 13(5), 77–90.

Ahmed, N. (2016). *Family, citizenship and Islam: The changing experiences of migrant women ageing in London*. Routledge.

All Party Parliamentary Group of British Muslims (APPG). (2018). *Islamophobia Defined: the inquiry into a working definition of Islamophobia*. https://static1.squarespace.com/static/599c3d2febbd1a90cffdd8a9/t/5bfd1ea3352f531a6170ceee/1543315109493/Islamophobia+Defined.pdf

Arbona, C. & Jimenez, C. (2014). Minority stress, ethnic identity, and depression among Latino/a college students. *Journal of Counselling Psychology*, 61(1), 162.

Au, K. H. (1993). *Literacy instruction in multicultural settings*. Wadsworth Publishing Company.

Beck, A. & Naz, S. (2019). The need for service change and community outreach work to support trans-cultural cognitive behaviour therapy with Black and Minority Ethnic communities. *The Cognitive Behaviour Therapist*, 12(1), 1–10.

Blakemore, S. J. (2019). Adolescence and mental health. *The lancet*, 393(10185), 2030–2031.

Bhui, K., Stansfeld, S., Hull, S., Priebe, S., Mole, F. & Feder, G. (2003). Ethnic variations in pathways to and use of specialist mental health services in the UK: Systematic review. *The British Journal of Psychiatry*, 182(2), 105–116.

Bhui, K., Khatib, Y., Viner, R., Klineberg, E., Clark, C., Head, J. & Stansfeld, S. (2008). Cultural identity, clothing and common mental disorder: A prospective school- based study of white British and Bangladeshi adolescents. *Journal of Epidemiology and Community Health*, 62(5), 435–441.

Biggart, A., O'Hare, L. & Connolly, P. (2013). A need to belong? The prevalence of experiences of belonging and exclusion in school among minority ethnic children living in the 'White hinterlands'. *Irish Educational Studies*, 32(2), 179–195.

Bowl, R., 2007. The need for change in UK mental health services: South Asian service users' views. *Ethnicity and Health*, 12(1), 1–19.

Brøndbo, P. H., Mathiassen, B., Martinussen, M., Heiervang, E., Eriksen, M., Moe, T. F. & Kvernmo, S. (2011). The strengths and difficulties questionnaire as a screening instrument for Norwegian child and adolescent mental health services, application of UK scoring algorithms. *Child and Adolescent Psychiatry and Mental Health*, 5(1), 32.

Cheng, H. L., Lin, S. P. & Cha, C. H. (2015). Perceived discrimination, intergenerational family conflicts, and depressive symptoms in foreign-born and US-born Asian American emerging adults. *Asian American Journal of Psychology*, 6(2), 107.

Connolly, P. & Keenan, M. (2002). Racist Harassment in the White Hinterlands: Minority ethnic children and parents' experiences of schooling in Northern Ireland. *British Journal of Sociology of Education*, 23(3), 341–355.

Cooper, C., Spiers, N., Livingston, G., Jenkins, R., Meltzer, H., Brugha, T., ... & Bebbington, P. (2013). Ethnic inequalities in the use of health services for common mental disorders in England. *Social Psychiatry and Psychiatric Epidemiology*, 48(5), 685–692.

Crozier, G. (2009). South Asian parents' aspirations versus teachers' expectations in the United Kingdom. *Theory Into Practice*, 48(4), 290–296.

Crozier, G. & Davies, J. (2007). Hard to reach parents or hard to reach schools? A discussion of home—school relations, with particular reference to Bangladeshi and Pakistani parents. *British Educational Research Journal*, 33(3), 295–313.

Dabbagh, N., Johnson, S., King, M. & Blizard, R. (2012). Muslim adolescent mental health in the UK: An exploratory cross-sectional school survey. *International Journal of Culture and Mental Health*, 5(3), 202–218.

Dorling, D. & Tomlinson, S. (2019). *Rule Britannia: Brexit and the End of Empire*. Biteback Publishing.

Every, D. & Perry, R. (2014). The relationship between perceived religious discrimination and self-esteem for Muslim Australians. *Australian Journal of Psychology*, 66(4), 241–248.

Furnham, A. & Adam-Saib, S. (2001). Abnormal eating attitudes and behaviours and perceived parental control: A study of white British and British-Asian school girls. *Social Psychiatry and Psychiatric Epidemiology*, 36(9), 462–470.

Gardner, K. (1995). *Global migrants, local lives: Travel and transformation in rural Bangladesh: Travel and transformation in rural Bangladesh*. Clarendon Press.

Gardner, K. (2009). Lives in motion: The life-course, movement and migration in Bangladesh. *Journal of south Asian development*, 4(2), 229–251.

Ghosh, A. (2006). *Power in print: Popular publishing and the politics of language and culture in a colonial society, 1778–1905*. Oxford University Press.

Goodfellow, M. (2018). *Race' and Racism in the UK. in* McFarlane, L. (ed.) *New Thinking for the British Economy*. Open Democracy. UK

Goodman, A. & Gregg, P. (Eds.). (2010). *Poorer children's educational attainment: How important are attitudes and behaviour?* (pp. 76–92). Joseph Rowntree Foundation.

Goodman, A., Patel, V. & Leon, D. A. (2008). Child mental health differences amongst ethnic groups in Britain: A systematic review. *BMC Public Health*, 8(1), 1–11.

Han, M. & Lee, M. (2011). Risk and protective factors contributing to depressive symptoms in Vietnamese American college students. *Journal of College Student Development*, 52(2), 154–166.

Hassan, M. (2020). *The relationship between Bangladeshi immigrant parents and their children in Portugal: Focus on education and sociability aspect* (Doctoral dissertation).

Hoque, A. (2017). Third-generation British-Bangladeshis from east London: Complex identities and a culturally responsive pedagogy. *British Journal of Sociology of Education*, 39(2), 182–196.

Houghton, L. C., Troisi, R., Sommer, M., Katki, H. A., Booth, M., Choudhury, O. A. & Hampshire, K. R. (2020). "I'm not a freshi": Culture shock, puberty and growing up as British-Bangladeshi girls. *Social Science & Medicine*, 258, 113058.

Islam, Z., Rabiee, F. & Singh, S. P. (2015). Black and minority ethnic groups' perception and experience of early intervention in psychosis services in the United Kingdom. *Journal of Cross-cultural Psychology*, 46(5), 737–753.

Jasperse, M., Ward, C., & Jose, P. E. (2012). Identity, perceived religious discrimination, and psychological well-being in Muslim immigrant women. *Applied Psychology*, 61(2), 250–271.

Khan, H. (2018). *'Mrs Bibi Syndrome', the medical stereotype undermining elderly Asian women*. Media Diversified. Retrieved on February 28, 2021, from https://mediadiversified.org/2018/09/14/mrs-bibi-syndrome-the-medical-stereotype-undermining-elderly-asian-women/

Kibria, N. (2008). The 'new Islam' and Bangladeshi youth in Britain and the US. *Ethnic and Racial Studies*, 31(2), 243–266.

Kulis, S., Marsiglia, F. F., Sicotte, D. & Nieri, T. (2007). Neighborhood effects on youth substance use in a southwestern city. *Sociological Perspectives*, 50(2), 273–301.

Lander, V. (2011). Race, culture and all that: An exploration of the perspectives of White secondary student teachers about race equality issues in their initial teacher education. *Race Ethnicity and Education*, *14*(3), 351–364.

Lee, Y. M. (2007). The immigration experience among elderly Korean immigrants. *Journal of Psychiatric and Mental Health Nursing*, 14(4), 403–410.

Main, G. & Bradshaw, J. (2016). Child poverty in the UK: Measures, prevalence and intra-household sharing. *Critical Social Policy*, *36*(1), 38–61.

Maynard, M. J. & Harding, S. (2010). Ethnic differences in psychological well-being in adolescence in the context of time spent in family activities. *Social Psychiatry and Psychiatric Epidemiology*, *45*(1), 115–123.

Mazhar, F. (2008). Language, ecology and knowledge practice, *The New Age*, 21 February. Dhaka.

Memon, A., Taylor, K., Mohebati, L. M., Sundin, J., Cooper, M., Scanlon, T. & de Visser, R. (2016). Perceived barriers to accessing mental health services among black and minority ethnic (BME) communities: A qualitative study in Southeast England. *BMJ Open*, 6(11), 1–9.

Miranda, R., Polanco-Roman, L., Tsypes, A. & Valderrama, J. (2013). Perceived discrimination, ruminative subtypes, and risk for depressive symptoms in emerging adulthood. *Cultural Diversity and Ethnic Minority Psychology*, 19(4), 395.

Nadal, K. L., Griffin, K. E., Wong, Y., Hamit, S. & Rasmus, M. (2014). The impact of racial microaggressions on mental health: Counseling implications for clients of color. *Journal of Counseling & Development*, 92(1), 57–66.

NIMH National Institute of Mental Health. (2013). Transforming the understanding and treatment of mental illness through research.

http://www.nimh.nih.gov/health/publications/the-numbers-count-mental-disorders-in-america/index.shtml.

Polanco-Roman, L. & Miranda, R. (2013). Culturally related stress, hopelessness, and vulnerability to depressive symptoms and suicidal ideation in emerging adulthood. *Behavior Therapy*, 44(1), 75–87.

Putnam, R. (1993). The prosperous community: Social capital and public life. *The American prospect*, 13(Spring), Vol. 4. Available online: http://www. prospect. org/print/vol/13 (accessed 7 April 2003).

Rahman, M. & Azim, F. (2015). Bangladeshi migrant parents' involvement in their children's schooling: Identifying the barriers. *International Journal of Education and Applied Sciences Research*, 2, 36–47.

Rippy, A. E. & Newman, E. (2006). Perceived religious discrimination and its relationship to anxiety and paranoia among Muslim Americans. *Journal of Muslim Mental Health*, 1(1), 5–20.

Roberts, R. E., Attkisson, C. C. & Rosenblatt, A. (1998). Prevalence of psychopathology among children and adolescents. *American Journal of Psychiatry*, 155(6), 715–725.

Rothon, C., Goodwin, L. & Stansfeld, S. (2012). Family social support, community "social capital" and adolescents' mental health and educational outcomes: A longitudinal study in England. *Social Psychiatry and Psychiatric Epidemiology*, 47(5), 697–709.

Shain, F. (2021). Navigating the unequal education space in post-9/11 England: British Muslim girls talk about their educational aspirations and future expectations. *Educational Philosophy and Theory*, 53(3), 270–287.

Sian, K. P. (2015). Spies, surveillance and stakeouts: Monitoring Muslim moves in British state schools. *Race Ethnicity and Education*, 18(2), 183–201.

Stevenson, J., Demack, S., Stiell, B., Abdi, M., Ghaffar, F. & Hassan, S. (2017). *The social mobility challenges faced by young Muslims*. Social Mobility Commission.

Strand, S., de Coulon, A., Meschi, E., Vorhaus, J., Frumkin, L., Ivins, C.,... & Rehman, H. (2010). *Drivers and challenges in raising the achievement of pupils from Bangladeshi, Somali and Turkish backgrounds*. DCSF.

Umaña-Taylor, A. J. & Updegraff, K. A. (2007). Latino adolescents' mental health: Exploring the interrelations among discrimination, ethnic identity, cultural orientation, self-esteem, and depressive symptoms. *Journal of Adolescence*, 30(4), 549–567.

Walters, S. (2007). How do you know that he's bright but lazy? Teachers' assessments of Bangladeshi English as an additional language pupils in two year three classrooms. *Oxford Review of Education*, 33(1), 87–101.

Willen, S. S. (2007). Toward a critical phenomenology of "illegality": State power, criminalization, and abjectivity among undocumented migrant workers in Tel Aviv, Israel. *International Migration*, 45(3), 8–38.

Williams, T. (2017). *Triple threat: Being a black muslim woman in the UK [Blog]*. Retrieved on February 28, 2021, from https://blackballad.co.uk/views- voices/ triple-threat-being-a-black-muslim-woman-in-the-uk

Ying, Y. W. & Han, M. (2007). Familism and mental health: Variation between Asian American children of refugees and immigrants. *International Journal of Applied Psychoanalytic Studies*, 4(4), 333–348.

4 Gypsy, Roma, and Traveller Pupils and Mental Wellbeing

Martin Myers

Synopsis

Gypsy, Roma, and Traveller[1] (GRT) communities suffer some of the worst health outcomes in the UK including low levels of life expectancy, high rates of infant mortality, and a high prevalence of chronic health conditions (McFadden et al., 2018; NHS, 2020). Less widely understood outside of GRT communities has been the prevalence of mental health issues, including anxiety, stress, and levels of suicide seven times that for the wider population amongst GRT men (Sweeney & Dolling, 2020). Young GRT people are often ill-equipped to deal with mental health challenges as within communities there has been a reluctance to talk about mental health. This is all the more problematic as GRT communities experience the very social conditions that exacerbate mental health issues, including poor and insecure accommodation, higher incidences of family bereavement and trauma, and higher rates of imprisonment (Cemlyn et al., 2009; HoC, 2019). Other specific circumstances including the exclusion of GRT identifying as LGBTQ+ has similarly exacerbated many young people's problems. Recently, there has been a concerted drive by GRT community and advocacy groups to promote accessible healthcare messages throughout their communities and in particular to younger community members. Schools also have an important role to play in delivering these messages. However, relationships between schools and GRT families are often shaped by misunderstandings about GRT culture, and this does result in teachers not always addressing pupil's needs (Bhopal & Myers, 2009; Hamilton, 2018). This chapter explores mental health issues within GRT communities and situates these within the community and social structures that have made this such a devastating area of daily life. It will then explore how schools can support young GRT people better in the future.

DOI: 10.4324/9781003160526-4

Background

Gypsies, Roma, and Travellers in the UK

Gypsies, Roma, and Travellers are distinct ethnic groups of people who have lived in all parts of the UK for over 500 years. This chapter discusses some of the social, political, and historical backgrounds that shape GRT lives before focusing on the impact of mental health and wellbeing on GRT groups and pupils in schools. Despite using GRT as a catch-all category for people who often share ethnic backgrounds, characteristics, and heritage, GRT is not a homogeneous category and there are significant differences within and between different groups of people.

One overarching similarity shared by most GRT people is the regular experience of racism towards their communities (Myers et al., 2010; HoC, 2019). These include populist stereotypes that GRTs are invariably criminals, vagrants, and unclean. These are not new stereotypes but rather they are a common currency prevalent for generations (Myers, 2018). The same stereotypes were included in the very first piece of legislation to directly target Gypsies in the UK. The Egyptians Act passed in the reign of Henry VIII identified Gypsy identity in terms of criminality, vagrancy, and dirtiness and required them to renounce their identity or face an escalating punitive regime from losing property rights, through deportation and, finally, the death sentence (Myers, 2019). Neither the Egyptians Act nor the other major building blocks of GRT history feature in the history curriculum. Consequently, there is little public recognition that GRT groups migrated from the North of India to Europe in the early Middle Ages; that they were often enslaved in Europe throughout the 19th and early 20th century; and that hundreds of thousands of Gypsies were exterminated in the Nazi holocaust (Myers, 2019; Spielhaus et al., 2020).

In Britain today, despite the enactment of policies such as the Equality Act 2010, it is widely acknowledged that GRT groups experience daily racism in all aspects of their daily lives (Cemlyn et al., 2008; Myers, 2018; Cromarty, 2019). In terms of the provision of social services, GRT communities are consistently identified as suffering a range of inequalities. Access to healthcare and poor health outcomes, access to schooling and poor educational outcomes, and access to good quality accommodation have all been acknowledged as longstanding failings of UK social policy (Myers et al., 2010; Bhopal & Myers, 2016; Cromarty, 2019). These failings generally sit together as a pattern of discriminatory behaviours that reflect structural racism within schools, healthcare providers, local authorities, and other state institutions, but they also reflect the widely held racist beliefs about GRTs in the UK. It is important to take a holistic view of how these discriminatory factors interlink. One factor that directly causes poor health outcomes and poor educational outcomes is the unacceptable levels of provision of accommodation available to many GRT families (Myers, 2018; HoC, 2019). A key driver of poor accommodation for GRT families has been the success of many local communities to campaign, with the support of their political representatives from all sides of the political spectrum, against the provision of new Traveller sites in their neighbourhoods. Poor social provision is often a direct reflection of public prejudice and not just a nebulous failing of an inept government or ill-informed policy. Cemlyn et al. note the multiple damaging effects this has on GRTs:

> A history of mistrust and suspicion between Gypsies and Travellers and authorities, arising from a history of institutionalised prejudice and mistreatment means that developing mutually beneficial relationships of trust and positive communication can sometimes be challenging.
>
> (Cemlyn et al., 2009 p. 4)

Gypsy, Roma, and Traveller communities and school

Such mistrust has been a feature of the relationship between many GRT families and schools. One notable success driven by policymakers has been the steep increase in school attendance. In 1967, the Plowden Report identified Gypsy children as "the most deprived in the country" and estimated only 4% of GRT children attended schools. By the 1990s, this figure had risen to around 70%, in large part reflecting the work of the Traveller Education Services (TES).[2] The TES were notable for approaching the problems GRT families faced while accessing education from a holistic perspective. In addition to working with schools, they acted as advocates for families using their resources to address accommodation problems or negotiate access to healthcare. TES officers often had close personal connections with families and also worked from the position of understanding GRT culture and the pressures under which many families lived. The success of such an approach, based on an understanding of both GRT culture and their experiences of discrimination, would be beneficial in classrooms to understand GRT pupils experiences of mental health.

Whilst the numbers of GRT children attending schools have increased, GRT children are still the group most likely to experience the worst educational outcomes amongst all ethnic groups (Cromarty, 2019). In 2020, Gypsy and Traveller children were still less likely than other children to attend school, more likely than any other ethnic group to be excluded from school, and have worst outcomes in terms of exam achievement and progression into higher education. It is worth noting that these educational outcomes are a backdrop to pupils' own mental health experiences but also relate to wider health issues within communities due to the poor provision of social care cuts across different services.

Unofficial exclusions or 'off-rolling' is the practice of schools persuading certain pupils they would be better suited to home education. Although off-rolling has only recently become a public issue, it is a practice that many GRT families have encountered for decades. Schools often explain GRT pupils' absence from school because they are nomadic and have 'moved on' (Bhopal & Myers, 2018; Myers, 2018). However, the majority of GRT families live in brick-and-mortar housing or on fixed Traveller sites, and their children are unlikely to move from place to place at short notice. Families are more likely to choose settled accommodation so that their children can access stable and secure education in one locality. If anything, for families who are mobile, the prospect of accessing education for their children is often a specific reason for choosing more settled accommodation.

As discussed previously, access to accommodation is often difficult for GRT communities because of public and political discourse which fails to address accommodation shortages. The impact of this failure of policy making includes significant educational and healthcare inequalities. In 2015, the DCLG (Department for Communities and Local Government) introduced planning policy that made it increasingly difficult for Gypsies to build new Traveller sites on land they owned. The policy defined GRT ethnicity as related to their mobility and nomadism; however, most GRT families are no longer nomadic (a fact readily identified in the House of Commons briefing paper (Cromarty, 2019) cited above). One consequence of this policy was that it increased the likelihood of GRT families being evicted from land they owned and made homeless. Being homeless, like other forms of insecurity, is a significant factor in undermining families' access to education and other social provision such as healthcare. It also has damaging consequences for families' mental health.

In the classroom, it is useful for teachers to understand the dynamics of GRT families' issues around securing accommodation. Firstly, to understand the pressure that evictions cause pupils is important because it will impact their educational performance and mental health. Secondly to acknowledge that such pupils are experiencing multiple inequalities, when they are made homeless, that sit within the broader patterns of racism that affect their lives. When GRT pupils have been made homeless, it is not necessarily an indication that they are nomadic or mobile but that they no longer have access to their home. Making such holistic judgements about GRT pupils and framing them from the perspective of those pupils is one of the most helpful ways teachers can work with GRT pupils. It is also one of the most helpful ways they can understand how mental health impacts on pupils' lives.

Mental and physical health outcomes

The NHS identifies that 'Gypsy, Roma, and Traveller communities experience some of the poorest health outcomes' of all people living in the UK (NHS, 2020). These include significantly lower life expectancy; higher maternal and infant mortality; higher incidence of accidental injury and infections amongst children; high rates of accident and emergency attendance; low uptake of childhood immunisations and consequent increasing risk of preventable disease; and poor dental health. A wide range of factors contribute to poorer health outcomes many of which relate to structural inequalities. Many GRT families live in poor accommodation, including poorly maintained local authority Traveller sites situated in inaccessible locations, and many others are effectively homeless as a consequence of discriminatory planning policies (Myers, 2018). In addition, poor educational outcomes, social exclusion, and discrimination encountered when accessing health services have been identified as directly contributing to poor health (McFadden et al., 2018). Whilst problems of accessing healthcare are often contextualised as being a consequence of GRT 'mobility' or nomadism this obscures the reality that most GRT families are not nomadic. As in the case of children absent from school, the suggestion of mobility often provides a smokescreen for service providers to explain poor outcomes (Myers, 2018). There is evidence of social service agencies relying on charitable agencies to assume the responsibility for working with GRTs citing their expertise; this offloading of casework has been identified when dealing with mental health issues.

Whilst the NHS is explicit in identifying worse health outcomes for GRTs than the population at large, it is largely silent on issues surrounding mental health. In 2019, the House of Commons Women and Equalities Committee highlighted the problems faced by GRTs when accessing mental health services and recommended the need for increased long-term funding (HoC, 2019). The Women and Equalities Committee drew upon the limited research that had been conducted around GRT and mental health and gathered evidence from a range of GRT advocacy groups including Friends, Families, and Travellers and The Traveller Movement. These identified a number of disturbing trends that together indicate the seriousness of mental health for many different GRT communities.

Comparisons between the general population and GRTs indicate there are much higher levels of poor mental health. GRT people are more than twice as likely to experience depression and three times more likely to suffer from anxiety (HoC, 2019). Suicide rates amongst GRT communities are extremely high. In particular, GRT men are seven times more likely to commit suicide than other men with a study in Ireland finding that suicide accounted for 11% of Traveller deaths (AITHS, 2010). Within GRT communities, the disproportionately high numbers of GRTs serving custodial prison sentences are at greater risk of suicide (Traveller Movement, 2019a). HM Inspectorate of Prisons found that 27% of GRT prisoners experienced mental health problems compared to 13% of the wider prison population (PPO, 2015). Young GRT boys are also disproportionately more likely to be sent to Young Offenders institutions. Those GRT groups who openly identify as LGBTQ+ are also at a high risk of mental health and suicide (Traveller Movement, 2019a). They often find their sexuality is incompatible with the religious and heteronormative culture of GRT communities causing them to be ostracised by both family and community.

Experiences of discrimination

To understand the causes of such high prevalence of mental health issues, it is important to relate this to the broader patterns of discrimination described above. GRT lives are often characterised by insecurity around their accommodation and poor access to healthcare. GRT pupils often find the experience of attending school difficult and traumatic with little recognition of their culture in the curriculum and very poor understandings of the issues affecting their lives. Discrimination and prejudice towards GRTs has been described as the "last acceptable form of racism" (Traveller Movement, 2017; HoC, 2019) highlighting how much of the British population may be complicit in such racist beliefs. Unfortunately, this includes pupils and teachers in schools, and this has a damaging effect on the mental health of GRT pupils. The impact of these structural inequalities is regularly exacerbated by racist hate crimes directed towards GRTs and "the persistent grinding and demoralising effect of hate crime/hate speech and discriminatory representations" (Greenfields & Rogers, 2020 p. 15). These have all shown to be directly associated with stress, anxiety, depression, PTSD, self-harm, and suicide.

Within many GRT communities, mental health carries stigmatising connotations of madness and commonly used healthcare terms such as 'anxiety' or 'stress' are often not readily understood (Matthews, 2008). School initiatives to educate young people about mental healthcare are likely to be less effective for GRT pupils due to high rates of school exclusions (Wilkin & Derrington, 2010; HoC, 2019). Pupils missing out on health education is also more likely to impact young GRT men who are more likely to leave school at an earlier age to start work (Myers et al., 2010).

There is also evidence to suggest that many family members, including pupils, experience multiple bereavements within their families (Rogers & Greenfields, 2017; NHS, 2020). This is partly a direct consequence of factors such as the overall poor health of GRTs. Rogers and Greenfield highlight how many GRT bereavements result from illnesses where the expectation amongst the general UK population would be that mortality was preventable. They also demonstrate how many bereavements are "sudden, unexpected and often traumatic, with high numbers of road traffic accidents, suicide and infant and childhood deaths" (2017, p. 97). For communities who often survive within hostile marginalised environments by maintaining tightly knit family bonds, with family members often living and working together, the impact of such losses can be devastating. Within GRT communities, the expressions of extended grief that are often considered normal are interpreted as 'pathological' or 'complicated grief' that requires treatment in a healthcare context (Shear et al., 2011; Rogers & Greenfields, 2017). Within GRT communities, the normalisation of extended grief is often believed to represent individuals or families coping with their loss. Many GRT pupils are likely to have encountered bereavements within their families and also experienced the very deep collectively felt impact of such loss. They are often ill-equipped at a young age and without wider support to deal well with their losses.

Other characteristics of GRT culture, often shaped by their marginalised status in society, also contribute to poor mental health. For GRT men and boys in particular, gendered roles and expectations often assume that they need to always present an image of being strong, in control and providing for their families (FFT, 2019). This often makes it difficult for GRT men to acknowledge or recognise they are suffering from mental health issues including depression, stress, and anxiety. By doing so, they may feel they are letting their families down. They are however often very susceptible to such problems not least because of the burdens they shoulder when faced with resolving insecurities in providing for their families. These include finding decent accommodation and generating regular income. Many GRT men choose self-employment and at times when it is difficult to generate work, or when the marginalised status of GRTs makes it difficult to secure work, this is often perceived as a personal failing to provide for the family.

In summary, GRTs experience racism and marginalisation in many aspects of their lives. This contributes to their likelihood of experiencing poorer mental health outcomes because of the difficulties they face. The same forms of marginalisation also tend to restrict access to healthcare services that might be able to offer solutions to poor mental health.

What can teachers do?

For teachers, the prevalence of mental health problems facing GRT pupils may not be as apparent or as approachable a subject as for other pupils in their classrooms. The main approach recommended from this chapter is that teachers should make themselves more aware of the issues and the background to what are often complex problems. There is a plethora of evidence which shows that GRT pupils do not feel their needs are met in schools. This reflects a wide range of longstanding problems that need to be understood individually and holistically. Mental health issues, both those of individual pupils and their experiences of mental health issues amongst family and friends are not isolated issues.

One practical measure which may have an impact on improving the mental health of GRT pupils is to acknowledge and address the discrimination they experience in schools. GRT pupils do experience racism and bullying in schools from other pupils, from parents, and from teachers; GRT culture is missing almost entirely in the curriculum and is rarely acknowledged or celebrated by schools; too many GRT children are excluded permanently from schools; and too many GRT pupils do not achieve satisfactory exam results which would help them progress to university. To be clear, these experiences form a backdrop to understanding about mental health and the racism that characterises GRT health outcomes. They are symptomatic of the racism GRT pupils experience in all aspects of their lives beyond the school gates. As teachers, it is important to think about how some of these issues can be addressed and how pupils can gain the most value from their educational experiences. In this respect, it is not an expectation that it is the role of teachers to change the world but rather that they contribute to some change. Small steps such as acknowledging the devastation of the Nazi holocaust on GRT lives in a history lesson or using accounts of hate crimes towards GRT families in a debate on what modern-day Britain looks like are small steps towards recognising GRT lives more clearly.

Of all the detrimental experiences faced by GRT pupils in schools, those of racism and bullying are the most consistently identified. These reflect the endemic racism encountered by many GRT outside the school gates. Unfortunately, some teachers also share the same racist attitudes, and this contributes to racism in schools going unaddressed. For GRT pupils, there is a direct correlation between experiencing racism or being bullied and feelings of anxiety, stress, and depression. If a GRT pupil feels unable to discuss these feelings, in school or at home, this will make their life much harder. It may be that at home it is difficult, particularly for young GRT men who feel they have to maintain an image of individual strength, to discuss mental health issues. If, at the same time, the school allows racism or bullying to persist, that leaves these young men with few options. They may feel it is better and easier not to attend school. As teachers, it is important to think about the reasons why GRT children are identified as 'others' and why the same racist tropes that were prevalent in Henry VIII's day maintain their resonance in schools today. These should be challenged, particularly when such views are held by senior school leaders.

Discussions about mental health in the classroom will often be framed within the context of mental health having become a normalised topic of conversation compared to 10 or 20 years ago. There may be an expectation that many pupils feel more comfortable to talk about mental health. In some quarters, it has even been suggested mental health issues have become trendy or glamourised. Not all GRT pupils fall within these expectations of how mental health is understood. Many GRT advocacy organisations and charities have made exceptional efforts to address mental health and foster conversations about mental health problems amongst different communities and different sections of those communities (Traveller Movement, 2019b). These are often led by younger GRT men and women. However, in classrooms, GRT pupils may be less comfortable with open discussions about mental health because of their own engagement with family culture. Often pupils feel torn by the contrary demands and expectations of what constitutes normative behaviours for school pupils and the expectations of their families. It would be unhelpful to exacerbate these very complicated personal dynamics by assuming the whole school approach to addressing mental health was necessarily the best for GRT pupils. GRT pupils may associate the school environment with the broader marginalisation and discrimination of GRT groups and not feel the school is a safe environment to discuss issues that affect them. This does not preclude having conversations with GRT pupils about mental health (their own or others), rather it is to suggest that getting to know pupils, their circumstances, and their perceptions of the world they live in, might be a better starting point.

Takeaway points

■ GRT groups have been British citizens for over 600 years. They have consistently been portrayed within a range of misrepresentative racist stereotypes including criminality, vagrancy, and dirtiness. One consequence has been their marginalisation throughout society. GRT pupils entering classrooms bear the burden of this history; they know that many pupils and teachers share those racist beliefs about them and their families.

■ Mental health issues are prevalent across all parts of GRT communities, and many pupils will experience individual problems and be affected by its impact on other family members. Supporting such pupils includes not just being aware of their individual needs but also understanding the broader social conditions that shape GRT pupils' lives.

■ GRTs experience some of the worst health outcomes of any group in the UK. This includes high mortality rates for illnesses that are often regarded as preventable in the wider population, high incidence of infant mortality, traumatic or violent deaths such as road traffic accidents, and suicides. Collective grief in response to these deaths can often be very deeply expressed throughout communities and families.

■ GRT pupils may not share the same attitudes and understandings of mental health as other pupils. It may be a more difficult subject for some GRT pupils, particularly young men, because they feel acknowledging mental health issues is a weakness.

■ Some GRT pupils may find particular aspects of their own identity are in conflict with their family's expectations and community values. Some LGBTQ+ GRT pupils may be scared their sexuality would not be accepted by other GRTs. However, this is changing and many more GRT young people do identify their sexuality openly.

Notes

1 Gypsies, Roma and Travellers or GRT is used in this chapter to reflect nomenclature used within official UK data collection and are also terms that would be recognised within the protected characteristic of 'race' in the Equality Act 2010. It should be noted that this collective grouping tends to obscure the individual differences between many different groups of people and how they identify themselves.
2 The Traveller Education Service was introduced in the 1970s to provide support for nomadic families. They were largely phased out following the 2010 Coalition government decision to cut funding.

Further reading

Online resources
The Traveller Movement https://travellermovement.org.uk/
Friends, Families, and Travellers https://www.gypsy-traveller.org/
Pavee Point https://www.paveepoint.ie/
Roma Support Group https://www.romasupportgroup.org.uk/
Texts and academic sources
Bhopal, K., and Myers, M. (2008). *Insiders, outsiders and others: Gypsies and identity*. Hatfield: University of Hertfordshire Press.
Greenfields, M. (2017). 'Good practice in working with Gypsy, Traveller and Roma communities', *Primary Health Care*, 27(10), 24–29.

Law, I., and Kovats, M. (2018). *Rethinking Roma. Identities, politicisation and new agendas–mapping global racism.* London: Palgrave MacMillan.

References

AITHS. (2010). *All Ireland traveller health study: Summary of findings.* Dublin: UCD.

Bhopal, K., and Myers, M. (2009). 'Gypsy, Roma and Traveller pupils in schools in the UK: Inclusion and 'good practice'', *International Journal of Inclusive Education*, *13*(3), 299–314.

Bhopal, K., and Myers, M. (2016). 'Marginal groups in marginal times: Gypsy and Traveller parents and home education in England, UK', *British Educational Research Journal*, 42(1), 5–20.

Bhopal, K., and Myers, M. (2018). *Home schooling and home education: Race, class and inequality.* London: Routledge.

Cemlyn, S., Greenfields, M., Burnett, S., Matthews, Z., and Whitwell, C. (2009). *Inequalities experienced by Gypsy and Traveller communities: A review. Equalities and Human Rights Commission Research Report 12.* Manchester, UK: Equalities and Human Rights Commission.

Cromarty, H. (2019). *Gypsies and Travellers house of commons briefing paper 08083.* London: House of Commons.

Equality Act. (2010). London: HMSO. https://www.legislation.gov.uk/ukpga/2010/15/contents accessed 02.02.21

Friends, Families and Travellers (FFT) (2017). *Lack of increase in Affordable Pitches for Gypsies and Travellers in England.* https://www.gypsy-traveller.org/wp-content/uploads/2017/12/Lack-of-increase-in-affordable-pitches-report-Dec-2017-FINAL.pdf

Greenfields, M., and Rogers, C. (2020). *Hate: "As regular as rain" A pilot research project into the psychological effects of hate crime on Gypsy, Traveller and Roma (GTR) communities.* London: Ministry of Housing, Communities and Local Government.

Hamilton, P. (2018). 'Engaging Gypsy and Traveller pupils in secondary education in Wales: Tensions and dilemmas of addressing difference', *International Studies in Sociology of Education*, 27(1), 4–22.

House of Commons (HoC). (2019). *Tackling inequalities faced by Gypsy, Roma and Traveller communities.* HC 360. London: HoC.

Matthews, Z. (2008). *The health of Gypsies and Travellers in the UK.* London: Race Equality Foundation.

McFadden, A., Siebelt, L., Jackson, C., Jones, H., Innes, N., MacGillivray, S., Bell, K., Corbacho, B., Gavine, A., Haggi, H. M. and Atkin, K. (2018). *Enhancing Gypsy, Roma and Traveller peoples' trust.* University of Dundee. https://doi.org/10.20933/100001117 accessed: 06.05.21

Myers, M. (2018). 'Gypsy students in the UK: The impact of 'mobility 'on education', *Race Ethnicity and Education*, *21*(3), 353–369.

Myers, M. (2019). 'Gypsies, mobilities, and schools in the United Kingdom'. In *Oxford research encyclopaedia of education.* https://doi.org/10.1093/acrefore/9780190264093.013.854 accessed: 05.02.21

Myers, M., McGhee, D., and Bhopal, K. (2010). 'At the crossroads: Gypsy and Traveller parents' perceptions of education, protection and social change', *Race Ethnicity and Education*, 13(4), 533–548.

NHS. (2020). *Improving uptake and delivery of health services to reduce health inequalities experienced by Gypsy, Roma, and Traveller people.* https://www.england.nhs.uk/ltphimenu/improving-access/improving-uptake-and-delivery-of-health-services-to-reduce-health-inequalities-experienced-by-gypsy-roma-and-traveller-people/ accessed: 05.02.21.

PPO (Prisons and Probation Ombudsman for England and Wales). (2015). *Deaths of Traveller in prisons.* http://www.ppo.gov.uk/app/uploads/2015/01/PPO_LLB_FII7_Final.pdf accessed 30.01.20.

Plowden Report. (1967). *Children and their primary schools: A report of the Central Advisory Council for Education (England).* London: HMSO.

Rogers, C. and Greenfields, M. (2017). 'Hidden losses and 'forgotten'suffering: the bereavement experiences of British Romany Gypsies and Travellers', *Bereavement Care*, 36(3), 94–102.

Shear, M. K., Simon, N., Wall, M., Zisook, S., Neimeyer, R., Duan, N.,... Keshaviah, A. (2011). 'Complicated grief and related bereavement issues for DSM-5', *Depression and Anxiety*, 28(2), 103–117.

Spielhaus, R., Szakács-Behling, S., Ailincai, A., Hopson, V., and Pecak, M. (2020*). The representation of Roma in European curricula and textbooks. Analytical report.* Strasbourg: Council of Europe.

Sweeney, S., and Dolling, B. (2020). *A research paper: Suicide Prevention in Gypsy and Traveller communities in England.* Brighton: Friends, Families and Travellers.

Traveller Movement. (2017). *The last acceptable face of racism?* London: Traveller Movement.

Traveller Movement. (2019a). *Traveller movement submission to Women and Equalities Committee inquiry into the mental health of men and boys.* London: Traveller Movement.

Traveller Movement. (2019b). *Support for Gypsy, Roma and Traveller LGBT+ people and their families.* London: Traveller Movement.

Wilkin, A. and Derrington, C. (2010). *Improving the outcomes for Gypsy, Roma and Traveller pupils.* https://dera.ioe.ac.uk/860/1/DFE-RR043.pdf

5 British Chinese Pupils' Mental Wellbeing

Bonnie Pang, Lizana Oberholzer, and Winnie Sin Wai Pui

Synopsis

This chapter is jointly written by a researcher, an independent educational consultant, and an English teacher, all of whom care about the wellbeing of British Chinese pupils. Each of these authors brings a wealth of knowledge through research and/or teaching and helps pupils gain insight into everyday challenges and struggles and develop resilience. The authors engage in reflective practice, and the consequent strategies are provided to inform teachers and parents on how to support pupils' needs and promote their wellbeing. The chapter aims to provide a three-dimensional understanding of pupils' experiences through the following: first, a researcher (Bonnie) explores empirical data collected from Chinese supplementary schools that are important social, cultural, and political contexts for British Chinese pupils to develop their linguistic identities and provide a safe space for them to escape from everyday struggles. Next, an independent educational consultant (Winnie) discusses how her work supports British Chinese pupils in coping with the tensions of cultural transition and how these conflicts have an impact on their mental wellbeing. Third, a teacher-practitioner (Lizana) examines her perceptions of, and teaching approaches to, an English classroom of British Chinese pupils, and how her work enables her pupils to manage new learning expectations, while promoting mental wellbeing.

Background

Researchers have long argued that the crude representations of the Chinese as the 'successful ethnic minority' is based on popular Western stereotypes of the Chinese as collectivist, deferent, and conforming to Confucian values, which ignores the specific Chinese British construction of ethnic identity (Parker, 2000). This stereotype is also fuelled by Chinese British pupils' high academic achievement in GCSE results and university entrance numbers (Archer & Francis, 2006). This educational success

 DOI: 10.4324/9781003160526-5

continues beyond compulsory schooling, as more than 60% of these pupils continue higher education (Census, 2011). Thus, the relatively high achievement of many British Chinese pupils signals that they do not constitute or experience any disadvantage and thereby are not requiring any specific attention or resources. However, their social needs, such as mental wellbeing, perhaps are overlooked.

Early in the 1990s, Lau noted that British professionals have been accused of failing to engage Chinese families in the transition process because of their limited understanding of Chinese family values. This meant that Chinese parents "feel their voices are not heard" (Lau, 1997, p. 26). Recently, it has been argued that there is a lack of support for Chinese pupils and families have suffered from double detachment and experienced isolation from both host and home country (Chau & Yu, 2001). When compared to other ethnic groups in the UK, the Chinese have been perceived as the 'minority among minorities', 'quiet', or 'reserved' (Pang, 2021). Often racism against Chinese communities locally and globally occurs without social recognition and without provoking any serious protest (Eng & Han, 2019). Archer and Francis (2005) noted that British Chinese pupils experienced racialised discourses that are based on the dual positionings of them as either "'*geeks*' (high achieving, clever, good at maths, but passive/repressed) or '*tags*' (associated with violence, martial arts, and Triadism)" (pp. 391–392). Living within this intersection of isolation and otherness created by the limited visibility, the British Chinese communities in the UK require more social recognition and support. Yet, even when social recognition is deemed to be favourable, with positive discourses, such as resilience, high achievements, and model minority, this can be, as others have argued, damaging through erasing experiences of racism and racial disadvantage, and thereby perpetuating marginalisation (Pang, 2021).

The effect of marginalisation and racial discrimination on one's mental wellbeing should not be underestimated. For example, Eng and Han (2019) explore the psychic and social conditions of Asian Americans. They argue that the pervasiveness of the 'model minority' stereotype works as an important 'melancholic mechanism' which promotes the erasure and repression of one's identities. It highlights that 'doing well' does not mean 'feeling well'. This effect of 'racial melancholy' is enacted when Asian Americans are forged into an ideal of whiteness that is unattainable and therefore experienced everyday struggles of internal conflicts related to loss, mimicry, ambivalence, sacrifice, and reparation. And the consequences on mental wellbeing could be intergeneration.

> If the losses suffered by first-generation immigrants are not resolved and mourned in the process of assimilation – if libido is not replenished by the investment in new objects, new communities, and new ideals – then the melancholia that ensues can be traumatically passed down to the second generation.
>
> (Eng & Han, 2000, p. 680)

The related racialised constructions of 'model minority' and the 'Chinese takeaway' phenomenon are no longer helpful in understanding the younger generation Chinese, with particularities and differences in their engagement in different kinds of activities across the UK and so further research is needed in this area. Research that has examined overseas Chinese communities' mental wellbeing mainly focused on international student population and is found in university contexts in Australia (e.g. Lu, Dear, Johnston, Wooton & Titov, 2014) and the United States (e.g. Yip, 2005). In view of the current academic landscape, which does not provide an adequate understanding of the situation of British Chinese pupil's mental wellbeing, we aim to offer our everyday experiences and practical advice to teachers conducive to interacting with these pupils while schooling.

Our experiences of working with British Chinese pupils

Bonnie: Building on the academic background described above, I have recently completed a two-year ethnographic[1] research project (supported by a Marie Skłodowska-Curie Fellowship 2019–2020) focused on the health-related experiences of British Chinese pupils in Leeds and Manchester (Pang, 2020, 2021). The research mainly took place within two Chinese supplementary schools over an 18-month period. Previous research has noted that some Chinese children found these spaces enabled them to express playful identities where they can talk more, wear their own clothes, and be 'noisy' and boisterous. However, little is known about the implications of promoting these pupils' wellbeing as they transverse different schooling, home, and community environments associated with identity, social isolation, emotions, cultural values, and learning. The study found that there were a few British Chinese pupils who have received racist comments at dayschools such as 'do you eat dogs?' or 'Ching Chong Chinaman' and these children have learned to manage it by 'turning the table', using similar jokes to put down their white peers or to ignore the comments and pretend they were alright with them. These situations can become worse when a child told their parents about these racist incidents, but the parents are not proficient in English and cannot speak up for the child, and the family could feel helpless. Often, the parents from a different generation and cultural upbringing have different perspectives from their children on career aspirations, leisure activities, and Chinese schooling. It is common to receive comments from children that they did not choose to attend Chinese supplementary schools on weekends, despite valuing the friendship with their Chinese friends. Some families with Chinese takeaway businesses have long working hours and have therefore much less quality time to spend with their children on the weekends. These children are often left on their own spending time above the takeaway shop or are asked to help the family business during leisure time. In contrast, those families whose parents are doctors seem to have more opportunities for outdoor activities and have more adult supervision from parents, grandparents, or au pairs conducive to wellbeing and development.

Next, Winnie, an experienced independent educational consultant draws our attention to the needs of British Chinese pupils, especially those residing in boarding schools, about their experiences of home and schooling environments. This will be followed by Lizana, an English teacher, as she talks about her teaching experiences in managing the pupils' new learning expectations alongside promoting their mental wellbeing.

Winnie: My main role is to guide pupils and parents to settle in as they relocate from their home country to the UK. The British Chinese pupils came from various Chinese cities (e.g. Hong Kong, Macau, Guangzhou), social and cultural backgrounds, and have various life trajectories that impact on their current experiences in the UK. Some pupils are boarders who left their home environment. These pupils often struggle with developing deeper friendships with those pupils born in the UK because of their cultural differences such as relating to the local movies, food, and pop stars. Often these Chinese pupils failed to belong to a friendship group despite putting in an effort to sharing their own cultures with their peers. This scenario is exacerbated when these British Chinese pupils are the minority among the minority (i.e. the only British Chinese person) within the school. The pupils feel that they do not have a platform to express their identities and interests as they find it challenging to anchor themselves with friends in a foreign country. Under peer pressure, some of the pupils disassociate their Chinese identity and pretend to be 'Western-like'. In extreme cases, some British Chinese pupils made friends with their abusers in order to prevent further bullying and to seek protection (Chan, 2010). It is worth noting that these pupils are liable to suffer intrinsic stress as the above behaviours are against their choice but for survival.

These situations can get worse if parents and teachers cannot develop adequate dialogues to alleviate their children's stress and to meet their needs. On the one hand, the children struggle to develop meaningful friendships for support, and on the other hand, their parents often fail to realise the importance of belongingness and engaging in the 'British culture' for their children. For example, parents complained about their daughters wearing short shirts in winter, wearing heavy makeup to school, and changing their career aspirations (e.g. from being a medical doctor to a fashion designer) to be different from traditional familial values. Some Chinese parents have a fixed mindset and believe that if their children get a prestigious job, for instance, being a lawyer or a doctor, they will live a happy life. As these children further develop and digress from their parents' traditional expectations, their parents express guilt and worry if they have made the right decision in spending their life savings for a 'better' education in the UK. The ongoing tensions between Chinese pupils, peers, and parents create a stressful environment for the children, and if unresolved, it could have a negative impact on the children's mental wellbeing and development.

Lizana: As an English teacher, teaching pupils in high attaining schools in England, I am often touched by how British Chinese pupils progress on their learning journeys. They are committed pupils, but often torn between two cultures. At home, they have to step in line with the requirements of their home expectations, and the traditional cultural expectations they had to adhere to, and at school, they have to work on the requirements of the British education system and fit in with their peers. I find that some British Chinese pupils are encouraged at home to engage in their learning and school in a competitive way. For example, some pupils felt that they wanted to focus on their own individual efforts and produce a piece of work reflecting their own abilities, opposed to engaging in group tasks, where they needed to rely on others to contribute. During discussions, my pupils revealed that they are encouraged at home to reflect their best efforts and they are often rewarded for being the best or getting the highest grades. Some pupils have reservations about collaborative tasks as it distracts from what they are expected to do and achieve from the home front. This approach therefore is not always compatible with the educational approaches within their learning environment which encourages collaboration and engagement with others. As an English teacher, I believe schools can teach pupils to learn how to integrate into a more collaborative learning environment, and to adopt a growth mindset approach (Dweck, 2017). Similar to Winnie's experience in working with British Chinese pupils, the tensions between perspectives at home and the classroom can often bring along greater levels of anxiety, and pupils often find themselves at odds with what they are expected to do. In turn, this impacts on the wellbeing of pupils, as they can become too anxious to please parents and teachers and to fit in with their peers (Wei et al., 2013).

When working with pupils between 14 and 16 years old, while preparing them for national examinations, these challenges become even more pronounced (Holmes, 2005). Some Chinese pupils aim and are encouraged to achieve the highest grades and are often in a situation where they have a full day at school, followed by extra-curricular activities, and further tuition when they get home. From conversations with these pupils, it is known that their parents have high expectations of them to make a success of the opportunities they now have in a new country. Pupils were encouraged at home to apply themselves, work tirelessly to achieve their goals, and to strive for a better outcome for themselves and their extended families. Often traditional perspectives, such as family honour, are also drawn on, to remind the children that they need to make their families proud. These children, therefore, exhibited higher levels of anxiety than their local peers, partly due to the drive for perfectionism (Wei et al., 2007).

I also observed that these pupils' characteristics have impacted on how they approached their work, their ability to open up to learning, and to adopt a growth mindset. In subjects like English, for example, which is more cumulative, I believe pupils need to explore a variety of perspectives and viewpoints critically. Pupils often want to know what the 'recipe' is for producing a perfect assignment, or to have a clear sense of what is the 'correct' way to respond to a question. The desire to wanting to get all answers correct could impair pupils from opening up to the key aspects that would help them progress intellectually. I appreciate pupils' drive for being the best; however, I also worry that this could have prevented them from refining their English skills as required. This in turn, in addition to being already anxious and worried, can escalate the situation, which could lead to even higher levels of anxiety among these pupils.

What can teachers do?

Bonnie: Based on my research experiences, I can offer three points for teacher-practitioners when working with British Chinese pupils.

1. Generally, in managing student diversity in schooling, we need to see schools as micro-publics of a racially and ethnically diverse UK. This means as teachers, it

is our responsibility to keep abreast of the socio-political environments locally and globally, which feeds into our everyday interactions with our pupils. With global population shifts, schools need policies and strategies to attend to the interests and needs of diverse student populations.

2. Next, we need to bear in mind that there is diversity within diversity, and therefore we need to be aware that pupils have different forms of adaptations according to their cultural upbringing. One example is that there are many different kinds of familial practices in relation to Chinese families, and this has implications on how teachers discuss aspirations with these pupils, choices, and leisure activities. In addition, pupils recently coming from Hong Kong, China, Singapore, or Taiwan would possibly have very different beliefs and practices.

3. Third, according to the last Census (2011), while most of the British Chinese pupils have been born in the UK, many of their parents are born overseas in East or South East Asia. Taking into account the diverse language and knowledge, these pupils bring with them from their home environment to schooling, teachers need to further reflect on questions such as whose knowledge are schools presenting, and be more sensitive to understanding that not all knowledge presented at schools from the syllabus have been given the same weighting. At appropriate times, teachers need to acknowledge the different ways of living and knowing in the world and sometimes there is no one correct answer to practices and beliefs. In understanding these three broad principles, we can then further explore specific examples from working with British Chinese pupils in everyday schooling.

Winnie: Based on the ongoing tensions, British Chinese pupils face with their peers and parents, I believe helping pupils discover one's core values, as well as strengths and weaknesses, through self-regulated strategies is important for their personal development (YetCheng, Friesen & Adekola, 2019; Pui, 2019). Especially in times of conflicts and expectations imposed by significant others, they will not neglect their own emotions and needs. Self-regulated strategies can support pupils when they need help with managing their emotions, handling frustration, and resisting impulsive behaviour, for instance, when pupils think that their teachers and parents do not understand their needs and feelings. Here, I provide a vignette that illustrates the success of helping a pupil adapt to his new environment through self-regulated strategies:

Wong is a very hard-working and independent pupil. Although he struggled with the English-language learning environment, he remained positive about his learning. Wong valued friendship very much and I could see that he tried hard to establish friendships in order to adapt to the English school culture in a new country. Wong was a popular pupil with a good academic record in Hong Kong. At the very beginning, Wong thought that he could try to do something that his peers liked in order to be part of the friendship circle. Wong even pushed himself to do some things he did not like, for example, joining the school football team. Although he started to make some friends, he did not seem very happy, and I could see that his emotions were unstable at times.

Wong struggled with his emotions and did not want to talk too much about his everyday life with his parents. As a result, his parents worried a lot about Wong. I observed that often conflicts occur when neither party has proper interaction with the other. Wong did not have a chance to express his feelings and he struggled to make friends and wished that his friends treated him like a superstar. And Wong's parents were mostly concerned about their son's academic results and wondered why he spent so much time playing football with his friends.

In trying to resolve the conflicts faced by Wong as well as his relationship with his parents, I started a conversation with Wong and learned that he missed the experience of being a leader within a friendship group he had in Hong Kong. Using self-regulated strategies, we worked out his strengths and weaknesses and likes and dislikes. In this process, he found out that he neither likes football very much nor his current friendships. After we practiced this self-reflective exercise several times, he started to learn to consider things more thoroughly before making a decision. I can see that he has become more patient and is willing to share his likes and dislikes with others. With Wong's parents, I encouraged them to learn about their son's situation, for example, by talking to the boarding house master in the school about their son and asking Wong questions not only about academic results but also about activities that he cares about. I believe effective communication and knowing oneself are the keys to reducing worries and promoting a child's wellbeing.

I also have ongoing conversations with Chinese parents in encouraging them to being more open-minded about Westernised attitudes and regarding their children's cultural practices. I often find that the topic of discrimination and racism and sexual relationship is not discussed openly within British Chinese communities. Yet, the children need a safe platform where they can express their struggles and experiences regarding exclusion and difficult subjects in schooling. While I worked as a teacher in an Asian country, I realised that there is a tendency for the pupils to avoid cultural taboo topics and subjects that they perceive as 'bad', such as sex (Zhang & Shah, 2007). I think there is a need for parents and pupils to have a better understanding of their own minds, concerns, and needs. They should also try to avoid communicating with each other via text message, as it always leads to misunderstandings. My advice to British Chinese parents and children is to appreciate the intergenerational and intercultural differences and to have ongoing dialogues to cope with dilemmas in new cultural settings.

Lizana: I have worked with a wide range of British Chinese pupils, and I always counted myself lucky to have such committed and dedicated pupils. However, I am also concerned about the tensions some pupils experience between their home expectations, cultural expectations, and the new culture they need to function within and make sense of. In my teaching experiences, I have developed an understanding of the cultural and personal challenges each child faces, which is in line with the expectations for all teachers as outlined by Teachers' Standard 5 (DfE, 2014). The subject I teach also requires of pupils to develop their inference skills, and their ability to explore a variety of perspectives, and I often worked closely with all pupils on this. Here, I offer a vignette to discuss a specific British Chinese pupil's learning journey in a high attaining school and how her anxieties have impacted on learning:

Chan is a talented pupil, gifted in English, and also a talented musician and dancer. She was born in the UK and her parents immigrated from China 16 years ago. She had high hopes of applying to Russell Group University one day and worked extremely hard on all aspects of her learning. She was a delight to teach, and she aimed to please her parents, teachers, and peers. It is fair to say that Chan left no stone unturned. However, I often found Chan resisting engagement with alternative perspectives, which would enable her to do very well in this subject. In a one-to-one conversation, it was explained to her that it is important to explore a range of views with the context in mind. Later I realised it is because Chan was very unsure how to do that, and also she felt that her home tutor and parents continued to stress that she needed to read and use the books she knew to guide her.

It was then decided that Chan will work with me and read through sample essays to see how other pupils explored a range of perspectives. We highlighted these key points, and we decided to develop key questions Chan could ask when she writes an essay, to help her become more explorative. As a next step, I asked Chan if she would be prepared to try answering classroom questions in a similar way, by using this sentence starter: 'it can be looked at in two different ways, firstly and then secondly we can also think about it in this way...' We worked on these strategies and techniques for three weeks, before moving into developing a full essay for Chan in which she was asked to present two paragraphs reflecting alternative views.

We gradually scaffolded this approach until she became more confident and consistent in her approach, and until she started to look at her reading more critically too. She became clearer that she needs to be more open and fluid and develop her argument with a range of views in mind. I also helped her map her work across the success criteria and this gave Chan a clearer understanding of what is expected of her to understand that she is on track with her learning, which was helpful (Pink, 2009).

I have also worked closely with Chan's parents and home tutor to share what they were doing with Chan to ensure that there was a shared understanding of how they could all work together to help her succeed. Once I had opened these communication channels, all parties were able to work in a supportive way, and Chan became less worried about how she could improve on her learning. Chan was extremely anxious at first, but as she grew in confidence and developed an understanding of what was required, she became more courageous, and happy to challenge key points more often. Her anxiety levels dropped, and she became more willing to share her ideas during class time too. As a result, her overall academic performance improved as well.

Takeaway points

- British Chinese pupils come from diverse social and cultural backgrounds and thus have an array of cultural dispositions and practices that are sometimes similar to dominant British cultural values.

- As teachers and parents, we can develop more awareness of our binary understandings of cultural dispositions and practices as one can be both competitive and collaborative depending on appropriate circumstances.

- Ongoing dialogues are therefore needed amongst pupils, parents, and teachers to understand the nuances of individual pupil's needs, feelings, and thoughts as prior academic knowledge about 'Chinese pupils', especially those conducted elsewhere could potentially perpetuate stereotypes or reify British Chinese pupil's diverse lived experiences.

- We believe there is no one best approach for promoting British Chinese pupils' mental wellbeing but a willingness to engage in ongoing dialogues amongst parents, children, and teachers to work through conflicts.

- Developing a growth mindset and discovering core values seem to be helpful in promoting British Chinese pupils' mental wellbeing.

Note

1 A research approach to understanding (sub)cultures using immersive techniques, where the researcher spends time with a group to better understand their perspectives.

Further reading

Eng, D. L., & Han, S. 2019. *Racial melancholia, racial dissociation: On the social and psychic lives of Asian Americans*. Durham: Duke University Press.

Pang, B. 2021. Problematising the (in) visibility of racialized and gendered British Chineseness in youth health and physical cultures. *Sport, Education and Society*, 26(3), pp. 228–238.

Pang, B. 2020. Beyond hypervisibility and fear: British Chinese communities' leisure and health-related experiences in the time of coronavirus. *Leisure Sciences*, 43 (1–2), pp. 111–117.

YetCheng, M., Friesen, A. & Adekola, O. 2019. Using emotion regulation to cope with challenges: A study of Chinese pupils in the United Kingdom. *Cambridge Journal of Education*, 49(2), pp. 133–145.

References

Archer, L. and Francis, B. 2005. 'They never go off the rails like other ethnic groups': Teachers' constructions of British Chinese pupils' gender identities and approaches to learning. *British Journal of Sociology of Education*, 26(2), pp. 165–182.

Archer, L. and Francis, B. 2006. Challenging classes? Exploring the role of social class within the identities and achievement of British Chinese pupils. *Sociology*, 40(1), pp. 29–49.

Census. 2011. *Chinese ethnic group: Facts and figures*. https://www.ethnicity-facts-figures.service.gov.uk/summaries/chinese-ethnic-group

Chan, Y. M. 2000. Self-esteem: A cross-cultural comparison of British-Chinese, white British and Hong Kong Chinese children. *Educational Psychology*, 20(1), pp. 59–74.

Chau, R. C. and Yu, S. W. 2001. Social exclusion of Chinese people in Britain. *Critical Social Policy*, 21(1), pp. 103–125.

DfE. 2014. *Teachers' standards*. London: DfE.

Dweck, C. 2017. *Growth mindset*. Edinburgh: Robinson.

Eng, D. L. and Han, S. 2000. A dialogue on racial melancholia. *Psychoanalytic Dialogues*, 10(4), pp. 667–700.

Eng, D. L. and Han, S. 2019. *Racial melancholia, racial dissociation: On the social and psychic lives of Asian Americans*. Durham: Duke University Press.

Holmes, P. 2005. Ethnic Chinese Pupils' Communication with cultural others in a New Zealand university. *Communication Education*, 54(4), pp. 289–311.

Lau, A. 1997. The mental health of Chinese children and young people in Britain. In L. Yee & S. Au (Eds.), *Chinese mental health issues in Britain: Perspectives from the Chinese mental health association* (pp. 22–28). London: Mental Health Foundation.

Lu, S. H., Dear, B. F., Johnston, L., Wootton, B. M. and Titov, N. 2014. An internet survey of emotional health, treatment seeking and barriers to accessing mental health treatment among Chinese-speaking international students in Australia. *Counselling Psychology Quarterly*, 27(1), pp. 96–108.

Pang, B. 2020. Beyond hypervisibility and fear: British Chinese communities' leisure and health-related experiences in the time of coronavirus. *Leisure Sciences*. 43 (1–2), pp. 111–117.

Pang, B. 2021. Problematising the (in) visibility of racialized and gendered British Chineseness in youth health and physical cultures. *Sport, Education and Society*, 26(3), pp. 228–238.

Parker, D. 2000. The Chinese takeaway and the diasporic habitus: Space, time and power geometries. In H. Barnor (Ed.), *Un/settled multiculturalisms: Diasporas, entanglements, transruptions* (pp. 73–95). London: Zed books.

Pui, W. S. W. 2019. Empowering voices of pupils with learning difficulties–Implementing self-regulated learning strategies in a special school through participatory action research. *Polish Journal of Educational Studies*, 72(1), pp. 125–144.

Wei, M., Heppner, P. P., Mallen, M. J., Ku, T.-Y., Liao, K. Y.-H. and Wu, T.-F. 2007. Acculturative stress, perfectionism, years in the United States, and depression among Chinese international pupils. *Journal of Counselling Psychology*, 54(4), p. 385.

Wei, M., Su, J. C., Carrera, S., Lin, S.-P. and Yi, F. 2013. Suppression and interpersonal harmony: A cross-cultural comparison between Chinese and European Americans. *Journal of Counselling Psychology*, 60(4), p. 625.

YetCheng, M., Friesen, A. and Adekola, O. 2019. Using emotion regulation to cope with challenges: A study of Chinese pupils in the United Kingdom. *Cambridge Journal of Education*, 49(2), pp. 133–145.

Yip, T. 2005. Sources of situational variation in ethnic identity and psychological well-being: A palm pilot study of Chinese American students. *Personality and Social Psychology Bulletin*, 31(12), pp. 1603–1616.

Zhang, L., Li, X. and Shah, I. H. 2007. Where do Chinese adolescents obtain knowledge of sex? Implications for sex education in China. *Health Education*, 107(4), pp. 351–363.

Educating White Working-Class Boys: Addressing Masculinity, Wellbeing, and Mental Health

Garth Stahl

Synopsis

In the United Kingdom, the academic underachievement and poor behaviour of white working-class boys remain pervasive problems as well as continual sources of frustration for educators. The reasons for this phenomenon are complex and include both generational poverty and the construction of masculinity. This chapter seeks to highlight an unexplored dimension of the educational experiences of white working-class boys through focusing on the social construction of mental health as well as mental health itself. I focus on how certain cultural behaviours of white working-class boys are often misread by educators and, at times, falsely psychologized. Descriptions of 'crazy' and 'barking mad' boys work to preclude educators seeing that some young men are struggling with their sense of self as learners. Drawing from research on boys and schooling, the chapter proposes three interrelated strategies that practising teachers can use to proactively foster positive learning cultures and promote the wellbeing of white working-class boys: (1) critiquing problematic gendered behaviours; (2) increasing awareness around deficit language; and (3) developing sustainable and trusting teacher–pupil relationships.

Background

The academic underachievement and poor behaviour of white British boys remains a pervasive problem and a continual source of frustration for educators as evidenced by the parliamentary hearing on the Underperformance of White Working-Class Children in February 2014 (Select Committee on Education, 2014). Demie and Lewis (2011) note that the white working class in the United Kingdom, as an ethnic group, often come from backgrounds of intergenerational poverty, furthermore; they are often associated with low aspirations, low literacy levels, and feelings of marginalization, which contribute to their experiences with education.

DOI: 10.4324/9781003160526-6

Educational researchers have continued to document that many white working-class boys suffer in their schooling, which contributes negatively to their sense of self-worth (Gillborn & Kirton, 2000; Reay, 2002; Kingdon & Cassen, 2010; Stahl, 2012). The policy agenda has noted that young white people "have lower educational aspirations than most other ethnic groups" and that, furthermore, "the educational attainment of white boys is failing to improve at the rates of most other ethnic groups" (Communities and Local Government and Department for Children, Schools and Families, 2008, p. 8).

This chapter presents some reflections on the mental health and wellbeing of white working-class boys, the academically lowest-performing ethnic group in the United Kingdom. While the majority of white working-class pupils appear to suffer in the education system, the gender gap "grows during secondary school for White British students with boys falling further behind girls" (Strand, 2014, p. 160). The demands of the increasingly robust agenda of testing and standards have led to a culture of performativity in schools, which I would argue only contributes to portrayals of the white working-class as the new race victims, though this is not without critique (see Gillborn, 2010; Keddie, 2015). With this in mind, this chapter makes some connections concerning the relationship between generational poverty, masculinities, and mental health and the social construction of mental health. The behaviours exhibited by many white working-class boys, which carry a certain currency in their family and peer groups, are often misread and problematically psychologized in modern schooling. It is easy to stereotype and dismiss certain pupil behaviours ('crazy boys', 'rebellious lads') in schools and more challenging to confront the ways in which poverty, class, and culture influence how pupils come to understand themselves as learners. This chapter explores some of the ways gender, social class, and mental health are articulated together in educational settings and what this may mean for educators seeking to promote the wellbeing of white working-class boys.

My expertise is not in mental health, and I do not approach the topic from a psychology background. Instead, I draw from a socio-cultural perspective to problematize some of the ways white working-class boys are pathologized in their formal schooling. It is important to consider school as increasingly pressurized and framed by high-stakes accountability. Furthermore, it is important to consider how stress, anxiety, and poverty manifest and lead to white working-class boys performing gendered and classed behaviours that are counterproductive to their success in school (e.g. 'laddish,' 'anti-social'; see Francis, 2006). Such gendered and classed behaviours are part of the struggle many white working-class boys engage in to establish themselves in their schooling, peer group, and family life. These behaviours have a long-standing history in the United Kingdom (Nayak, 2003; Willis, 1977); furthermore, misunderstandings of these classed and gender performances serve as a barrier to properly addressing the wellbeing of this disadvantaged group.

I have argued before that white working-class boys are often thrice marginalized in their education in terms of race, class, and gender (see Stahl, 2015, 2017). Central to this argument is the fact that, in my experience, many white working-class boys struggle to express their emotions especially when feeling vulnerable in relation to academic pressures. There exists an emotional labour of doing 'boy work', where boys need to negotiate the management and regulation of feelings, performances, and expressions associated with the expectations around adolescent masculinities (Stahl & Keddie, 2020, p. 881). With this in mind, I intend for this chapter to serve as a provocation to think about the relationship between masculinities and wellbeing and what schools can do to positively contribute to a healthier school experience. The chapter proceeds in three sections. First, I consider the historic fraught relationship between working-class masculinities and education, with a focus on poverty, masculinities, and mental health. This serves as a foundation for the second part where I reflect upon and problematize some of the commonplace experiences I have observed when researching, teaching, and working with white working-class boys. The chapter concludes by proposing three interrelated strategies that practising teachers can use to proactively foster positive learning cultures and promote the wellbeing of white working-class boys, specifically: (1) critiquing problematic gendered identity performances; (2) increasing awareness around deficit language; and (3) developing sustainable and trusting teacher–pupil relationships.

Working-class masculinity and education

As Mills and Keddie (2007) assert, a significant percentage of boys "are not served well by many aspects of the schooling process" (p. 337). Primarily influenced by their economic situation, working-class boys have historically had an uneasy and problematic relationship with their education. As working-class young men in the United Kingdom were destined for work in factories and on the docklands for much of the 19th and 20th centuries, schooling was often seen as unnecessary and largely irrelevant. Within studies of working-class masculinity, Willis's (1977) landmark study 'Learning to labour' addressed how a group of young men became disaffected from their education and engaged in laddish behaviour both inside and outside the classroom. Willis's main argument concerns the contribution of the working-class 'lad' culture – affirmed through physicality, toughness, hedonism, and opposition to authority – to their educational failure (Willis, 2004). The work of Willis highlights the relationship between class background, culture, and masculinity.

More recent scholarship has documented the ways in which working-class boys acquire working-class behaviours in their primary socialisation (Evans, 2006), which greatly influences the learner and social identities they negotiate in the classroom as early as primary school (Swain, 2006). It has been documented that working-class boys display signs of 'disaffection' as early as the age of seven (Noble, 2000). Their initial socialisation within the family structure can position some working-class boys at a significant disadvantage and, from their first entry into the school environment, many working-class boys feel a sense of "educational worthlessness" (Reay, 2009, p. 25), which can often lead to underperformance. Teachers play an important role here and Entwisle, Alexander, and Olson (2007) explain that "because most teachers are middle class they may find the behaviour of middle-SES [Socio-Economic Status] boys to be more compatible with their standards than the behaviour of low-SES boys" (p. 117).

In the United Kingdom today, white working-class males often find themselves in school cultures that are overly focused on academic achievement, which invokes stress and anxiety (Stahl, 2015). Furthermore, many of their parents have experienced sustained periods of unemployment. As a result, the lifeworlds of many white working-class boys are deeply affected by both poverty and robust pressures from the school to succeed academically. This has led researchers to document the ways in which aspects of white working-class masculinities are evolving in the face of uncertainty, where there are new searches for 'respectability' and 'authenticity' (McDowell, 2003; Dolby & Dimitriadis, 2004) alongside reaffirmations of traditional identity practices (Stahl, 2018). With this in mind, it is understandable that many white working-class boys "perceive troublesome, oppositional and resistant behaviour within school as a social good" (Reay, 2009, p. 27), a necessary exercise in identity construction, and an outlet that elevates their status both in their families and in their all-powerful peer group.

Poverty, masculinities, and mental health

What has remained unexplored in research on white working-class boys is the relationship between poverty, masculinities, mental health, and the social construction of mental health. Research in psychology and health has linked poverty to one's mental health, where a lack of material resources (e.g. food security, housing) and very little control over one's life (e.g. a feeling of helplessness) can lead to chronic stress, which can be detrimental and present in a variety of ways (Welsh et al., 2015). In surveying the relationship between poverty and child mental health, Fitzsimons, Goodman, Kelly, and Smith (2017) found that low "socioeconomic status creates stress within the household" (p. 43) and that parental mental health correlates significantly with child mental health.

Research on masculinities and mental health for school-age children remains surprisingly rare. When mental health is considered alongside schoolboy masculinities, it is often associated with criminality or suicide rather than more common forms of mental illness such as depression, social anxiety, and others. Data from the Information Centre for Health and Social Care (2007) suggest that boys under ten are twice as likely to experience behavioural, emotional, and mental health issues than girls. This is an alarming statistic, and the reasons remain unclear.

The importance of understanding mental health as a gendered phenomenon cannot be discounted. We know there exists a relationship between gender normativity and mental health in adolescence (see Landstedt, Asplund & Gillander-Gadin, 2009). Masculinity, specifically traditional masculinity norms and values of strength, resiliency, and toughness, may serve as a barrier to men wanting to understand their own mental health and wellbeing (Mahalik & Dagirmanjian, 2019; Mac an Ghaill &

Haywood, 2012). Mahalik and Dagirmanjian (2019) note that working-class men, who often see themselves as invulnerable, view seeking help as weak and associated with femininity; their participants "described stigma through their anticipation of negative judgments from others, and threat to manhood status through failure to meet the masculine ideal of being strong and able to bear up when in pain" (p. 9).

Highlighting another dimension, research on masculinities and mental health has outlined several risk factors including social isolation and long-term unemployment, though mental health is also shaped by lifestyle choices and collective social norms about what it is to be a man. While the research remains limited, what is clear is that many men struggling with mental health are not only reluctant to seek support but they may also not recognize their issues as legitimate (Smith, Richardson & Robertson, 2016). In research on the social construction of male suicide, Mac an Ghaill and Haywood (2012) call for educators and counsellors to "consider how gender identities may be differently constructed, organized and cohered" depending on context. They also note that this may be paradoxical work because the endeavour to recognize "the gendered nature of suicidality" involves "simultaneously questioning dominant explanations of gender identity formation" (p. 483).

Reflections on the educational experience of white working-class boys

I now reflect on some of my observations from researching, teaching, and working with white working-class boys in the United Kingdom over the course of nine years. As I have discussed in my previous work, the notion of pupil capability is shaped by staffroom chatter where white working-class boys are often pathologized, and described as 'thick', 'feral', 'crazy', or 'fucked up' (Stahl, 2017). I am not only interested in how such labels significantly influence the relationships between pupils and educators, but also how notions of teenage rebellion, as a normative stage in adolescent development, are oftentimes falsely psychologized within the school environment. The casual or flippant reference to boys being mentally ill serves to normalize certain behaviours rather than problematize such behaviours. Furthermore, such an approach may influence the level of support provided to those young men who may be suffering from real mental health issues, which are often prevalent in populations experiencing abject poverty.

Faced with pathologization and labels which are counterproductive, I found that white working-class boys look for areas in their schooling where they can be valued (Stahl, 2017). Feeling powerless in their education, they will look to empower themselves and gain respect in the eyes of their peers. They may often engage in 'laddish' or 'loutish' behaviours (see Francis, 1999) that can be socially empowering but also transgress boundaries of what is considered acceptable in a school context. Warrington, Younger, and Williams' (2000) study shows that "individually, or in small groups, boys could see that [laddish] behaviour was not in their long-term interest; in the classroom, situation, however, they often found it difficult to deviate from an accepted group norm" (p. 405). Furthermore, for young men, the failure to gain respect can lead to strong feelings of shame, which can contribute to feeling uncomfortable with a certain level of expressiveness (Randell et al., 2015). This overlaps with research regarding masculinity and performing an identity involving emotional unavailability and stoicism (Allen, 2005).

During my time researching white working-class boys and their experiences with schooling, I rarely witnessed efforts to proactively support young men to critique their behaviours or handle such behaviours constructively. Schools need to be spaces where pupils feel safe, especially those pupils exhibiting challenging behaviours. Instead, I frequently saw efforts to discipline and punish such behaviours. Labelling and punishing behaviour only perpetuates the notion of the 'naughty boy' (the 'unteachable boy', Stahl, 2017) instead of finding curriculum-based and pedagogically innovative ways to problematize and critically reflect on constructions of masculinity (Mills & Keddie, 2007).

What can teachers do?

There exists uncertainty about how best to respond to the emotional labour of boys doing "boy work" (Stahl & Keddie, 2020, p. 881). In the case of white working-class boys, there has clearly been an overemphasis on their lack of achievement and poor behaviour and less exploration of how white working-class boys can experience their schooling in positive ways. Educators need to develop context-specific strategies to assist boys in negotiating the management and regulation of feelings, performances, and expressions associated with expectations concerning adolescent masculinities. While these strategies will not counteract the effects of poverty on mental health or alter the entrenched masculine norms which in many cases hold young men back, the proposed strategies would work to reduce the pathologizing of boys based on the behaviours they exhibit rather than the individuals that they are. These strategies, which are focused on diversifying the ways in which boys can be boys, are powerful if adopted by the whole school (Martino & Pallotta-Chiarolli, 2003). I will now propose three interrelated strategies that practising teachers can use to foster positive learning cultures and promote the wellbeing of white working-class boys: (1) critiquing problematic gendered behaviours; (2) increasing awareness around deficit language; and (3) developing sustainable and trusting teacher–pupil relationships.

Critiquing problematic gendered behaviours

In their work on gender justice, a pedagogy which seeks to dismantle harmful structures including patriarchy, misogyny, and homophobia, Mills and Keddie (2007) found that boys are more often than not their own worst enemy, specifically in reference to the 'laddish' behaviours they become caught up in. However, in considering the capacity of gender justice pedagogies, Mills and Keddie (2007) assert the "differences amongst boys thus make it very difficult to identify a pedagogy that is appropriate for all boys" (p. 337). Still, to advance the wellbeing and engagement of white working-class boys, it is essential to integrate pedagogical approaches which require boys to problematize the behaviours they accept as normative as well as to question the privileges associated with their masculinity. Such pedagogies should not only foreground critique, but they should also actively work to cast boys as activists for gender equity (Shefer, Hearn, Ratele & Boonzaier, 2018).

In addition, educators should also find ways to open up important spaces for boys to be vulnerable. Randell et al. (2015) write: "For boys who are oriented towards toughness, emotions are managed by concealment of emotional pain, which leads to emotional restriction in expressing difficult emotions such as fear, sadness and shame" (p. 491). Martino and Pallotta-Chiarolli (2003) note that boys are often aware of their own gendered behaviour and, more specifically, the "heteronormative and gendernormative constructions of emotions such as anger, aggression, grief and sensitivity" (p. 184). Furthermore, they document the ways in which boys are "able to interrogate normative masculinity and to discuss its power and hierarchical domination" (p. 200) in both their school and daily lives. Allen (2005) states that vulnerability must be "managed" (p. 46) in relation to masculinity, where divulging "insecurities renders masculinity vulnerable and may necessitate the reinstatement of a hegemonic masculine self" (p. 44). She refers to masculinity as having a "slippery nature"; in her focus groups, Allen observed "staunchly masculine subjects" who presented "softer" masculinities, "were not immune to feelings of inadequacy" and "harboured aspirations of romance and emotional attachment" (p. 48).

Increasing awareness around deficit language

The schooling experiences of white working-class boys are often shaped by low expectations from educators as well as deficit discourses, which affect their identities as learners. According to Comber and Kamler (2007), deficit discourses are dangerous and harmful belief systems that "blame certain groups in society as lacking and responsible for their lack [...] the poor, the wilful, the disabled, the non-English speaking, the slow, the bottom 10%" (p. 293). Haydn (2014) argues that deficit models contribute to a poor classroom climate and widespread behaviour issues in UK schools and that these deficit models lead to the construction of many white working-class boys as 'unteachable' (Stahl, 2017). Experiencing pathologization in both schooling, and arguably wider society, the white working-class boys I studied have limited spaces where they can feel a sense of worth.

I acknowledge that the labelling of young boys as 'thick', 'feral', 'crazy', or 'fucked up' (see Stahl, 2017) is an expression of the frustration educators may feel when attempting to educate these young men. However, describing boys as 'crazy' and 'out of control' also demonstrates how discourses of mental health are co-opted in ways which are very counterproductive. The labelling precludes educators from thinking critically about the behaviour of some white working-class young men, which is informed by white working-class cultural values; furthermore, it may make boys less likely to seek help when they need it. Careful attention to the language used to describe vulnerable groups in our schools is essential.

Developing sustainable and trusting teacher–pupil relationships

Mills and Keddie (2007) note that boys desire a school culture that is supportive, where difference is understood and where they feel a strong sense of connectedness. Research has sought to capture the importance – and the productivity – of pupil–teacher relationships specifically in regard to unsettling the pervasive deficit discourses which shape the experiences of pupils from underprivileged backgrounds (Comber & Kamler, 2007; Hattam & Prosser, 2008). There has been renewed attention in recent years to studying boys as relational learners and the importance of pupil–teacher relationships for boys from disadvantaged backgrounds (Reichert & Hawley, 2014; Nelson, 2016). Reichert and Hawley (2014) have composed a Relational Teaching Framework that comprises strategies to engage boys relationally towards their learning and has been utilized by middle-school teachers to support the engagement and learning of low-income Black boys in America. They highlight that boys perceive 'relationally effective teachers' as demonstrating the following qualities: (1) reaching out and going beyond; (2) personal advocacy; (3) establishing common ground; and (4) accommodating opposition.

Pupil–teacher relationships may mediate some of the emotional labour of doing 'boy work' (Stahl, 2015; Stahl & Keddie, 2020). As boys struggle with the management of feelings as well as the expectations around adolescent masculinities, many find such relationships can open up spaces to express their emotions and vulnerabilities, which is an integral part of fostering healthy masculinities (Harris, Kruger & Scott, 2020). As previously noted, educators who want to foster productive relationships with working-class young men need to be aware of young men's anxiety around feeling vulnerable and, as a result, their struggle to express themselves emotionally (see Allen, 2005). In their research, Mahalik and Dagirmanjian (2019) call attention to men's concerns about stigma, the importance of safety, and masculinity as a hindrance to men seeking help. With this in mind, teachers need to proactively build relationships over time. In their work on boyhood and the management of masculinities and emotion, Randell et al. (2015) note: "*To be able to be open* requires security in relationships" (p. 492, emphasis in original).

Research continues to document that schools need to be better equipped to address the needs of young men. Not discounting the incredible complexity of working as an educator today, it is important that teachers and school leaders actively maintain school communities which take mental health seriously and recognize its gendered dimension. It is clear that as the responsibilities of schools around mental health awareness continue to take shape, educators have an important role to play both in recognizing that populations experiencing abject poverty suffer from authentic mental health issues, and in challenging how boys are socially constructed within the school environment. For white working-class boys, the focus should be on what factors contribute to their engagement as they struggle with their sense of self and the effects of poverty. Proactively maintaining a school culture which regularly critiques gender stereotypes and foregrounds the importance of building relationships with boys perceived as 'troublesome' or 'problematic' is paramount.

Takeaway points

- The educational experiences of white working-class British boys are often shaped by intergenerational poverty, low literacy levels, and feelings of marginalization.

- There is an established relationship between poverty and mental health which needs to be included in discussions of consistently underperforming populations.

- Boys' and men's understanding of masculinity (e.g. resiliency, toughness) may serve as a barrier to seeking help for mental health issues.

- The cultural behaviours of white working-class boys which carry a certain currency in their family and peer groups, are often misread and problematically psychologized in modern schooling.

- Interrogating masculine norms and creating safe spaces for young men who present challenging behaviours is essential pedagogical practice.

- Teachers have a responsibility to guard against deficit discourses and labelling pupils and instead focus on building positive relationships.

Further reading

Demie, F. and Lewis, K. (2011). White working class achievement: An ethnographic study of barriers to learning in schools. *Educational Studies*, 37(3), 245–264.

Entwisle, D. R., Alexander, K. L. and Olson, L. S. (2007). Early schooling: The handicap of being poor and male. *Sociology of Education*, 80, 114–138.

Keddie, A. (2015). 'We haven't done enough for White working-class children': Issues of distributive justice and ethnic identity politics. *Race Ethnicity and Education*, 18(4), 515–534.

Select Committee on Education. (2014). *Underachievement in education by white working class children: First report*. London: UK Parliament. Available at: <http://www.publications.parliament.uk/pa/cm201415/cmselect/cmeduc/142/14202.htm>.

Stahl, G. (2012). Aspiration and a good life among white working-class boys in London. *Journal of Qualitative and Ethnographic Research*, 7(1), 8–19.

References

Allen, L. (2005). Managing masculinity: Young men's identity work in focus groups. *Qualitative Research*, 5(1), 35–57.

Comber, B. and Kamler, B. (2007). Getting out of deficit: Pedagogies of reconnection. *Teaching Education*, 15(3), 293–310.

Communities and Local Government and Department for Children, Schools and Families. (2008). *Aspiration and attainment amongst young people in deprived communities.* London: Cabinet Office.

Demie, F. and Lewis, K. (2011). White working class achievement: An ethnographic study of barriers to learning in schools. *Educational Studies,* 37(3), 245–264.

Dolby, N. and Dimitriadis, G. (2004). Learning to labor in new times: An introduction. In N. Dolby, G. Dimitriadis and P. Willis (eds), *Learning to labor in new times.* New York: RoutledgeFalmer, pp. 1–14.

Entwisle, D. R., Alexander, K. L. and Olson, L. S. (2007). Early schooling: The handicap of being poor and male. *Sociology of Education,* 80, 114–138.

Evans, G. (2006). *Educational failure and working class white children in Britain.* Basingstoke: Palgrave Macmillan.

Fitzsimons, E., Goodman, A., Kelly, E. and Smith, J. P. (2017). Poverty dynamics and parental mental health: Determinants of childhood mental health in the UK. *Social Science & Medicine,* 175, 43–51.

Francis, B. (1999). Lads, lasses, and (new) labour: 14–16-year-old students' responses to the 'laddish behaviour and boys' underachievement' debate. *British Journal of Sociology of Education,* 20(3), 355–371.

Francis, B. (2006). Heroes or zeroes? The discursive positioning of 'underachieving boys' in English neo-liberal education policy. *Journal of Education Policy,* 21(2), 187–200.

Gillborn, D. (2010). The white working class, racism and respectability: Victims, degenerates and interest-convergence. *British Journal of Educational Studies,* 58(1), 3–25.

Gillborn, D. and Kirton, A. (2000). WHITE HEAT: Racism, under-achievement and white working-class boys. *Inclusion and Special Educational Needs,* 4(4), 271–288.

Hattam, R. and Prosser, B. (2008). Unsettling deficit views of students and their communities. *Australian Educational Researcher,* 35(2), 89–106.

Harris, J., Kruger, A. and Scott, E. (2020). 'Sometimes I wish I was a girl, 'cause they do shit like cry': An exploration into Black boys' thinking about emotions. *Urban Education.* https://doi.org/10.1177/0042085920933327.

Haydn, T. (2014). To what extent is behaviour a problem in English schools? Exploring the scale and prevalence of deficits in classroom climate. *Review of Education,* 2(1), 31–64.

Information Centre for Health and Social Care. (2007). *Hospital episode statistics (admitted patient care): England.* London: ONS.

Keddie, A. (2015). 'We haven't done enough for White working-class children': Issues of distributive justice and ethnic identity politics. *Race Ethnicity and Education,* 18(4), 515–534.

Kingdon, G. and Cassen, R. (2010). Ethnicity and low achievement in English schools. *British Educational Research Journal,* 36(3), 403–431.

Landstedt, E., Asplund, K. and Gillander-Gadin, K. (2009). Understanding adolescent mental health: The influence of social processes, doing gender and gendered power. *Sociology of Health & Illness,* 31(7), 962–978.

Mac an Ghaill, M. and Haywood, C. (2012). Understanding boys': Thinking through boys, masculinity and suicide. *Social Science & Medicine,* 74(4), 482–489.

Mahalik, J. R. and Dagirmanjian, F. R. (2019). Working-class men's constructions of help-seeking when feeling depressed or sad. *American Journal of Men's Health,* 13(3), 1–13.

Martino, W. and Pallotta-Chiarolli, M. (2003). *So what's a boy?* Maidenhead: Open University Press.

McDowell, L. (2003). *Redundant masculinities?: Employment change and white working class youth.* Malden, MA: Blackwell Pub.

Mills, M. and Keddie, A. (2007). Teaching boys and gender justice. *International Journal of Inclusive Education*, 11(3), 335–354.

Nayak, A. (2003). 'Boyz to men': Masculinities, schooling and labour transitions in de-industrial times. *Educational Review*, 55(2), 147–159.

Nelson, J. D. (2016). Relational teaching with black boys: Strategies for learning at a single-sex middle school for boys of color. *Teachers College Record*, 118(6), 1–30

Noble, C. (2000). Helping boys do better in their primary schools. In K. Bleach (ed), *Raising boys' achievement in schools*. London: Trentham Books, pp. 21–37.

Randell, E., Jerdén, L., Öhman, A., Starrin, B. and Flacking, R. (2015). Tough, sensitive and sincere: How adolescent boys manage masculinities and emotions. *International Journal of Adolescence and Youth*, 21(4), 486–498.

Reay, D. (2002). Shaun's story: Troubling discourses on white working-class masculinities. *Gender and Education*, 14(3), 221–234.

Reay, D. (2009). Making sense of white working class educational underachievement. In K. P. Sveinsson (ed), *Who cares about the white working class?* London: Runnymede Perspectives, pp. 22–28.

Reichert, M. and Hawley, R. (2014). *I can learn from you: Boys as relational learners*. Cambridge, MA: Harvard Education Press.

Select Committee on Education. (2014). *Underachievement in education by white working class children: First report*. London: UK Parliament. Available at: <http://www.publications.parliament.uk/pa/cm201415/cmselect/cmeduc/142/14202.htm>.

Shefer, T., Hearn, J., Ratele, K. and Boonzaier, F. (2018). *Engaging youth in activism, research, and pedagogical praxis: Transnational and intersectional perspectives on gender, sex, and race*. Abingdon, Oxon: Routledge.

Smith, J. A., Richardson, N. and Robertson, S. (2016). Applying a genders lens to public health discourses on men's health. In J. Gideon (ed), *Handbook on gender and health*. Cheltenham: Edward Elgar, pp. 117–133.

Stahl, G. (2012). Aspiration and a good life among white working-class boys in London. *Journal of Qualitative and Ethnographic Research*, 7(1), 8–19.

Stahl, G. (2015). *Aspiration, identity and neoliberalism: Educating white working-class boys*. London: Routledge.

Stahl, G. (2017). Pathologizing the white 'unteachable': South London's working-class boys' experiences with schooling and discipline. In N. Okilwa, M. Khalife and F. Briscoe (eds), *The school to prison pipeline: The role of culture and discipline in school*. Bingley, UK: Emerald Publishing, pp. 91–112.

Stahl, G. (2018). Narratives in reconstituting, reaffirming, and (re)traditionalizing identities: Othering the nonnormative. *Men and Masculinities*, 21(5), 709–728.

Stahl, G. and Keddie, A. (2020). The emotional labor of doing 'boy work': Considering affective economies of boyhood in schooling. *Educational Philosophy and Theory*, 52(8), 880–890.

Strand, S. (2014). Ethnicity, gender, social class and achievement gaps at age 16: Intersectionality and 'getting it' for the white working class. *Research Papers in Education*, 29(2), 131–171.

Swain, J. (2006). Reflections on patterns of masculinity in school settings. *Men and Masculinities*, 8(3), 331–349.

Warrington, M., Younger, M. and Williams, J. (2000). Student attitudes, image and the gender gap. *British Educational Research Journal*, 26(3), 393–407.

Welsh, J., Strazdins, L., Ford, L., Friel, S., O'Rourke, K., Carbone, S. and Carlon, L. (2015). Promoting equity in the mental wellbeing of children and young people: A scoping review. *Health Promotion International*, 30(S2), 36–76.

Willis, P. (1977). *Learning to labour: How working class kids get working class jobs*. New York: Columbia University Press.

Willis, P. (2004). Twenty-five years on: Old books, new times. In N. Dolby, G. Dimitriadis and P. Willis (eds), *Learning to labor in new times*. New York: RoutledgeFalmer, pp. 167–196.

7 Teenage Girls and Mental Health and Wellbeing Within and Beyond School Spaces

Victoria Cann and Catherine Thomas

Synopsis

This chapter provides an overview of the everyday experiences girls encounter that have an impact on their mental health. Focusing on girls' encounters within the school space, such as the policing of their bodies, experiences of sexual assault, inequalities in sport, and the broader impact of social media on their lives, a rich tapestry is painted of the multiplicity of stressors that impact their mental health. By identifying these stressors, a series of propositions are made for those who work with girls both inside and outside of the school context, with the aim of cultivating spaces for girls that nourish their mental health. These include but are not limited to, punishing instances of sexual harassment, incorporating girls into organisational decision-making processes, and ensuring that girls are taken seriously.

Background

Girls Studies has steadily grown as a field of academic enquiry over the past 30 years, with themes such as heteronormativity (assumed straightness), sexuality, empowerment, and sexism all recurring in the works that examine the lives of teenage girls. While the predominance of scholarly works have focused on white girls in Western English-speaking contexts, work that explores girls from the global majority both inside and outside of the English-speaking West is starting to gain funding and recognition. In this chapter, we provide an overview of some of the literature that has emerged in this field that sheds light on the lived experiences of teenage girls within the UK context. We aim to reflect the diversity of these girls' experiences, highlighting some of the key challenges they face, and the impact that these challenges have on their mental health. Alongside works from the academic field, we also highlight some of the findings from important policy reports, where the most up-to-date findings of girls' experiences can often be found.[1]

DOI: 10.4324/9781003160526-7

A dichotomy has emerged in how girls are talked about in policy discourse and the mainstream media. This dichotomy places girls in an either/or position of innocent-victims-in-need-of-saving or as overtly-sexual-and-in-need-of-punishment. Both of these discourses are experienced differently by girls based on the different intersecting identities that they have. For example, white working-class, Black girls (of all classes, see Chapter 2), and girls from Gypsy and traveller communities (see Chapter 4) are more likely to be positioned as overtly sexual, likely to be the recipient of unwanted sexual attention whilst also being chastised for 'asking for it' in their presentation of femininity. Black girls find themselves the victim of racism as well as sexism (usefully described by Moya Bailey (2013) as 'misogynoir'), as school uniform codes unduly punish them for wearing their hair naturally. Racism frames, in different and nuanced ways, the lives of Asian girls (in all their multiplicities). Muslim girls are routinely positioned as 'threat' and/or 'victim' and the recipients of harassment both in schools and on the street (see Chapter 12). Meanwhile, the subjectivities of lesbian, bisexual, and transgirls (see Chapters 8 and 9) of all race and class backgrounds are (according to the girls we have spoken to in our work) not taken seriously and/or dismissed as attempts to get attention. Disabled and neurodiverse girls meanwhile are regularly denied their sexuality through outdated ideas of consent and bodily autonomy (see Chapter 14). Even cis white girls from what would otherwise be considered privileged backgrounds cite experiences of street harassment, social media bullying, and unfair treatment at school. What is clear then is that whatever 'sort' of girl you are, you're likely to encounter any number of challenges of any given day, both inside and outside of the school context.

Following the 'crisis' of boys' underachievement in UK schools (see Chapter 6), it has been suggested that the "equal opportunities initiatives of the 1980s have 'gone too far' in empowering girls" (Francis, 2005, p. 9). Therefore, even when girls do well, it is said to be to the detriment of the success of boys, and evidence that feminism has 'gone too far'. It seems that whatever their background, whatever their lived experiences, girls simply cannot win. All of this matters of course because each tension, micro-aggression, and act of violence has an impact on the mental health of teenage girls.

Taking seriously girls' mental health and wellbeing

Promotion of mental health initiatives means that young people are much more aware of their own mental health and wellbeing, and discourses of femininity mean that girls are generally expected to be more often in tune and able to respond to their mental health needs. For example, a study by Childline found that "75 per cent of counseling sessions were provided to girls – four times as many as boys (18 per cent)" (NSPCC, 2018, p. 34). While such statistics may also indicate the limits that toxic masculinity places on boys' ability to ask for help, they nevertheless signal a demand in service for girls. Furthermore, Childline notes that over a quarter of girls' concerns when they call for counseling or advice is mental/emotional support (NSPCC, 2018).

Across the board, girls describe not being taken seriously when they discuss their mental health struggles, including practices such as self-harm. The Plan UK report has found that girls who are open about mental-health problems are often dismissed by teachers and health professionals as 'attention-seeking' and 'exaggerating' (Plan UK, 2020). Furthermore, if and when girls *are* able to convince a professional of their need for support, long waiting lists and short-term provision leaves them with precarious futures. Mental health and wellbeing is also an area intersected by race and class. Racist discourses of the 'angry Black woman' impact the ways in which Black girls are able to react to distressing situations, and when they are able to seek help, there remains a scarcity of Black therapists – particularly in more rural areas. Another significant intersection that impacts on the mental health of girls is neurodiversity. For example, girls with conditions such as ASD (Autism Spectrum Disorder) and ADHD (Attention Deficit Hyperactivity Disorder) are much less likely to be diagnosed with these conditions (Moldavsky et al., 2013), leading to assumptions that they are simply troublemakers, and when those with these conditions do suffer mental breakdowns, they are more often labelled as a symptom of their condition rather than a separate issue that requires attention. This lack of recognition can lead girls to feel isolated from adults in their community and lead to the development of longer-term mental health issues that remain untreated or undiagnosed.

We now turn to some of the challenging spaces that girls find themselves occupying and reflect on how some of these require serious consideration when we are talking about the mental health of teenage girls in the UK.

Bodies in school

For many girls, the school that they attend is where they spend the vast majority of their time and is therefore a key space for cultivating their mental and emotional wellbeing. However, work in the field that has explored girls' school lives has revealed the multiplicity of challenges that girls face. Broadly speaking, these challenges include experiences of sexism, sexual assault, menstrual inequality, and double standards. Organisations such as Plan UK and Girlguiding have produced rich reports that highlight these school-based challenges (Plan UK, 2020; Girlguiding, 2019), and an overview of these will be provided here alongside work that exists in the academic field.

Joseph Remi-Salisbury and Laura Connolly (2018) have written about the experiences of Black girls at school, citing that their natural hair has become a site of contestation between girls, their families, and teachers. They write that "school uniform policy [...] operates to limit the expression of Blackness" (2018, p. 2) and, in particular, when it comes to Black hair, Remi-Salisbury and Connolly note a number of instances where young people have had their hair cut or suffered punishments for coming to school with their natural hair. The authors write that the school-level tension over the hair of Black pupils is a significant iteration of white supremacy within British schools (2018). Furthermore, Victoria Showunmi (2017) has found that Black girls struggle with issues of sexualised and racialised embodiment within the school space and Ringrose, Tolman, and Ragonese comment that Black girls need to cover their bodies to "avoid punitive treatment by authority figures" (2019, p. 79). Lamb and Plocha (citing Collins, 2000) highlight the dichotomous discourse encountered by Black girls whereby there is "pride in the voluptuous female body, and a long-standing punishing discourse suggesting that girls of colour, particularly black girls, are over-sexed and need to be controlled" (2015, pp. 86–87). This is an additional site of bodily surveillance on top of the micro-management of girls' bodies regardless of their racial background. For example, girls of all races talk of being punished for having painted nails, wearing make-up, or dyeing their hair. If we consider this form of surveillance in the context of girls' wider lives that are marked by fatphobia in the media, unrealistic beauty standards, and diet culture, further forms of punishment on the grounds of self-expression are likely to affect the self-esteem and wellbeing of girls. It is also worth noting that for poor girls, being able to wear appropriate clothes (either in terms of school uniform fashions and/or school uniform codes) is a further site of stress and perceived failure to conform. Many girls have expressed their frustration that the need to 'hide their bodies' from the world to avoid punishment in the school setting (Plan UK, 2020).

It is also worth considering experiences of menstruation in school when discussing the mental health and wellbeing of teenage girls. It has been found that 56% of menstruators feel embarrassed by their period and only 20% say that they feel comfortable discussing their period with their school teachers or staff (Plan UK, 2018). The regularity of menstruation (for most cisgirls, menstruating non-binary teens and transboys) means that the stigma of menstruation and the shame that it brings are an ongoing challenge for mental health and wellbeing. The *Break the Barriers* report has also found when menstruating, girls feel different as "their confidence drops and they become 'self-conscious'" (2018, p. 34) and this is compounded by those who suffer with gender dysphoria, endometriosis, and other related conditions. The inability to afford menstrual products, worsened by recent austerity measures, means that girls are at an even higher risk of experiencing mental ill-health when menstruating. According to some of the girls we have spoken to in our research, the potential visibility of menstruation also contributed to their experiences of verbal and sexual harassment from boys in school. For example, these girls reported that boys remove menstrual products from girls' bags to identify them as on their period and having to endure bullying and body-shaming comments when getting up to go to the toilet during class (if indeed, the teacher permits them to do so). The premise of such comments comes from a much broader policing of girls' agency over their own bodies, of which menstruation is a part.

This further demonstrates how the construct of femininity, specifically within the school environment, is rooted in a heteronormative binary that perpetuates a patriarchal power imbalance.

Experiencing sexual harassment

An NSPCC report noted that girls were more likely to experience sexual abuse than boys and it therefore follows that "a higher proportion of girls have counselling about sexual abuse and self-harm" (NSPCC, 2018) than boys. We understand that all forms of verbal and sexual harassment are, in fact, tools to reinforce girls' place in the world (as objects rather than active agents in their own lives). According to gender theorist Judith Butler, this is affirmed through the everyday 'production' of gender, which is to say that as social beings, we observe how others 'do' gender and equate that back to what we expect of them based on their gender presentation (so as boys or girls, for example). Butler (1990) argues that this is framed within what they call the 'heterosexual matrix', or in other words, an assumption (that is rendered common sense), that all those who present as male are sexually interested in girls and therefore produce identities of 'heterosexual masculinity', which is considered acceptable by their friends and peers, teachers, and family.[2] Sexual harassment itself is one of the acts synonymous with this form of masculinity, which means that young girls' experiences of everyday harassment and even forms of violence that span sexting, groping, sharing images, and physical and sexual violence are normalised under the trope of 'boys will be boys'. As noted above, navigating such forms of violence (either as individual acts or cumulative) acts as a primary stressor on girls' mental health.

It is worth recognising that girls and young women are attempting to navigate the discourses of successful femininity, where their agency is diluted and interrupted by the polarisation of who they want to be and the reality of who they *have* to be in this 'heterosexual matrix'. This manifests in coercive relationship cultures, sexual harassment, sexual assault, and abuse with the onus and emphasis on the girls themselves to augment their behaviour in order to keep themselves safe (Gådin, 2012; Paechter, 2017; Renold, 2005; Renold & Ringrose; 2008; Ringrose & Renold, 2010). Girls carry the weight of this responsibility on a daily basis, from choosing what to wear that will limit the objectification they receive, elevating or achieving social status with a heteronormative relationship, and/or changing their route home to avoid being verbally harassed or targeted by large groups of boys.

Of course, the policing of gender encompasses all sexualities and identities, which means that experiences of violence and harassment are prevalent in any space that exists outside of the gender binary or those who do not subscribe to (hetero) gendered norms, referred to by Butler as 'othering'. For Butler "sexual harassment of gay people may well take place not in the service of shoring up gender hierarchy, but in promoting gender normativity" (1990, p. xxiii). It is therefore crucial in our work with girls that we look not only to boys as the perpetrators of sexual violence and harassment but to other girls too.

Throw like a girl

One site for the development of good mental health for girls in school is sport, not least because sport can be fun and offers a space to 'get away' from the classroom. A study into American girls and young women has found that engagement in sport has benefits that extend well beyond individual fitness levels. Researchers found that physical activity in most instances acted as a form of antidepressant and reduced instances of suicidal ideation and thoughts (Staurowsky et al., 2009). However, some of the studies that have looked into girls' experiences of P.E. have found that this potential is rarely being met for the majority of teenage girls at school in the UK. This is one of the main areas where girls talk about the frustrations of double standards. For example, girls find themselves *again* to be micromanaged with their P.E. kit, with a number of schools refusing to let girls wear shorts, leggings, or trousers. Girls also express dismay at being told they cannot play outside when it's raining even though boys still do, highlighting how fragile they are seen to be. Assuming that girls cannot 'take' the elements or perform in the same sort of conditions as their male counterparts are notions that girls see as being upheld by both teachers and their male peers.

A further consequence of segregating sports along gender lines is that transgirls who may be very early in their transition process (or not even 'out') will be forced to share changing rooms with boys, to play on all boy sports teams further compounding their dysphoric feelings and impacting their mental health. Given that suicide remains a significant issue for LGBTQ+ health (McDermott, 2015), and trans suicide in particular a major concern, the (often unintentional) exclusion of trans youth from sport, given all of its potential for mental wellness is a point of concern for us. We encourage you to read the chapter on trans-youth in this volume (see Chapter 9) to better understand the unique challenges presented to trans youth in terms of their mental health.

Social media

While our focus for this chapter is on girls' experiences in school, it would be remiss to talk of the mental health of teenage girls without citing their engagement with social media, and thus while we do not give this significant attention, we provide an overview of the main issues here. A study by Kelly et al. (2018) has found that depressive symptoms linked to social media use are higher among girls. The study notes that overall depressive symptoms linked to social media usage have connections to sleep. This is, they argue because young people sleep close to their phones, regularly checking their devices throughout the night due to the FOMO ('fear of missing out'). Kelly et al. (2018) note that this insistence on checking their phone throughout the night and light from their screens impacts melatonin production and circadian rhythm (sleep cycle/pattern). The authors also found that harassment and reputational damage through sharing of materials also contributes to potential depressive episodes, making social media usage a key site for understanding the mental health of teenage girls. Amy Shields Dobson has written that "[c]ultural commentators quite often treat girls' and young women's media practices and self-representations not only with panic but also with disdain and contempt" (2015, p. 1). While social media can play a very positive role in girls' lives, providing access to networks of likeminded people and countering feelings of loneliness, it can also become a site of emotional stress and low self-esteem. For example, endless scrolling on social media can have an impact on their body confidence, particularly when so many images have filters (see Plan UK, 2020). In addition to feeling that their bodies are not 'good enough', girls also experience considerable sexual abuse in online spaces, with requests for 'nudes' and receiving criticism whether they deliver or not. For example, in their research into American girls' social media habits, Julia Lippman and Scott Campbell found that "girls were commonly judged harshly whether they sexted (e.g., 'slut') or not (e.g., 'prude'), whereas boys were virtually immune from criticism regardless" (2014, p. 371) and this certainly reflects the feelings of the girls that we have worked with in the UK. Relating back to the issues of policing bodies discussed above, social media has also been found to exacerbate these problems with Ringrose, Harvey, and Livingstone writing "such sexual double standards are hardly new, [but] the technology provides new ways for value to circulate through images" (2013, p. 317). In many ways, this encapsulates the ways in which social media, including spaces such as TikTok, Snapchat, and Instagram extend many of the pressures that girls experience in school to their homes and private lives.

What can teachers do?

Working with girls in schools as researchers has shown us the complex challenges they face when it comes to grasping and realising their own agency. Whilst information on increased gender equity is presented within the pursuit of individual freedom, rights, and autonomy to be and do whatever they choose, the path to this equality is littered and lined with everyday sexism, verbal and sexual harassment, and the ongoing reduction of space that comes with life under patriarchy. The impact of these experiences on girls' mental health is profound and not yet fully recognised, theorised, or understood. We therefore urge that schools provide intersectionally sensitive, consciousness-raising spaces for girls that extend beyond specialist school groups.

We advocate for the creation of spaces that allow girls and genderqueer young people to share their experiences of oppression, but we urge teachers to ensure a commitment to extending the safety of these spaces across the school more widely. For example, there are now a number of schools that provide space for feminist groups or inclusivity for the LGBTQ+ community (and these are much valued by those who engage with them) yet do little to advocate for and enforce this space more broadly in the school halls or playgrounds. Punishing boys (and girls) who transgress respectable conduct could be undertaken through more traditional means like detention or, as we encourage, could be more creative, like asking the boy to write a report or create a video on sexism and the way it harms individuals and society.

The language of equality is being spoken within the confines of a classroom or specialist group; meanwhile, male pupils congregate outside to pull faces, bang on the doors, and make comments. In this way, the very armour the school is trying to provide these girls with falls away as soon as they open the door, leaving in its place a target on their backs with no one or nothing to protect them. This also serves to perpetuate the masculine and feminine binary, which further marginalises and alienates members of the LGBTQ+ community who associate the freedom of their individual expression as associated with increased risk of harm. The levels of harassment that girls experience from boys is normalised as a product of performative masculinity, which is an iteration of pervasive heteronormativity, which simply identifies heterosexuality as the norm. This imbalance perpetuates stereotypical masculine and feminine norms that further reduce girls' space for action at the risk of alienation, isolation, and 'othering'. Girls who self-identify as feminist are often celebrated by schools yet experience increased verbal and sexual harassment such as threats of female genital mutilation (FGM) and sexual violence. The visibility of their feminism brings with it a performative pressure of its own, which one girl we have spoken to likened to being sent out to war on a daily basis with everyone watching to see if you win or lose. She relayed practicing her 'come backs' to the verbal abuse she experienced every morning in front of the mirror to make sure she didn't show 'any weakness'. This pressure resulted in high anxiety, which made going into school a daily battle.

There are a number of things that teachers and practitioners can do to ease this pressure and create more space for girls to exercise their rights and learn to operationalise the discourse of equality beyond specialist feminist groups. It is important to identify here what we mean by space; even though we recognise the value of holding specialist groups, if a safe space for girls to discuss feminism, or members of the LGBTQ+ community only exists within the four walls of a classroom every Tuesday between 1 and 2 pm, it is not doing anywhere near enough to increase their space for action outside of that room or designated time. Therefore, for the purposes of this chapter and for girls' mental health, when we refer to space, we mean the physical, mental, and emotional space an individual girl can fill throughout her day in a way that is not inhibited, reduced, oppressed, marginalised, assaulted, or abused due to her gender or sexuality.

To aid teachers in the production of these sorts of spaces, we provide recommendations around the following themes of accountability and agency.

Accountability

Say it with us: Accountability Is Everything. The most prolific message we received loud and clear from girls over and over was one of silence. Silence to the everyday sexism, misogynoir, or to homophobia in the halls. Silence to the boys who engage in period shaming, slut shaming, and ongoing 'low level' harassment, all with the objectives of reducing girls' movements and reminding them that their bodies are public property. Silence when it comes to challenging all forms of gender stereotyping, from gendered spaces in schools (such as the football field) to celebrating boys for their 'strength' and dismissing their behaviour as 'banter'.

This silence is not only deafening, but it is complicit, and it contributes to inequalities and all forms of violence and abuse against girls, which can create a sense of hyper-vigilance, increased anxiety, vulnerability, and powerlessness. In short, unless accountability is upheld in *every* space, the time allocated to the existing feminist groups may only serve to increase marginalisation and risk of harm, mentally and physically. Below are some examples of the level of accountability girls have told us they need in order to make a real difference to their daily lives:

- A zero-tolerance policy to ALL racist, sexist, or homophobic language. Offenders need to be punished at the first instance to ensure that the whole of the school environment is a safe space for all.

- Demonstrate the impact and harm of everyday sexism to everyone, and how it can be challenged.

- Challenge those policies that are oppressive to girls, which includes when girls are penalised for incorrect uniform – instead, start a discussion on what girls and boys want from their uniform and how they feel it separates them.

- Challenge gendered spaces in schools and be mindful of how much 'space' is taken up by gendered sports. Think about how this can be overcome – work with the pupils to tackle this.

- Take opportunities to discuss media or themes that perpetuate gender stereotypes.

- Ensure that the resources being used reflect intersectional equality – if they do not, ask pupils who or what is missing and why do they think that is?

Remember that language is extremely important, as it is the building blocks of the walls we all create in order to feel safe. If the language around you promotes a sexist, homophobic, or racist environment, the walls will become thicker and higher reducing movement and space.

Agency

Girls know what they want. They know what they need, and they recognise the inequalities around them. They are hungry and adamant for change, they have the voice and the will to advocate for it, but what they do not have is agency. They crave space in both their socio-cultural norms and the physicality of their daily routines. If this space is not provided, facilitated, and protected, why should girls believe practitioners when they say that they can and will achieve whatever they set their minds to?

As researchers, we are fundamentally aware that we are not the experts in girls' mental health, girls are, and as Jørgensen et al. (2019) write, girls provide that expertise readily and enthusiastically as soon as they have the agency to do so. They inform us of their challenges, fears, and frustrations and to be in a position to listen, engage with, and learn is one of privilege. This agency needs to exist outside of an hour a week in a classroom over lunch time, because if agency is marginalised it becomes tokenistic and diluted.

Experiences of abuse, harassment, and violence are not inevitable. They are not norms girls simply have to survive. It is not a question of some of us, some of the time, speaking out and challenging a construct that is oppressive; it is our responsibility as individuals and a community to actively pursue our rights and empower others to do so. We therefore encourage teachers and youth work practitioners to create a meaningful space within which girls can feed into the decisions that impact them. Below are some examples of what girls have told us they would like this to look like:

- Consistency in classes and sessions that focus on the impact of inequality, everyday sexism, and gender stereotyping. Most of the girls we have spoken to only access this type of content and debate when researchers or specialist facilitators come into the schools and every group has demonstrated a desire to continue.

- Activism is a natural progression from increased agency, which means that a pathway to school policy or politics needs to be established that is engaged with and reactive to the voices of girls.

- This pathway must be wholly supported by accountability (see above).

Takeaway points

- Girls' accounts of their lives and mental health (from disclosures of sexual assault to instances of self-harm) should be taken seriously.

- See girls in all their multiplicities, see the sexist racism they encounter, see their disability, see their class, but do not define them wholly on these identities.

- Punish behaviour that is harmful to girls.

- Ask girls what changes they want to see and then include them in the implementation of changes.

Notes

1 Those with an interest in girls' experiences would be interested in the reports that come from charities and thinktanks such as Plan International UK; Girlguiding; Childline; Mermaids.
2 It is important to note that Butler does not believe this is inherent or acceptable, but rather that this is the context in which gender is experienced and produced. This has negative consequences for girls which come in the form of sexual violence and harassment as we discuss, but also for boys who are not straight and also for non-binary folks.

Further reading

AGENDA (n.d.) *A young people's guide to making positive relationships matter*, available at: http://agenda.wales/

Girlguiding (2019) *Girls' attitudes survey 2019*, London: GirlGuiding.

Halo Collective (n.d.) *Understanding Black British hair discrimination,* available at: https://halocollective.co.uk/

Integrate UK (2020) *Charity fighting to end #FGM and empowering young people*, video resources available at: https://integrateuk.org/what-we-do/projects-videos/

Okanlawon, Kafayat. (2019) *This is us: Black British women and girls*, London: Break The Habit Press.

Plan UK (2018) *Break the barriers: Girls' experiences of menstruation in the UK*, London: Plan International UK.

Plan UK (2020) *The State of Girls Rights 2019–2020*, London: Plan International UK.

Renold, E. J. (2019) *Primary agenda: Supporting children in making positive relationships matter*. Cardiff: Cardiff University, Children's Commissioner for Wales, NSPCC Cymru/Wales, and Welsh Women's Aid.

References

Bailey, M. (2013) 'New terms of resistance: A response to Zenzele Isoke' *Souls*, 15 (4), 341–343.

Butler, J. (1990) *Gender Trouble*, London: Routledge.

Francis, B. (2005) 'Not/knowing their place: Girls' classroom behaviour' in Gwynedd Lloyd (ed.) *Problem girls: Understanding and supporting troubled and troublesome girls and young women*, Abingdon: RoutledgeFalmer.

Gådin, K. G. (2012) 'Sexual harassment of girls in elementary school: A concealed phenomenon within a heterosexual romantic discourse' *Journal of Interpersonal Violence*, 27 (9), 1762–1779.

Girlguiding. (2019) *Girls' attitudes survey 2019*, London: GirlGuiding.

Jørgensen, C. R., Weckesser, A., Turner, J., and Wade, A. (2019) 'Young people's views on sexting education and support needs: Findings and recommendations from a UK-based study' *Sex Education*, 19 (1), 25–40.

Joseph-Salisbury, R. and Connelly, L. (2018) '"If your hair is relaxed, white people are relaxed. If your hair is nappy, they're not happy": Black hair as a site of 'post-racial' social control in English schools' *Social Sciences*, 7 (11) 1–13.

Kelly, Y., Zilanawala, A., Booker, C., and Sacker, A. (2018) 'Social media use and adolescent mental health: Findings from the UK millennium cohort study' *EClinical Medicine*, 6, 59–68.

Lamb, S., and Plocha, A. (2015) 'Pride and sexiness: Girls of color discuss race, body image and sexualization' *Girlhood Studies*, 8 (2), 86–102.

McDermott, E. (2015) 'Asking for help online: Lesbian, gay, bisexual and trans youth, self-harm and articulating the 'failed' self' *Health: An Interdisciplinary Journal for the Social Study of Health, Illness and Medicine*, 19 (6), 561–577.

Moldavsky, M., Groenewald, C., Owen, V. and Sayal, K. (2013) 'Teachers' recognition of children with ADHD: Role of subtype and gender' *Child Adolescent Mental Health*, 18, 18–23.

NSPCC. (2018) *The courage to talk: Childline annual review 2017/18* available at: https://learning.nspcc.org.uk/media/1596/courage-talk-childline-annual-review-2017-18.pdf

Paechter, C. (2017) 'Young children, gender and the heterosexual matrix' *Discourse: Studies in the Cultural Politics of Education,* 38 (2), 277–291.

Plan UK. (2018) *Break the barriers: Girls' experiences of menstruation in the UK*, London: Plan International UK.

Plan UK. (2020) *The state of girls rights 2019–2020*, London: Plan International UK.

Renold, E.J. (2005) *Girls, boys, and junior sexualities: Exploring children's gender and sexual relations in the primary school,* New York: RoutledgeFalmer.

Renold, E.J., and Ringrose, J. (2008) 'Regulation and rupture Mapping tween and teenage girls' resistance to the heterosexual matrix' *Feminist Theory,* 9 (3), 313–338.

Ringrose, J., and Renold, E.J. (2010) 'Normative cruelties and gender deviants: The performative effects of bully discourses for girls and boys in school' *British Educational Research Journal,* 36 (4), 573–596.

Ringrose, J., Harvey, L., Gill, R., and Livingstone, S. (2013) 'Teen girls, sexual double standards and 'sexting': Gendered value in digital image exchange' *Feminist Theory,* 14 (3), 305–323.

Ringrose, J., Tolman, D., and Ragonese, M. (2019) 'Hot right now: Diverse girls navigating technologies of racialized sexy femininity' *Feminism & Psychology*, 29 (1), 76–95.

Shields Dobson, A. (2015) *Postfeminist digital cultures: Femininity, social media, and self-representation*, New York: Palgrave Macmillan.

Showunmi, V. (2017) 'The role of the black girls club: Challenging the status quo' in Martin, J. L., Nickels, A. E., Sharp-Grier, M. (eds) *Feminist pedagogy, practice, and activism: Improving lives for girls and women*, New York, NY: Routledge, pp. 229–246.

Staurowsky, E. J., DeSousa, M. J., Ducher, G., Gentner, N., Miller, K. E., Shakib, S., Theberge, N., and Williams, N. (2009) *Her life depends on it II: Sport, physical activity, and the health and well-being of American girls and women.* East Meadow, NY: Women's Sports Foundation.

8 Including Pupils Who Identify as Lesbian, Gay, Bisexual, Transgender, or Queer (LGBTQ+)

Jonathan Glazzard and Samuel Stones

Synopsis

This chapter will explore the experiences of pupils who identify as lesbian, gay, bisexual, or queer (LGBTQ+). It will draw on Meyer's (2003) theory of minority stress to explore their experiences of discrimination, concealment, internalised homophobia, and poor mental health outcomes. It will argue that addressing prejudice-based bullying in isolation is a reactive approach, which often fails to address prejudice. Instead, the chapter will outline the aspects of a whole-school approach to LGBTQ+ inclusion with specific emphasis on ways of working partnership with children and parents. We will explore ways of embedding LGBTQ+ experiences and identities into the curriculum and we will consider the role of the physical and emotional environment in the school. Central to the whole-school approach is the role of the school leadership team. This chapter will therefore explore the roles and responsibilities of school leaders in relation to LGBTQ+ inclusion. We will also explore how the 2020 statutory guidance for relationships and sex education can be addressed in relation to LGBTQ+ identities and relationships.

Background

Research suggests that LGBTQ+ young people experience higher rates of depression, anxiety, and self-harm compared to their heterosexual and cisgender peers (Goldbach & Gibbs, 2017). Evidence also indicates that they are more likely to attempt suicide (Marshal et al., 2011) and experience eating disorders (Austin et al., 2013). Research indicates that stigmatising experiences during adolescence can reduce academic achievement and result in negative outcomes later in life (Radkowsky & Siegel, 1997).

DOI: 10.4324/9781003160526-8

The Stonewall *School Report* (see Bradlow et al., 2017) identified that:

- Nearly half of lesbian, gay, bi, and transgender pupils (45%) – including 64% of transgender pupils – are bullied for being LGBTQ+ at school.

- Half of LGBTQ+ pupils (52%) hear homophobic language 'frequently' or 'often' at school, more than a third (36%) hear biphobic language 'frequently' or 'often', and almost half (46%) hear transphobic language 'frequently' or 'often'.

- The majority of LGBTQ+ pupils (86%) regularly hear phrases including 'that's so gay' or 'you're so gay' in school.

- Nearly one in ten transgender pupils (9%) are subjected to death threats at school.

- Almost half of LGBTQ+ pupils (45%) who are bullied for being LGBTQ+ never tell anyone about the bullying.

- Less than a third of bullied LGBTQ+ pupils (29%) reported that teachers intervened when they were present during the bullying.

- Two in five LGBTQ+ young people (40%) have been the target of homophobic, biphobic, and transphobic abuse online.

- Nearly all LGBTQ+ young people (97%) reported that they had seen homophobic, biphobic, and transphobic content online.

- Two in three LGBTQ+ young people (65%) thought that online platforms are unlikely to do anything about tackling homophobic, biphobic, and transphobic content or incidents when it is reported to them.

Minority stress

Minority stress theory (Meyer, 2003) considers how stress can affect the mental health outcomes in individuals with a minority status. The theory suggests that individuals with a minority status experience three stressors:

General stressors. These are stressors which result from environmental circumstances. They could include family factors such as parental conflict, parental separation, abuse and neglect, and community-related factors such as social deprivation.

Distal stressors. These are stressors which arise from the experience of prejudice, discrimination, and violence.

Proximal stressors. These are stressors which arise from the expectations of rejection, prejudice, discrimination, and violence. That is, an individual with a minority status does not have to actually experience distal stressors, but the anticipation that they might encounter these stressors in different social and environmental contexts can result in internalised stress. For example, they may anticipate that they will encounter prejudice if they disclose their sexual or gender identity. This can lead to pupils concealing their identities, which can result in internalised stigma.

Negative experiences when disclosing their identities (distal stress) may increase expectations of further rejection (proximal stress) in different contexts (Goldbach & Gibbs, 2017). Additionally, concealing one's identity due to fear of rejection (proximal stress) can reduce the likelihood of experiencing prejudice, discrimination, and violence (distal stress). Thus, the stressors are inter-related and bi-directional.

Meyer's (2003) theory posits that stressors can be moderated by social support systems that are specifically established to foster both group solidarity and positively affirm minority identities. Many secondary schools now provide 'safe spaces' for pupils who identify as LGBTQ+ to meet informally. Such groups enable pupils to provide each other with mutual support and advice. Some groups also adopt a proactive approach to LGBTQ+ inclusion within the school by developing initiatives to embed LGBTQ+ inclusion across the whole school. Providing opportunities for LGBTQ+ pupils to meet as a group can enhance social connectivity, reduce internalised stigma, and increase resilience. However, there is also a risk that separating out one group of pupils in this way can also result in internal exclusion though the creation of an 'othered' group. One way of addressing this is to allow membership of the group to heterosexual allies who are deeply committed to LGBTQ+ inclusion.

What can teachers do?

The following sections outline practical strategies that schools can implement to support young people who identify as LGBTQ+.

Consult with stakeholders: develop a vision

Before developing LGBTQ+ provision schools should consult with parents and carers to ensure that they understand the reasons why this strand of inclusion is a priority for the school. Schools need to support parents to help them understand the school's legal position in relation to the Equality Act 2010 and the Public Sector Equality Duty (Section 149 of the Equality Act 2010) which requires schools to foster good relations between different groups of people. Leaders also need to emphasise to parents that regardless of personal beliefs, schools have a responsibility to promote a culture of respect.

Meeting with parents prior to undertaking this work will help address any misconceptions and provide reassurance that the school is, in no way, promoting one type of sexuality or gender identity over another. Parents may also need reassurance that schools have a statutory responsibility to teach inclusive relationships education. Parents should be given an opportunity to contribute to the vision.

If the school has pupils who are openly LGBTQ+, they should also be invited to contribute to the school vision statement. They will have useful insights to share, and they will probably be aware of which aspects of provision need to be developed or improved. Schools may also wish to involve community organisations (such as LGBTQ+ youth groups), charities, and universities in shaping the vision.

Mitigating stress

As LGBTQ+ pupils move between spaces in school, there is potential for them to experience both proximal and distal stressors. They may not feel safe in the school grounds, in the changing rooms, or in the toilets. They may be worried about interactions in specific lessons with pupils who are openly homophobic, biphobic, or transphobic. They may perceive that some teachers hold negative attitudes towards their sexual or gender identities, particularly if LGBTQ+ inclusion is never addressed in their lessons. They may interpret stares, giggles, and jokes to be microaggressions. Teachers can reduce minority stress using a range of approaches. These include:

- Displaying the LGBTQ+ flags in their classrooms to represent a commitment to LGBTQ+ inclusion.

- Developing lessons and resources which are LGBTQ+ inclusive.

- Displaying signs in classrooms, changing rooms, dining spaces, and toilets which communicate a zero-tolerance approach to LGBTQ+ bullying.

- Challenging homophobic 'banter' in sport and in the school grounds.

- Making visible the school's commitment to LGBTQ+ inclusion on the website, across the school social media platforms, and in the school entrance.

- Celebrating events such as LGBT history month and Pride.

- Making visible the work and achievements of the school LGBTQ+ group.

- Making visible the commitment of the school's leadership team to LGBTQ+ inclusion.

- Including a section on the school newsletters to share the actions taken to promote LGBTQ+ inclusion.

- Making it explicit to all pupils, staff, and parents how LGBTQ+ bullying will be addressed.

Positively affirming sexual and gender identities

Schools can reduce minority stress by positively affirming non-normative sexual and gender identities. An affirmative model encourages pupils to be proud of their identities. It views diversity as positive, energising, and enriching. It rejects attempts which seek to 'normalise' individuals and removes those with minority identities from their positions as victims within a normalising society.

An affirmative model embraces diversity as a positive aspect of someone's identity. Schools can use a variety of approaches in adopting this model. These include:

- Celebrating the work of famous LGBTQ+ people across all subjects.

- Celebrating Pride, LGBTQ+ history month, and other special events.

- Displaying the LGBTQ+ flags in major areas of the school.

- Celebrating same-sex marriages and civil partnerships among staff, governors, and parents.

- Wearing rainbow lanyards.

- Introducing a sports kit in the colours of the rainbow for pupils to wear during LGBT history month.

- Making trans identities as visible in the school as LGB identities.

- Embedding LGBTQ+ identities into the curriculum.

It is interesting how language which was once directed towards the LGBTQ+ community as an insult has now been re-claimed by the community and is used to describe people's identity. The use of the word 'Queer' was once intended as an insult. It was a derogatory term used to belittle people who identified as LGBTQ+. Many LGBTQ+ people now define themselves as 'Queer'. The word has been re-claimed and no longer has negative connotations. This represents an example of resistance by the LGBTQ+ community and the term is now used as a positive affirmation of identity.

Disclosure: coming out

The process of 'coming out' can result in both proximal and distal stressors for young people. Prior to disclosure, LGBTQ+ young people may have experienced psychological distress from internalised stigma, particularly as they are coming to terms with their sexuality or gender identities. The anticipation that their disclosure might be met with hostility or disgust can result in fear of disclosure (proximal stress) which can result in young people concealing their identity. This can be stressful because it results in 'cognitive burden' (Goldbach & Gibbs, 2017, p. 47). When young people are met with prejudice and discrimination following a disclosure (distal stressors) this can result in further psychological distress.

The process of coming out can also be liberating and empowering for young people, particularly, if they encounter positive responses to their disclosures. If their LGBTQ+ status is positively affirmed, this can help build confidence and self-worth, and it can reduce stress. Coming out is a deeply personal decision and young people will do this when they feel ready to do so. However, schools can support pupils to feel proud of their sexuality and gender identities in a range of ways. These could include:

- Providing guidance on the school website to support pupils through the process of coming out.

- Providing guidance to all pupils on how to support their friends when they come out.

- Asking former LGBTQ+ pupils to come to school to talk about their own experiences of coming out and other life experiences.

- LGBTQ+ teachers being open about their sexuality gender identities.

- Signposting pupils to services in the community, including LGBTQ+ youth groups.

- Using peer-mentoring schemes to enable older LGBTQ+ pupils to support younger pupils through the process of coming out.

- Requesting that LGBTQ+ pupils write their own coming out stories and poems to produce an anthology – these could be anonymous.

- Involving role models in sharing their own coming out stories with pupils, for example, local sports players.

- Displaying positive messages about LGBTQ+ people around the school.

In many cases, young people will disclose their sexuality gender identities to their friends before they make a disclosure to family members. They may fear rejection by their parents and carers, and this may result in proximal stress. They may be worried that they will not be accepted by their families or communities, and this can lead to psychological distress. It is critical that schools do not intentionally or unintentionally 'out' pupils to anyone. A person's sexuality gender identity is a private matter and young people do worry greatly about being 'outed' consent.

Schools can introduce briefing sessions to parents and carers to inform them about the LGBTQ+ inclusion work that is taking place in the school. In these sessions, teachers can provide information to parents and carers about how they can support their child if they make a disclosure. Many parents are keen to understand more about LGBTQ+ experiences and want to respond appropriately if their child comes out. Information could also be placed on the school website or circulated across the school social media platforms to provide advice to parents on how to support their child if a disclosure is made. Parents may benefit from an LGBTQ+ myth-busting guide and schools may also wish to provide an LGBTQ+ fact guide as well.

Supporting pupils who come out

Staff may experience pupils making disclosures of their sexuality. These conversations are extremely important because the pupil may have had to build up a significant amount of courage to make the disclosure. The following points are important:

- Do not tell the child that they are going through a 'phase'.

- Thank them for telling you and make assurances of confidentiality. The only exception to this rule is if the child is at risk of harm.

- Ask them if they have spoken to anyone else about their sexuality.

- Listen to what they say.

- Reassure them that their feelings are normal and that their sexuality is valid. Positively affirm their identity. You may even wish to share personal information with the child, for example, if you have friends or family members who identify as LGBTQ+.

- Encourage the child to talk about their concerns or anxieties.

- Ask the child what they want to do next.

- Ask the child what, if anything, they would like you to do next.

- Avoid making comments such as 'we are all the same'. This is not true. People are different and the aim of the conversation should be to positively affirm difference.

(NAHT, 2018)

During this conversation, it is important to be alert to signs which may indicate that the pupil is experiencing mental ill-health. If you are concerned that they need additional pastoral or school-based counselling support, discuss this with the pupil and seek their consent.

Building resilience

Resilience is context-specific and multi-dimensional. It is possible to be highly resilient in some contexts and to demonstrate less resilience in other contexts. For example, young people may demonstrate resilience in sports but lack resilience in mathematics when they encounter a complex mathematical problem. Some may be more resilient at home than they are in school and vice versa. It is typically linked with the ability to bounce-back or recover from adverse experiences so that the impact of these experiences is lessened.

Positive psychology focuses on the character strengths within individuals. One way that schools can build resilience in LGBTQ+ pupils is to emphasise their character strengths. By increasing pupils' awareness of their character strengths, this will increase their self-worth and confidence. When they encounter stressors, they can reflect on their character strengths which contribute to their identity. Schools also need to reassure LGBTQ+ pupils that there is nothing wrong with them, they do not need to change, and that others who subject them to prejudice, discrimination, and abuse need support to help them change their attitudes. They need to be given reassurances that they are not the problem; the perpetrators need support to help them re-shape their attitudes and values. Prejudice, discrimination, and bullying are not acceptable in any society. Schools are a microcosm of the society they serve.

If LGBTQ+ young people are supported to recognise that perpetrators need support, this can increase their resilience. Schools can also support LGBTQ+ young people to understand the origins of prejudice. Negative attitudes and values are shaped via a process of socialisation through interactions with others including families, cultures, communities, and peers. Schools can support LGBTQ+ pupils to understand that prejudice is rarely personal; it is the result of many years of socialisation by others. Schools can adopt a systemic approach to intervention by working with pupils, families, and community organisations to help break down prejudice. Schools need to ensure that young people know what help is available to support them and how to access it when they need it.

It is important to remember that resilience is not just an innate character trait within individuals. It is relational. Therefore, when people have support from friends, teachers, family members, and the wider community, they can be more resilient in the face of adversity. Sadly, when some young people come out, these support networks are cut off from them and they are subjected to prejudice and discrimination. This impacts detrimentally on their resilience. Teachers should be aware of young people who may need extra support in school due to external support networks being cut off. In these cases, pastoral support can play a critical role in ensuring positive mental health outcomes for young people.

Developing digital resilience and digital citizenship

Through the digital curriculum, schools need to support LGBTQ+ pupils to be resilient online. Pupils need to be taught about the dangers associated with being online and schools need to ensure that they have the appropriate digital literacy skills to protect themselves from harm. According to the Stonewall report (Bradlow et al., 2017):

- Just two in five LGBTQ+ young people (40%) have an adult at home they can talk to about being LGBTQ+.

- Nearly all LGBTQ+ young people (96%) say the Internet has helped them understand more about their sexual orientation and/or gender identity.

- Two in five LGBTQ+ young people (40%) have been the target of homophobic, biphobic, and transphobic abuse online.

- Nearly all LGBTQ+ young people (97%) see homophobic, biphobic, and transphobic content online.

- Two in three LGBTQ+ young people (65%) think that online platforms are unlikely to do anything about tackling homophobic, biphobic, and transphobic content or incidents when it is reported to them.

All pupils also need to be taught about the concept of digital citizenship so that they know how to conduct themselves appropriately online. Schools need to prepare LGBTQ+ pupils for the types of abuse that they are likely to experience online and provide them with appropriate ways of responding to this, for example, by blocking accounts and reporting abuse. All pupils also need to be aware of the dangers of online grooming and sexting. Schools need to provide pupils with opportunities to seek help if they experience online abuse. Some schools operate digital ambassador schemes. Digital ambassadors are usually older pupils with advanced digital skills. Digital ambassadors can easily be trained to become skilled listeners. When LGBTQ+ pupils experience something negative online, they can talk to a digital ambassador. Some schools train pupils to be LGBTQ+ ambassadors and this scheme could operate in exactly the same way. LGBTQ+ pupils may be less willing to talk to a teacher or to a parent, particularly if they do not wish to disclose their sexuality gender identities so it is important that mechanisms are established through which they can talk to a peer.

A critical component of building resilience is to ensure that LGBTQ+ young people know where they can get support and advice. Resilience is not just about 'bouncing-back' from a negative experience. If young people know where to turn to for support and advice, they can overcome adversity more easily. Schools therefore play an important role in signposting LGBTQ+ pupils to local support organisations, including LGBTQ+ youth clubs, charity helplines, and services within the school including counselling and pastoral support.

Addressing homophobic, biphobic, and transphobic bullying

Homophobic language includes phrases including *'that's so gay'* or *'you're so gay'*. Young people may excuse this language as harmless banter but there are two key issues for schools to address here. Firstly, often the word 'gay' is being used as a synonym to replace 'rubbish'. For example, *'those trainers are so gay'* can be used to mean *'those trainers are rubbish'*. The association of 'gay' with 'rubbish' is dangerous link because it can result in the marginalisation of LGBTQ+ people. Secondly, regardless of whether language was intended as harmful banter, if it is perceived as homophobic, biphobic, or transphobic by a victim, then it should be addressed as a homophobic, biphobic, or transphobic incident. All schools should therefore have a zero-tolerance policy on the use of this type of language and this should be reinforced through clear, visible notices which are displayed around the school. All staff should be prepared to challenge the inappropriate use of language and banter and therefore professional development for all members of staff will empower staff to recognise bullying and to challenge it. This can be done calmly and in a non-confrontational way by explaining to young people why it is wrong, hurtful, and damaging. Educating young people is more effective than using punishment. It is important to remember that many young people will be exposed to this type of language and banter at home, and they may have internalised it. If the use of homophobic, biphobic, or transphobic language has never been challenged, young people may not understand why it is wrong to use these terms or phrases. Helping young people understand why they must not use prejudice-based terminology is essential rather than resorting to punishment.

Sadly, some pupils will hear prejudice at home and therefore schools play a critical role in re-educating them about this, thus helping to re-shape their attitudes and values. It is important to help young people understand the harmful effects of prejudice, language, and discrimination on individuals and on society as a whole. This is difficult work because, in some cases, schools are directly challenging parental, community, or religious values. However, it is crucial work because young people need to understand that prejudice is never tolerated in society, further or higher education, or employment. In order to function successfully as a productive member of society, young people need to learn to adjust their behaviours. However, merely adjusting behaviours is not sufficient in itself. Schools need to support young people to actually believe that prejudice and discrimination are wrong so that these behaviours do not occur in contexts outside of school.

Young people may become victims of bullying online outside of school. Schools should educate pupils to block the accounts of perpetrators and to take screenshots of bullying. These can be used as sources of evidence. Victims of cyber bullying need to be encouraged to talk to friends, parents, or teachers about their experiences. Schools play a key role in ensuring that young people know that they should not feel ashamed or embarrassed if they become a victim of bullying and they should highlight the importance of seeking help by talking to others. Victims of bullying should be encouraged to resist replying to comments because this can fuel the situation. The digital curriculum should provide all young people with the digital literacy skills that they need to keep themselves safe online. In addition, it should introduce pupils to the concept of digital citizenship, i.e. that young people need to be taught how to be good digital citizens. They need to learn that behaviour which is not tolerated in the offline world is also not acceptable in the online world. As good digital citizens, they need to learn to treat each other with respect, compassion, and empathy. These behaviours constitute good citizenship both offline and online.

Encouraging perpetrators and victims to meet and talk together can be effective. Restorative approaches support both victims and perpetrators. The victim is supported by a mediator to explain to the perpetrator how bullying has impacted on them. They can talk about the impact of bullying on their feelings, their mental health, and their daily life. The perpetrator should be supported to listen to the victim's account and can then be supported to explain why they chose to bully the victim and what they have learned from listening to their account. They can also be supported by a mediator to explain how they will modify their behaviour in the future. The approach is designed to provide reassurance to the victim that there will not be a repeat incident so that they feel safer.

Developing an LGBTQ+ pupils' group

Developing an LGBTQ+ pupils' group is an effective way of empowering pupils. The group can provide LGBTQ+ pupils with a safe, informal space to gain mutual support. However, effective LGBTQ+ pupil groups achieve far more than providing members with mutual support; they advance LGBTQ+ inclusion, challenge prejudice and discrimination, and change attitudes. It is important to allow non-LGBTQ+ pupils to join the group because this creates a powerful message that the group is inclusive and has support from the heterosexual student body. These pupils can act as LGBTQ+ allies and their membership of the group helps to demonstrate that the group is not separate from the rest of the school community.

The group may be initiated by a staff member, or it may be completely pupil-initiated. When developing the group, it will be useful to refer to the guidance that Stonewall has developed (Stonewall, 2018). In the first meeting:

- Establish the aims, focus, and aspirations of the group. The group members will need to decide what exactly they want the group to achieve within a specific time-scale and how they are going to achieve this.

- Ensure that the group is pupil-led right from the start.

- Gain support from the senior leadership team. One way of achieving this is for a member of the leadership team to voice their commitment to the group in the first meeting.

- Allow non-LGBTQ+ pupils to join the group.

- Name the group: the pupils will need to decide on a name and logo for the group so that the group has a brand.

- Consider how the group will be advertised.

- Create ground rules: one of the most important things to establish in the initial meeting is that the group provides a confidential space for members to discuss their concerns. In addition, disagreements between members of the group should be kept outside of the group and not brought into meetings.

■ Create a plan for the year. Members will need to decide what they want to achieve over the course of the year. Decisions will need to be made about what activities the group will develop to address key calendar dates. These include LGBTQ+ history month, anti-bullying week, and mental health awareness week.

The pupil members should be empowered to take responsibility for making decisions in relation to the above points. It is important that the group has a visible presence in the school and is not hidden away. One way of achieving this is to assign a space for the group to display their achievements and to advertise key events. The student members will need to decide if there will be a Chair and Deputy Chair and, if so, how these will be elected. This is a good way of teaching pupils about democracy and addressing one of the Fundamental British Values. The group will also need to decide how often meetings will be held and whether minutes of meetings will be recorded. Fundamentally, the group will need to be given opportunities to organise events. Pupil members need to be kept busy by working on worthwhile projects. This will help members stay motivated.

Members may wish to consider creating a newsletter, leaflets, social media platforms, or a website to promote the group and to provide helpful advice for other pupils. Guidance on coming to terms with one's sexuality gender identity as well as advice on 'coming out' is more likely to be taken seriously if it has been written by other pupils who have also experienced the same issues.

It is more effective to distribute different tasks to different pupils so that there is a fair allocation of workload. Pupil members will have different strengths. Some will have strengths in oral communication; others may have strengths in event organising, and others will have technological expertise. It is important to draw on different people's talents and experiences.

LGBTQ+ pupil groups may also want to be 'outward facing'. One way of achieving this is for the group to gain support from community organisations, parents, and carers. Some parents will resist the group and be suspicious of its motives. This is a matter for staff members to address. Parents' and carers' concerns need to be listened to, but leadership teams should communicate a clear message to parents that the school is committed to equality and that the school has a legal obligation to support the LGBTQ+ student body. Pupil members may wish to consider gaining support from parents and carers who are willing to participate in the group.

Senior leadership teams will need to consider how they are going to measure the impact of the LGBTQ+ group. Impact can be measured both qualitatively and quantitatively. Examples of impact measure include:

■ Quotes from pupil members of the group which illustrate how the group has benefitted them individually.

■ More detailed case studies of pupil members, for example, one page pen portraits.

- Attendance data or achievement data of pupil members.

- Impact on the number of incidents of LGBTQ+ bullying.

Staff members will also need to be encouraged to promote the group by signposting pupils to the group who may benefit from being members. Members need to view themselves as agentic individuals who have the power to effect positive change. The group should not be viewed solely as a means of support. However, this should fall within its remit. Essentially, it is a key element of the whole-school approach to LGBTQ+ inclusion in that it represents the *student partnership* strand. However, it can also bare influence on other aspects of the whole school approach to LGBTQ+ inclusion. This may include the curriculum, teaching and learning, and staff development. These roles are outlined below.

Visibility through the curriculum

Traditionally, schools and colleges have sought to promote LGBTQ+ inclusivity through curriculum drop-down days, extra-curricular events, and themed assemblies. However, in recent years, schools and colleges have begun to embed LGBTQ+ inclusion throughout their core curriculum offer. This illustrates a cultural shift in the promotion of LGBTQ+ inclusion whereby standalone activities are seen as insufficient in promoting and developing a culture of LGBTQ+ inclusion.

Takeaway points

- Schools play a critical role in eradicating homophobic, biphobic, and transphobic bullying.

- Schools also play an even more critical role in transforming pupils' attitudes towards non-normative gender and sexual identities.

- It is not sufficient for pupils to *know* that prejudice-based bullying is wrong and against the law. They must also *believe* that it is wrong to think about LGBTQ+ people in a negative way.

- Schools have a duty to prevent harm, but they also have a duty to foster good relationships between different groups of people. It is therefore crucial that the curriculum is used effectively to educate pupils about LGBTQ+ identities, experiences and achievements.

References

Austin, S. B., Nelson, L. A., Birkett, M. A., Calzo, J. P., and Everett, B. (2013), 'Eating disorder symptoms and obesity at the intersections of gender, ethnicity, and sexual orientation in US high school students', *American Journal of Public Health*, 103, (2), 16–22.

Bradlow, J., Bartram, F., Guasp, A., and Jadva, V. (2017), *School report: The experiences of lesbian, gay, bi and trans young people in Britain's schools in 2017*, Stonewall.

Equality Act 2010, c.1. Available at: http://www.legislation.gov.uk/ukpga/2010/15/contents (Accessed: 13 May 2020).

Goldbach, J. T., and Gibbs, J. J. (2017), 'A developmentally informed adaptation of minority stress for sexual minority adolescents', *Journal of Adolescence*, 55, 36–50.

Marshal, M. P., Dietz, L. J., Friedman, M. S., Stall, R., Smith, H. A., McGinley, J., et al. (2011), 'Suicidality and depression disparities between sexual minority and heterosexual youth: A meta-analytic review', *Journal of Adolescent Health*, 49, (2), 115–123.

Meyer, I. H. (2003), 'Prejudice, social stress, and mental health in lesbian, gay, and bisexual populations: Conceptual issues and research evidence', *Psychological Bulletin*, 129, (5), 674–697.

National Association of Head Teachers (NAHT). (2018), *LGBT inclusion in schools: Advice and guidance,* NAHT.

Radkowsky, M., and Siegel, L. J. (1997), 'The gay adolescent: Stressors, adaptations, and psychosocial interventions', *Clinical Psychology Review*, 17, (2), 191–216.

Stonewall. (2018), *Student voice: Setting up a student LGBT group in secondary schools and colleges*, Stonewall.

Supporting Pupils Who Identify as Trans*

Matt Leonard

Synopsis

This chapter explores some of the school experiences of trans* young people and focuses on some of the strategies and programmes that have already been implemented in schools to help teachers support trans* pupils in the classroom and create a safer, more nurturing, and more inclusive learning environment for them and their peers.

To date, there has been little research conducted on the school experiences of trans* young people, especially within the UK. Current research highlights that these pupils often face a significantly more hostile educational environment than their cisgender, and even Lesbian, Gay, or Bisexual (LGB), peers. However, it also demonstrates that for many young people, a safe and supportive school environment can protect against some of these hostile factors; having teachers who understand and support them can be hugely influential in allowing for the safe expression of their identities.

Throughout this chapter, the term trans* will be used to encompass the whole community of gender-variant people and includes all gender identities which are different from the ones assigned at birth.

Background

There are no official records of the number of trans* individuals in the UK, although it is estimated that around 1% of the population is transgender (Reed, Rhodes, Schofield & Wylie, 2009). Children are thought to develop their awareness of gender constancy at around the age of four (Szkrybalo & Ruble, 1999), and it is from this age that young people may begin to question their gender identity. Indeed, Kennedy and Hellen (2010) highlight that 76% of their participants had questioned their gender identity by the end of primary school, and only 4% of participants first questioned their gender identity after the age of 18.

 DOI: 10.4324/9781003160526-9

However, while many young people may have questioned their gender identity at this age, access to support with regard to the transition process has previously been limited. Over the past decade, this has changed. The number of young people being referred to the Gender Identity Clinic (GIC) in the Tavistock and Portman Trust (a national centre supporting transgender children and young people in the UK) for assessment has increased by almost 3,500% over the past ten years, rising from 77 assessment referrals in 2009/2010 to 2,728 referrals in 2019/2020 (NHS, 2019, 2020a). Perhaps reflecting this growth, the GIC highlights that the current waiting time for new referrals is approximately 33–36 months (NHS, 2020b), meaning that many trans* young people of school age may not be getting the emotional, social, and physical support they need.

The potential impact of this lack of support is, unfortunately, well documented. Trans* young people are consistently found to be at greater risk of mental-health difficulties, including anxiety and depression (Chodzen, Hidalgo, Chen & Garofalo, 2019; Connolly, Zervos, Barone, Johnson & Joseph, 2016), and have been shown to be at higher risk of suicide than their cisgender (those whose gender identity matches their gender assigned at birth) and LGB peers (Johns et al., 2019; McDermott, Hughes & Rawlings, 2018; Stieglitz, 2010). Perhaps relating to this, trans* young people have also been found to be at greater risk of illegal-substance misuse and other self-hazardous behaviours, such as smoking and drinking, and sexual risk-taking (Coulter, Bersamin, Russell & Mair, 2018; Day, Fish, Perez-Brumer, Hatzenbuehler & Russell, 2017; Johns et al. 2019).

Negative experiences of school and outcomes

Schools are often cited as a source of negative experiences for trans* young people, and indeed, as highlighted by Formby (2014), this has led to an environment where trans* young people *expect* to be bullied due to their gender identity. A consistently high percentage of trans* young people report experiencing transphobic or gender-related bullying in school, and this has been directly linked to higher levels of self-reported anxiety, depression, and low self-esteem (Hellen, 2009; Witcomb et al., 2019). As well as the detrimental effects on their mental health, these negative experiences have also been linked to school avoidance, poor academic achievement, reduced engagement in extracurricular activities, and an overall reduction in their confidence in themselves and their trust in others (Bradlow, Bartram, Guasp & Jadva, 2017; Department for Children, Schools and Families, 2009; Hellen, 2009).

One of the most common negative experiences relates to verbal harassment. Trans* young people report being frequently subjected to negative remarks about their gender expression, as well as homophobic language and personal attacks, and are more likely to experience verbal harassment than their cisgender and LGB peers (Day, Perez-Brumer & Russell, 2018; Formby, 2014; Jones et al., 2016; Kosciw, Greytak, Zongrone, Clark & Truong, 2018; McGuire, Anderson, Toomey & Russell, 2010). As well as verbal harassment, trans* young people are also subject to greater incidents of physical and sexual assaults (Jones & Hillier, 2013; Jones et al., 2016; McGuire et al., 2010; Sausa, 2005; Wyss, 2004).

In addition to explicit bullying or harassment, however, trans* pupils face significant difficulties and barriers relating to the structure of schools as a system. Schools are traditionally mapped on to cisgender binary norms (i.e. Frohard-Dourlent, 2016). In primary schools, boys and girls may be asked to line up separately, and throughout education, young people observe gender-based segregation through uniforms, lessons, facilities, and sports. Even the lessons themselves are typically geared towards binary cisgenderism; and it was only from September 2020 that LGBTQ+ representation in Relationships Education in primary schools and Sex Education in secondary schools became a requirement, and to the extent that it is "fully integrated into their programmes of study for this area of the curriculum rather than delivered as a stand-alone unit or lesson" (DfE, 2019, p. 15).

One of the biggest systemic challenges faced by trans* young people, however, is a perceived lack of support from school staff. In some instances, prejudices are reported to come directly from school staff (Austin & Craig, 2015; Kosciw et al., 2018), and institutions as a whole (Austin, Craig & McInroy, 2016; Formby, 2014), in terms of verbal harassment and blaming the pupils themselves for, or dismissing, the issues they raise. However, in most instances, it is the *unintentional* prejudices, such as non-intervention in observed harassment or lack of awareness around gender issues, which is viewed as the biggest barrier to support for trans* young people (Formby, 2014; Grossman et al., 2009; Jones & Hillier, 2013; Jones et al., 2016; McGuire et al., 2010).

School staff often recognise these unintentional episodes themselves, and report feeling unprepared or unsupported in managing gender issues within a classroom, and wanting additional training in and around LGBTQ+ and gender-identity support (e.g. Formby, 2014; Payne & Smith, 2014). Some local authorities are now producing guidance for schools on supporting trans* young people (e.g. Brighton and Hove City Council, 2018; Lancashire County Council, 2013), but while these often focus on schoolwide policies, they may not always offer an insight into individual teacher support and strategies.

Positive experiences and outcomes

What happens when trans* young people feel supported in their identities, then? School staff have been highlighted as playing a pivotal role in creating a nurturing environment for trans* pupils (Luecke, 2011). Leonard (2019) explored the positive school experiences of trans* young people, highlighting the importance of language, the role of individual teachers and whole-school approaches, as well as support from the wider community (including family, friends, and other role models) and the role the young people themselves played in maintaining their well-being.

Interestingly, Leonard's (2019) research highlighted that, more often than not, it was the relationships with individual teachers and the role they played that had the greatest impact on trans* young people, rather than the school as a system. Individual teachers were lauded for their respect of language, including names and pronouns, and their willingness to step in when they witnessed others – both pupils and staff – misusing these, either intentionally or unintentionally. Indeed, teachers being able to confront and stop observed incidents of harassment is frequently cited by trans* young people as something they recognise, appreciate, and value in school staff, and this is something that makes them feel safer, more accepted, and supported within schools (e.g. Leonard, 2019; McGuire et al., 2010).

Additionally, individual teachers were praised for their role in driving positive change within the school system and providing a safe space for trans* young people to be themselves. Evans and Rawlings (2019) have also found similar themes, highlighting the importance of relationships with staff members and friends in creating a safe and supportive school environment for trans* young people.

In contrast to the outcomes following negative experiences discussed above, having a supportive and trusted adult in school has been linked to lower rates of absenteeism and dropping out of school (Greytak, Kosciw & Boesen, 2013; Kosciw et al., 2018; Sausa, 2005), increased feelings of safety (Kosciw et al., 2018; McGuire et al., 2010), greater academic achievement (Kosciw et al., 2018), and a more positive overall academic experience (Goodrich, 2012). In terms of mental health, trans* young people who feel supported in school have been found to demonstrate greater positive self-esteem (Dessel, Kulick, Wernick & Sullivan, 2017), and their levels of depression and anxiety are on par with their cisgender peers (Olson, Durwood, DeMeules & McLaughlin, 2016).

Supportive teachers and schools

When we explore these areas of support and the impact they may have on trans* young people, the most important message is consistency, particularly in relation to language (Bowskill, 2017). Language, and the way we use language to explore and understand ourselves, is felt to be a pre-requisite for gender development, self-identity, and the initial coming-out process (Schimmel-Bristow et al., 2018). Having access to language which can question and deviate from a binary representation of sex and gender can be a source of both power and resistance for trans* young people (McGlashan & Fitzpatrick, 2018). Indeed, being able to include and explore a range of gender identities, binary and non-binary, within classroom learning and resources has been recommended as one of the key areas in which school staff can create an inclusive and acceptive culture for trans* pupils (Bartholomaeus & Riggs, 2017).

When exploring the impact of language, and names in particular, it must be considered that, for many trans* young people, it is not just finding a name that matches their gender identity, but rather finding their "true name", a name which "embodies the essence of who they are" (VanderSchans, 2016, p. 1), and therefore appropriate name and pronoun use is intrinsically linked to acceptance and respect. Turban, Ferraiolo, Martin, and Olezeski (2017) highlight that having schools recognise, use, and officially record pupils' preferred name and gender in school was one of the top ten recommendations made by trans* young people to colleges and healthcare providers, and, when this is done by the school and staff, is highlighted as one of the most important and affirming actions a school can take (Leonard, 2019; McCormack, 2012).

However, while recognition and adoption of appropriate language may be considered an immediate sign of respect, as highlighted by Leonard's (2019) participants, this has to be part of a wider course of action, so as not to be viewed as mere lip service. Along with inclusive language being adopted throughout the curriculum, to cultivate a truly supportive school environment, Bartholomaeus and Riggs (2017) recommend a schoolwide approach, including explorations into school philosophy and ethos; policies, procedures and guidelines; leadership; record keeping; practices and language use; resources and training; support for the school community; curriculum teaching and learning; and transgender-specific initiatives.

When exploring some of these recommendations, perhaps the first thing a school should consider is establishing policies to support and protect trans* pupils. Having policies in place, and enforcing them, sets precedence and guidelines for staff and pupils, and also results in trans* pupils worrying less about bullying, facing less discrimination overall, and feeling more confident when bullying and discrimination does occur (Bradlow et al., 2017; Kosciw et al., 2018).

Further, considering schoolwide initiatives, another way of supporting trans* young people within a school environment that is becoming increasing prevalent within the UK, although perhaps still more common in the US, is access to supportive clubs and societies. Known in the US as GSAs (Gay-Straight Alliances), these LGBTQ+-inclusive clubs have been demonstrated to improve overall school climate for trans* young people, identify supportive members of staff, and both empower trans* pupils and provide them access to resources to advocate for their own rights and the rights of others (Jones & Hillier, 2013; Kosciw et al., 2018; McGuire et al., 2010).

In order to create an inclusive and supportive classroom environment, having books, posters, and learning resources which include a range of genders and identities within the classroom and school (e.g. within the library) can help trans* young people explore, recognise, and understand their own gender identities, and can support cisgender peers' understanding of gender identities as well (Bartholomaeus & Riggs, 2017; Riley, 2018; Sadowski, 2016). Further, projects such as No Outsiders can support teachers and schools in mapping values of tolerance, including the concept of gender identity, on to the curriculum (DePalma & Jennett, 2010).

Perhaps the most contentious of the issues faced by schools, however, will be access to gendered activities and provisions. This includes provisions, such as toilets, uniforms and changing rooms, as well as lessons such as PE, Drama, Music, and activities like choir (where there may be gendered roles and voices), and school trips. The literature currently available and local authority guidance highlight that schools should work with trans* young people to enable them to access the resources and provisions appropriate to their gender in a manner which makes them feel safe (e.g., Bartholomaeus & Riggs, 2017; Brighton and Hove City Council, 2018; Lancashire County Council, 2013; Sausa, 2005), and, indeed, these rights are enshrined within the Equality Act (2010).

It is important that this is considered carefully, however. Regarding bathrooms and changing rooms, for instance, a common strategy is for schools to utilise disabled bathrooms for trans* young people, but this practice has been received as helpful in some instances, but wholly inappropriate and humiliating in others (e.g. Jones et al., 2016; Leonard, 2019). The most important thing is to speak with the pupil themselves and explore what they would feel most comfortable with, and how this can be provided.

Indeed, while everything listed above may support the school as a system to become a more inclusive and supportive environment for trans* young people, it is important that we remember that every young person is unique, and the best way forward will always be from a child-centred approach, considering and including what is required for each individual pupil (Mangin, 2020).

What can teachers do?

While this is not meant to be an exhaustive list, below are some key recommendations to support teachers and school staff in ensuring their schools are safe and inclusive environments for trans* young people.

Adopt language, names, and pronouns

As discussed, language can play a pivotal role in the formation and acceptance of identity, so it will be important to speak to your pupils and explore how they would like to be addressed, both in terms of name and pronouns. It is important to consider that not all trans* young people will want to change their names or pronouns, and that the language used may not always fit on to the he/she binary. Some individuals will prefer neutral pronouns, such as they/zie, and others, who are gender fluid, will express their gender identity differently on different days. Always speak to your pupils about their preferences, and remember, if you make an honest mistake, that's okay! If you can admit when you have made a mistake and apologise, you are still demonstrating that you respect and support them.

While it is important to use appropriate language in school, however, it will be useful to speak to your pupils about how to discuss them with their families. Muñoz-Plaza, Quinn, and Rounds (2002) highlight that for some trans* young people, while they may have socially transitioned at school, they may not have disclosed their gender identity at home. As highlighted by one of Leonard's (2019) participants: "They asked my permission [...] I'm so happy they didn't just go 'your son' [...] 'cause, y'know you wouldn't want to be outed because your parents may not be as accepting?" (p. 63).

A final consideration around language is that for many trans* young people, there may be a disparity between what they prefer to be called and their government-recorded name, and this may raise issues in terms of examinations and official documentation. Unfortunately, exam boards require the individual's unique pupil number or unique learner number, which is linked to their legal name. Therefore, unless the young person has changed their name by deed poll, all official documentation will be in their government-recorded name.

However, in school, the individual's name can be changed in systems such as SIMS before an official name change has taken place, and this can provide not only prompts for school staff, but also a schoolwide commitment to support the pupil.

Challenge all occurrences of misgendering and harassment

As highlighted earlier, individual staff members are often recognised as being key sources of support for trans* pupils. Much of this is rooted in using the correct language, as discussed above, but also teachers addressing harassment, improper language use, and inequality if it is observed – be it from pupils or other staff members – is vital in demonstrating they can both talk the talk *and* walk the walk.

While some of these incidents will be accidental, in which a gentle reminder may be all that is needed to correct and support the individual in question and continue to highlight your support for the trans* young person, it is also possible you will hear and/or witness episodes of intentional harassment, bullying, and abuse. When this occurs, it will be important to address it immediately. One way to do this might be through school policy, as will be discussed further below. For example, could a guide be produced (Brighton and Hove City Council, 2018, provides a fantastic starting point) to help school staff offer a consistent approach to challenging prejudice and harassment should it occur?

Perhaps the hardest part of this will be challenging your own peers. However, again, is there something in the school policy which can support you with this? Are there ways you can do this constructively so that the young person remains at the centre of any discussions and planning?

Create a trans*-inclusive school environment

The first step in establishing a supportive space for trans* pupils within school will likely be through exploring your own classroom. Consider whether you can make it more inclusive:

- Are there displays or posters which could signify to any trans* pupils that your classroom is a safe and supportive space?

- Are there books and resources which could help a trans*-questioning pupil explore their gender identity, or be used as a class discussion around different gender identities?

- Are there resources you can use within your lesson plans to incorporate different gender identities, or celebrate works and ideas by individuals whose gender identity does not fit the typical gender binary?

Most importantly, however, are you able to provide a safe space for a trans* pupil just by being there? Freedman's (2019) participants highlight the importance of having a trusted person with whom trans* young people can talk to and be listened to without judgement, and how even this small act of providing a quiet space can have a huge impact on feelings of safety and inclusion. As one of Freedman's participants shared; "she just listens to me and she doesn't say much which I think is good 'cos it just gives me a safe space where I can tell my opinions and just be heard" (p. 74).

Additionally, are there other ways in which you can establish a trans* inclusive environment in school? For example, is there an extracurricular club that promotes equality or LGBTQ+ inclusion? If not, and you aren't able to set one up, are there any clubs or resources in your local community that you can signpost trans* young people to?

Explore school policy and guidance

School policies and guidelines are there to support not only pupils in school, but also you as teachers. Get to know your schools! What policies are there that deal with incidents of harassment and bullying? Are there any policies that support trans* pupils with regard to access to different provisions and activities?

- If your school does not have specific policies and guidelines that support trans* young people, how can this be addressed?

- Are there other schools in your local area with specific guidelines who can assist you in developing them?

- Can you invite a guest speaker to the school who can lead discussions or explore additional training for all staff?

Again, the Brighton and Hove City Council (2018) guidelines provide a good starting point for this, and all policies agreed on should respect the young person's rights as enshrined in the Equality Act 2010.

Adopt a person-centred approach

Finally, one of the key things to remember is that not all trans* pupils will present the same way, or even want the same things. Some pupils will be just starting their transition, while others would have been living in their transitioned gender for a number of years. Similarly, some trans* young people may transition socially but not want physical transition support (e.g. hormone treatment or gender-reassignment surgery), whereas others will. It will be important to get to know your pupils, what they want, and how you can help.

As highlighted by Brighton and Hove City Council (2018), it may be helpful to support individual pupils to explore how they share their gender identity within the school, and to help them develop scripts and responses to questions they frequently receive. If a pupil is just starting their transition, be a part of that and ask them what *they* think it is important that you know, and what *they* feel they may need support with.

Takeaway points

- Trans* pupils often face a number of challenges in school, both physical and social, all of which can have a significant impact on their social, emotional, and physical well-being, as well as their academic engagement and achievement.

- Schools should be a place of safety and support for trans* pupils, with relationships with individual teachers being highlighted as one of the most reassuring, helpful, and empowering resources within the school environment.

- There are many ways to create a safe and supportive space for trans* pupils, but most importantly: respect and adopt appropriate language, including names and pronouns; be confident in challenging any harassment you see, no matter who it comes from; and talk to your pupil(s) and explore with them the best way you might help.

Further reading

Bartholomaeus, C. and Riggs, D.W. (2017). *Whole-of-School Approaches to Supporting Transgender Students, Staff, and Parents*.

Brighton and Hove City Council. (2018). https://www.brighton-hove.gov.uk/families-children-and-learning/information-about-our-trans-inclusion-schools-toolkit

Leonard, M. (2019). *Growing Up Trans: Exploring the Positive School Experiences of Transgender Children and Young People* (Doctoral dissertation, University of East London).

References

Austin, A. and Craig, S.L. (2015). Empirically supported interventions for sexual and gender minority youth: A stakeholder driven model. *Journal of Evidence-Based Social Work*, 12(6), 567–578.

Austin, A., Craig, S.L. and McInroy, L. (2016). Toward transgender affirmative social work education. *Journal of Social Work Education*, 52(3), 297–310.

Bartholomaeus, C. and Riggs, D.W. (2017). Whole-of-school approaches to supporting transgender students, staff, and parents. *International Journal of Transgenderism*, 18(4), 361–366.

Bowskill, T. (2017). How educational professionals can improve the outcomes for transgender children and young people. *Educational and Child Psychology*, 34(3), 96–108.

Bradlow, J., Bartram, F., Guasp, A. and Jadva, V. (2017). *School Report: The Experiences of Lesbian, Gay, Bi and Trans Young People in Britain's Schools in 2017*. London, UK: Stonewall.

Brighton and Hove City Council. (2018). *Trans* Inclusion School Kit: Supporting Trans, Non-Binary and Gender Questioning Children and Young People in Brighton and Hove Educational Settings*. Brighton, UK: Brighton and Hove City Council's Standards and Achievement Team and Allsorts Youth Project. Retrieved from: https://new.brighton-hove.gov.uk/news/2018/trans-guidance-schools-helps-tackle-stereotyping-and-keep-children-safe.

Chodzen, G., Hidalgo, M.A., Chen, D. and Garofalo, R. (2019). Minority stress factors associated with depression and anxiety among transgender and gender-nonconforming youth. *The Journal of Adolescent Health*, 64(4), 467–471.

Connolly, M.D., Zervos, M.J., Barone, C.J., Johnson, C.C. and Joseph, C.L.M. (2016). The mental health of transgender youth: Advances in understanding. *The Journal of Adolescent Health*, 59, 489–95.

Coulter, R.W., Bersamin, M., Russell, S.T. and Mair, C. (2018). The effects of gender-and sexuality-based harassment on lesbian, gay, bisexual, and transgender substance use disparities. *Journal of Adolescent Health*, 62(6), 688–700.

Day, J., Perez-Brumer, A. and Russell, S.T. (2018). Safe schools? Transgender youth's school experiences and perceptions of school climate. *Journal of Youth and Adolescence*, 47(8), 1731–1742.

Day, J.K., Fish, J.N., Perez-Brumer, A. Hatzenbuehler, M.L. and Russell, S.T. (2017). Transgender youth substance use disparities: Results from a population-based sample. *Journal of Adolescent Health*, 61(6), 729–735.

DePalma, R. and Jennett, M. (2010). Homophobia, transphobia and culture: Deconstructing heteronormativity in English primary schools. *Intercultural Education*, 21, 15–26.

Department for Children, Schools and Families. (2009). *Guidance for Schools on Preventing and Responding to Sexist, Sexual and Transphobic Bullying: Safe to Learn: Embedding Anti-Bullying Work in Schools*. London, UK: Department for Children, Schools and Families. Retrieved from: https://www.gires.org.uk/wp-content/uploads/2014/10/DCSF-01136-2009.pdf.

Department for Education. (2019). *Relationships Education, Relationships and Sex Education (RSE) and Health Education: Statutory Guidance for Governing Bodies, Proprietors, Head Teachers, Principals, Senior Leadership Teams, Teachers*. London, UK: Department of Education.

Dessel, A.B., Kulick, A., Wernick, L.J. and Sullivan, D. (2017). The importance of teacher support: Differential impacts by gender and sexuality. *Journal of Adolescence*, 56, 136–144.

Evans, I. and Rawlings, V. (2019). "It was just one less thing that I had to worry about": Positive experiences of schooling for gender diverse and transgender students. *Journal of Homosexuality*, 68(9), 1–20.

Formby, E. (2014). *(Trans)gender Identity Awareness and Support in Rotherham*. Sheffield, UK: Centre for Education and Inclusion Research, Sheffield Hallam University.

Freedman, A. (2019). *The Experiences of Transgender Young People and Their Parents: Informing the Work of Educational Psychologists* (unpublished doctoral dissertation). London, UK: University College London.

Frohard-Dourlent, H. (2016). *Muddling Through Together: Educators Navigating Cisnormativity While Working With Trans and Gender-Nonconforming Students* (unpublished doctoral dissertation). Vancouver, Canada: University of British Columbia. Retrieved from: https://open.library.ubc.ca/cIRcle/collections/ubctheses/24/items/1.0228782.

Goodrich, K.M. (2012). Lived experiences of college-age transsexual individuals. *Journal of College Counseling*, 15(3), 215–23.

Greytak, E.A., Kosciw, J.G. and Boesen, M.J. (2013). Putting the "T" in "resource": The benefits of LGBT-related school resources for transgender youth. *Journal of LGBT Youth*, 10(1–2), 45–63.

Grossman, A.H., Haney, A., Edwards, P., Alessi, E., Ardon, M. and Howell, T.J. (2009). Lesbian, gay, bisexual and transgender youth talk about experiencing and coping with school violence: A qualitative study. *Journal of LGBT Youth*, 6(1), 24–46.

Hellen, M. (2009). Transgender children in schools. *Liminalis: Journal for Sex/Gender Emancipation and Resistance*, 9(3), 81–99.

Johns, M.M., Lowry, R., Andrzejewski, J., Barrios, L.C., Demissie, Z., McManus, T. … and Underwood, J.M. (2019). Transgender identity and experiences of violence victimization, substance use, suicide risk, and sexual risk behaviors among high school students—19 states and large urban school districts, 2017. *Morbidity and Mortality Weekly Report*, 68(3), 67–71.

Jones, T. and Hillier, L. (2013). Comparing trans-spectrum and same-sex-attracted youth in Australia: Increased risks, increased activisms. *Journal of LGBT Youth*, 10(4), 287–307.

Jones, T., Smith, E., Ward, R., Dixon, J., Hillier, L. and Mitchell, A. (2016). School experiences of transgender and gender diverse students in Australia. *Sex Education*, 16(2), 156–171.

Kennedy, N. and Hellen, M. (2010). Transgender children: More than a theoretical challenge. *Graduate Journal of Social Science*, 7(2), 25–43.

Kosciw, J.G., Greytak, E.A., Zongrone, A.D., Clark, C.M. and Truong, N.L. (2018). *The 2017 National School Climate Survey: The Experiences of Lesbian, Gay, Bisexual, Transgender, and Queer Youth in Our Nation's Schools*. New York, NY: GLSEN.

Lancashire County Council. (2013). *Transgender Guidance*. Lancashire, UK: Lancashire County Council.

Leonard, M. (2019). *Growing Up Trans*: Exploring the Positive School Experiences of Transgender Children and Young People* (unpublished doctoral dissertation). London, UK: University of East London.

Luecke, J.C. (2011). Working with transgender children and their classmates in pre-adolescence: Just be supportive. *Journal of LGBT Youth*, 8(2), 116–156.

Mangin, M.M. (2020). Transgender students in elementary schools: How supportive principals lead. *Educational Administration Quarterly*, 56(2), 255–288.

McCormack, M. (2012). The positive experiences of openly gay, lesbian, bisexual and transgendered students in a Christian sixth form college. *Sociological Research Online*, 17(3), 5–32.

McDermott, E., Hughes, E. and Rawlings, V. (2018). The social determinants of lesbian, gay, bisexual and transgender youth suicidality in England: A mixed methods study. *Journal of Public Health*, 40(3), e244–e251.

McGlashan, H. and Fitzpatrick, K. (2018). "I use any pronouns, and I'm questioning everything else": Transgender youth and the issue of gender pronouns. *Sex Education*, 18(3), 239–252.

McGuire, J.K., Anderson, C.R., Toomey, R.B. and Russell, S.T. (2010). School climate for transgender youth: A mixed method investigation of student experiences and school responses. *Journal of Youth and Adolescence*, 39(10), 1175–1188.

Muñoz-Plaza, C., Quinn, S.C. and Rounds, K.A. (2002). Lesbian, gay, bisexual and transgender students: Perceived social support in the high school environment. *The High School Journal*, 85(4), 52–63.

NHS. (2019). Referrals to the Gender Identity Development Service (GIDS) level off in 2018–19. The Tavistock and Portman NHS Foundation Trust. Retrieved from: https://tavistockand-portman.nhs.uk/about-us/news/stories/referrals-gender-identity-development-service-gids-level-2018-19/.

NHS. (2020a). Referrals to GIDS, financial years 2015–16 to 2019–20. The Tavistock and Portman NHS Foundation Trust. Retrieved from: https://gids.nhs.uk/number-referrals.

NHS. (2020b). Waiting times. The Tavistock and Portman NHS Foundation Trust. Retrieved from: https://gic.hns.uk/appointments/waiting-times/.

Olson, K.R., Durwood, L., DeMeules, M. and McLaughlin, K.A. (2016). Mental health of transgender children who are supported in their identities. *Pediatrics*, 137(3). Retrieved from: http://pediatrics.aappublications.org/content/137/3/e20153223.

Payne, E. and Smith, M. (2014). The big freak out: Educator fear in response to the presence of transgender elementary school students. *Journal of Homosexuality*, 61, 399–418.

Reed, B., Rhodes, S., Schofield, P. and Wylie, K. (2009). *Gender Variance in the UK: Prevalence, Incidence, Growth and Geographic Distribution*. London, UK: Gender Identity Research and Education Society.

Riley, E. (2018). Bullies, blades, and barricades: Practical considerations for working with adolescents expressing concerns regarding gender and identity. *International Journal of Transgenderism*, 19(2), 1–9.

Sadowski, M. (2016). *Safe is Not Enough: Better Schools for LGBTQ Students*. Cambridge, MA: Harvard Education Press.

Sausa, L.A. (2005). Translating research into practice: Trans youth recommendations for improving school systems. *Journal of Gay and Lesbian Issues in Education*, 3(1), 15–28.

Schimmel-Bristow, A., Haley, S.G., Crouch, J.M., Evans, Y.N., Ahrens, K.R., McCarty, C.A. and Inwards-Breland, D.J. (2018). Youth and caregiver experiences of gender identity transition: A qualitative study. *Psychology of Sexual Orientation and Gender Diversity*, 5(2), 273–281.

Stieglitz, K.A. (2010). Development, risk, and resilience of transgender youth. *Journal of the Association of Nurses in AIDS Care*, 21(3), 192–206.

Szkrybalo, J. and Ruble, D.N. (1999). God made me a girl: Sex-category constancy judgments and explanations revisited. *Developmental Psychology*, 35(2), 392–402.

Turban, J., Ferraiolo, T., Martin, A. and Olezeski, C. (2017). Ten things transgender and gender nonconforming youth want their doctors to know. *Journal of the American Academy of Child and Adolescent Psychiatry*, 56(4), 275–277.

VanderSchans, A. (2016). The role of name choice in the construction of transgender identities. *Western Papers in Linguistics/Cahiers linguistiques de Western*, 1(2), 1–21.

Witcomb, G.L., Claes, L., Bouman, W.P., Nixon, E., Motmans, J. and Arcelus, J. (2019). Experiences and psychological wellbeing outcomes associated with bullying in treatment-seeking transgender and gender-diverse youth. *LGBT Health*, 6(5), 216–226.

Wyss, S.E. (2004). "This was my hell": The violence experienced by gender non-conforming youth in US high schools. *International Journal of Qualitative Studies in Education*, 17(5), 709–730.

Mental Wellbeing of Children Looked After (CLA) in Schools

Amy Warhurst

Synopsis

Children who are Looked After (CLA) are not a homogeneous group; however, they often share similar stories of disrupted home lives and multiple school changes. Indeed, 71% of CLA, in a pilot study, experienced at least one change across any measure (i.e. any change in home-placement, school placement, or social worker) within the previous 12 months (Children's Commissioner, 2017).

Many more CLA have Special Educational Needs (SEN) (58%) than their peers (17%) and that, added to the instability of their home and school placements, means many CLA significantly underperform academically when compared to their peers. Schools that do well at reducing the gap between CLA and their peers seem to do so by offering discrete social and emotional support, having high aspirations for their CLA, encouraging them to take control of their own learning, participating in wider school and community activities, and liaising regularly with their carers. CLA themselves value having a trusted adult in school with whom they can share their thoughts and experiences, often require additional support with transitions (start/ends of lessons, school days, school terms, school years), and have more limited access to internet-enabled technology, so appreciate it when their teachers recognise this and take this into account when setting homework tasks.

Background

Many schoolchildren are defined as being CLA, who are children in public care, placed with foster carers, in residential homes, or with other relatives. Children are looked after when their parents cannot provide ongoing care. Children may be placed with family members, friends, or foster carers depending on individual circumstances. Some children and young people who become looked after may eventually return home (Isle of Wight Council, 2021).

 DOI: 10.4324/9781003160526-10

As of March 2020, there were just over 80,000 CLA in England (DfE, 2020). These children as individuals have many differences; however, they often share similar stories of disrupted home lives and multiple school changes. As a group, they are more likely to have higher rates of SEN, higher rates of bullying, higher rates of mental health issues, and higher rates of disruptive behaviours. They are also more likely to have lower academic success, fewer friendships, and less trust in their relationships with peers and adults (see below for more details on these aspects).

Moving placements

Data from DfE (2019b) show that the majority of CLA (68%) had just one placement in the past 12 months, but a significant minority (10%, just over 8000 children) had three or more placement moves within the same year. This means that the child has had several changes of carer and home, not necessarily in close geographical proximity. Indeed, it should also be noted that only 73% of CLA were placed within 20 miles of their home. This will, of course, have consequences for school attendance, with several school placements being necessary for many CLA within their whole schooling journey, but this means some CLA move schools more than once within a single school year. Research has shown that children who undergo one home-placement move are almost three times more likely to experience a mid-year school move than those who do not move, compared to children who have multiple home-placement moves who become almost four times more likely to move schools mid-year (Children's Commissioner, 2017).

These movements and educational disruptions, such as missing important aspects of the curriculum, reduced chances of attending extra-curricular groups and completing home-based project work and more, all add up to difficulties CLA might face in keeping up with their peers. When this is combined with their much higher rates of SEN, the attainment figures for CLA make for very worrying reading. Indeed, CLA themselves report that changing foster parents and social workers results in anxiety and reduces their performance in general schooling and exams (Children's Commissioner for England, 2015). Furthermore, placement moves are associated with lower GCSE attainment and increased levels of psychiatric disorders, whilst conversely, stable care placements (for 18 months or more) are associated with improved mental health for CLA (Conn et al., 2015; Ford et al., 2007).

School attainment

The government (Department for Education) figures for 2018–2019 show a marked difference between CLA and their peers, with CLA underperforming across all subjects. For example, during Key Stage 1, CLA are 24–28% less likely to be achieving at an expected level across the four key subjects of reading, writing, maths, and science, when compared to non-CLA peers. This deficit remains similar during Key Stage 2, where they are 29% less likely to achieve at an expected level.

Unfortunately, the gap does not narrow significantly during Key Stage 4, where, again, CLA are 25% less likely than their non-CLA peers to achieve an average level of qualifications based on the governments' attainment eight measures (the average achievement of pupils in up to eight qualifications including English (double weighted if both language and literature are taken), maths (double weighted), three further qualifications that count in the English Baccalaureate (EBacc) and three further qualifications that can be GCSE qualifications (including EBacc subjects or any other non-GCSE qualifications on the DfE approved list).

The data also showed that 58% of looked after children at the end of Key Stage 2 had a special educational need identified, compared to 17% of non-looked after children, and predictably, attainment rates for children with a SEN are also much lower than for their peers.

Peer, home, and social worker relationships

During childhood and adolescence, friendship can be a source of emotional support and those with close friends have shown better psychological health and adjustment (Bukowski et al., 1996) and friendships contribute to happiness and identity development (Demir et al., 2011). Van Harmelen et al. (2017) found friendship support to positively influence both immediate, and later, psycho-social functioning. Research into CLA's experiences of friendship, however, is limited. They are less likely than their non-CLA peers to have friends although most do have at least one friend (Smith, 1995). These friendships are highly valued as a source of practical and emotional support; however, a number of challenges can create difficulties forming and maintaining close friendships. These include frequent placement moves, stigma or feeling different to their peers, limited support from foster carers to maintain friendships, and rules and regulations about visiting friend's homes (Emond, 2014; McMahon & Curtin, 2013; Ridge & Millar, 2000; Rogers, 2017; Selwyn et al., 2010). Making friends can be hard for children in care when they first arrive at a new school. Some children report having to lie when making new friends, so that their friends would not realise that they were in care. This can prevent children from getting close to new friends or being able to turn to them when things are difficult (Children's Commissioner, 2019).

Many researchers have found that Looked After children are up to twice as likely to experience bullying as other young people (e.g. Daly & Gilligan, 2005) 24% of care leavers reported being bullied for being in care (Ofsted, 2012). This is made more difficult for these children as they are less likely to have a strong social support network, less likely to have a trusted adult to confide in, and are more easily isolated from their peers (Children's Commissioner, 2019). Victims of bullying have elevated levels of anxiety, depression, self-harm, and suicidal thoughts with the effects of childhood bullying often extending even into later adulthood (beyond 50 years of age). Bullying has a negative impact on the victims' quality of life and social relationships, causing misery and a loss of self-esteem (Boulton &

Smith, 1994). Worried or upset children do not learn well, they find it hard to concentrate or solve problems effectively (Turkel & Eth, 1990). Victims of bullying often truant to avoid being bullied, feel physically ill after being bullied, and experience sleeping difficulties as a direct result of bullying (Sharp & Thompson, 1992).

Many CLA find that having many different social workers can reduce their ability and/or willingness to make the effort to get to know and trust the next social worker. It can feel frustrating, repetitive, and exhausting to build that same relationship over and over. In some cases, it leads to apathy or indifference towards changes of social worker. Contrastingly, where they have had a constant social worker over a long period of time, children report feeling very upset or distraught if the social worker then has to move on. Unfortunately, changes in social workers are frequent, with 25% of CLA having two or more changes in social workers within one year, and 10% having three or more changes in social workers (Children's Commissioner, 2017). This change in social worker can lead to very high levels of distress, anxiety, a feeling of rejection, a lack of control, and predictability in their life and a sense of chaos. Additionally, they may be expected to discuss past, traumatic, life events with their new social worker, adding another barrier to them achieving a sense of normality and having moved on from that experience.

All of these aspects: changes to home, school, or social worker, increased chances of bullying, and more difficulties in maintaining friendships are further exacerbated by a high prevalence of mental health issues experienced by CLA. Figures show that among CLA aged 5–17 years, 45% were assessed as having a mental disorder: 37% had clinically significant conduct disorders; 12% were assessed as having anxiety and/or depression, and 7% were diagnosed as hyperactive (Meltzer et al., 2003). The same researchers also found that CLA with any mental health issue were four times less likely than those without to report spending any time with their friends.

Additionally, a study of three UK Local Authorities found a relationship between problematic behaviours and low educational attainment for all children. In comparison to the non-CLA group, however, the CLA sample were perceived by teachers as having more problem behaviours in a range of social situations. In addition, teachers seemed less likely to use resilience interventions where pupils displayed higher levels of behavioural difficulties. Teachers frequently undervalued their own influence in fostering pupils' resiliency. They also perceived CLA to be more resilient than non-CLA. Teachers identified CLA's relationships with adults and peers, including their challenging behaviours, as barriers that sometimes prohibited educational progress (Boorn, 2008).

Traumatic experiences

CLA have often had early traumatic experiences, either as abuse or neglect from their first care-givers and/or multiple placement moves. These early experiences often affect their ability to form relationships and attachments. Where a child has an insecure attachment, this can lead to unfortunate consequences. If they cannot rely on an adult to respond to their needs in times of stress, they are unable to learn how to soothe themselves, manage their emotions and frustrations, develop self-confidence, and engage in reciprocal relationships. Research has inextricably linked attachment to school readiness and school success (e.g. Commodari, 2013; Geddes, 2006; Zarrella et al., 2018). Insecure attachments can also lead to regulatory disorders, thus creating challenging behaviour. Toxic stress, where there are high levels of stress hormones leading to hyperarousal (fight-flight-freeze) and dissociation (zoning out) can lead to an inability to manage their own behaviour. They may experience shame, be hypersensitive to criticism, and/or show an apparent lack of remorse for their behaviours. They may experience social function disorders, thus creating social difficulties, or be unable to interpret or understand their own or others' emotions, thereby creating difficulty with empathy. This may lead to feelings of worthlessness, low self-esteem, and a lack of capacity for joy (Cairns, 2006).

Furthermore, traumatic experiences (in the absence of caring, stable relationships with adults) especially during periods of early development, can be toxic to brain architecture and other developing organ systems due to constant activation of the body's stress systems. This results in fewer neural connections in the brain, which means it is more difficult to utilise the brain capacity and to learn effectively. This disruption to brain development can also lead to regulatory systems becoming primed towards arousal and fear, rather than being relaxed and ready to learn. Additionally, these children can also show impaired predictions of the behaviour of others, and can misinterpret neutral behaviours as threats, thus exacerbating social difficulties (Cozolino, 2013; Siegel, 2013).

Having a trusted teacher, or member of school staff, that remains constant, can really support a child to make a secure attachment, and can also make a big difference to their experience of going through difficult transitions outside of school (Children's Commissioner, 2019).

Due to disruptions and trauma in their early relationships and development, CLA are often not readily able to learn well within school (Burleson & Thoron, 2017). Maslow (1943) postulated that everyone has needs, and that some needs must be met before others. At the most basic levels, these include physiological needs (food, water, sleep, etc.) over which teachers have very little control, other than referring to other services, and safety and security needs (health, family, and social stability), which teachers can help with by providing predictable and orderly routines, and a feeling of safety within school. Once physiological and safety needs have been adequately addressed, then the child's need for love and belongingness (friendship, family, sense of connection) comes next. This can be fostered by their teacher via encouraging their CLA to participate in clubs and other after-school activities with their peers, showing them they are valued as a learner and class member, and praising their efforts. Once these needs have been met, then the child can become ready to learn, and from this, the child will be able to build self-esteem, the fourth level of need (Maslow, 1943).

What can teachers do?

Listen and support

CLA are a disparate group of children; so, it is important that you treat any child as an individual and listen to what they need. Designated teachers for CLA have statutory guidance to follow (DfE, 2018) but the key points for listening to your CLA can be summed up as:

- Making yourself available and taking the time to get to know your CLA.

- Noticing when they are upset and listening to them when they need help, considering giving them some emotional coaching or ELSA support.

- Understanding that they may not need to be treated differently.

- Trying to understand their experiences of being Looked After and remembering that these experiences will affect their present and future in ways they themselves may not notice or be aware of.

Be discrete

CLA themselves have requested that teachers support them discreetly so as to reduce the likelihood of bullying. They would like to be asked how they would like to refer to their foster family (e.g. as Aunty and Uncle), again to reduce the dissimilarity between them and their peers (Wilson et al., 2004). They would also like meetings between them and their social worker to take place outside of school, preferably in their home, again to lessen the sense of being different from their peers (Children's Commissioner, 2019). Sometimes laptops/PCs need to be shared within the foster care setting and so teachers should be sensitive to the limitations this can have when setting homework tasks, etc. (Boffey, 2013).

Support with transitions

CLA would like teachers to understand that transitions are very difficult and exhausting and that a change of school may also coincide with (another) change in care family, so lots of support may be needed especially at beginnings and end of lessons, school days, and school terms/years (Hertfordshire County Council, 2007).

Help them develop wider skills

They would also like teachers to help them tolerate stress, build up a sense of identity and self-efficacy, learn to problem-solve, and know to whom and how to ask for help and support (Cairns & Fursland; 2008). CLA, and their carers, also appreciate being given the opportunity to participate in outside-of-school activities such as after-school clubs and community groups, which helps to bolster their resilience and creates a stronger sense of self-identity (Gilligan, 2009). They would also encourage teachers to involve carers in their schooling and encourage good links in their home and school-based learning opportunities (APPG, 2012).

In a small-scale study of best-practice, OfSTED (2007) found that within 20 schools rated "excellent", those managing to reduce the gap between CLA outcomes and their peers were: holding a recognition that CLA may be Gifted and Talented; encouraging CLA to be responsible for their own learning; closely monitoring progress in academia, social relationships and personal aspects; including CLA in after-school activities and learning outside of the classroom; supporting CLA within school in a low-profile manner; ensuring swift and early intervention for any emerging issues with attendance or behaviour, etc.; and engaging carers and parents with the teaching staff wherever possible.

Teachers can help CLA by recognising that there may be significant gaps in their learning through attending multiple schools, so a robust assessment of strengths and gaps will be necessary and setting high expectations for your CLA pupils will help them to achieve their full potential (Rees, 2015). Educational achievements are interconnected to pupils' self-esteem, future career opportunities, lifestyle, and relationship successes (Jackson, 2001); so, it is essential that you, as their teacher, do not knock their confidence but instead highlight their strengths, recognise their achievements, and have high aspirations for them.

CLA need an environment where they are encouraged to focus on their learning (Barr & Parrett, 2001), where they can make choices for themselves, where peers are supportive, and where they are given responsibilities for helping others (Allen, 2003). Clear, predictable routines help with a sense of safety and stability and give a sense of personal control to your CLA (Burleson & Thoron, 2017).

Takeaway points

- CLA are generally more likely to have SEN, be bullied, have mental health issues, and display disruptive behaviours.

- CLA are also more likely to have lower academic success, fewer friendships, and less trust in their relationships with peers and adults.

- As their teacher, you can help by providing a stable and supportive relationship with CLA, a clear and reliable routine, and helping them to quickly integrate with their peers and the wider school community.

- Celebrate CLA academic success and efforts and provide discrete support with any areas of difficulty.

Further reading

Cairns, K. (2006) *Attachment, Trauma and Resilience*. London: British Agencies for Adoption and Fostering

Children's Commissioner for England (2019) *Children's Voices: Children's Experiences of Instability in the Care System*. London: Children's Commissioner

Jackson, S. (Ed.). (2001) N*obody Ever Told Us School Mattered: Raising the Educational Attainments of Children in Care*. London: British Agencies for Adoption and Fostering

Rogers, J. (2017) 'Different' and 'Devalued': Managing the Stigma of Foster-Care With the Benefit of Peer Support. *British Journal of Social Work, 47*(4), 1078-1093

References

Allen, B. (2003) Pupils' Perspectives on Learning Mathematics. In Allen, B and Johnston-Wilder, S (ed) *Mathematics education: Exploring the Culture of Learning*. London: Routledge.

APPG for Looked After Children and Care Leavers. (2012) *Education Matters in Care*. London: Crown Copyright.

Barr, R. D., and Parrett, W. (2001) *Hope Fulfilled for At-Risk and Violent Youth: K-12 Programs That Work*. New Jersey: Prentice Hall.

Boffey, M. (2013) *Fostering in a Digital World*. London: The Fostering Network.

Boulton, M. J., and Smith, P. K. (1994) Bully/Victim Problems in Middle-School Children: Stability, Self-Perceived Competence, Peer Perceptions and Peer Acceptance. *British Journal of Developmental Psychology, 12*(3), 315–329.

Bukowski, W. M., Motzoi, C., and Meyer, F. (2009) Friendship as Process, Function, and Outcome. In Rubin, K. H, Bukowski, W. M and Laursen, B (eds) *Handbook of Peer Interactions, Relationships, and Groups*. London: The Guilford Press.

Burleson, S. E., and Thoron, A. C. (2017) *Maslow's Hierarchy of Needs and Its Relation to Learning and Achievement*. USA: University of Florida http://knowen-production. s3.amazonaws.com/uploads/attachment/file/2007/Maslow_E2_80_99s%2BHierarchy%2Bof%2BNeeds%2Band%2BIts%2BRelation%2Bto%2BLearning.pdf

Cairns, K. (2006) *Attachment, Trauma and Resilience*. London: British Agencies for Adoption and Fostering.

Cairns, K., and Fursland, E. (2008) *Transitions and Endings: A Training Programme*. London: British Agencies for Adoption and Fostering.

Children's Commissioner for England. (2015) *State of the Nation Report 1: Children in Care and Care Leavers*. London: Children's Commissioner.

Children's Commissioner for England. (2017) *Stability Index for Children in Care*. London: Children's Commissioner.

Children's Commissioner for England. (2019) *Children's Voices: Children's Experiences of Instability in the Care System*. London: Children's Commissioner.

Commodari, E. (2013) Preschool Teacher Attachment, School Readiness and Risk of Learning Difficulties. *Early Childhood Research Quarterly, 28*(1), 123–133.

Conn, A. M., Szilagyi, M. A., Jee, S. H., Blumkin, A. K., and Szilagyi, P. G. (2015) Mental Health Outcomes Among Child Welfare Investigated Children: In-Home Versus Out-Of-Home Care. *Children and Youth Services Review, 57*, 106–111.

Cozolino, L. (2013) *The Social Neuroscience of Education: Optimizing Attachment and Learning in the Classroom.* London: Norton and Co.

Daly, F., and Gilligan, R. (2005) *Lives in Foster Care – The Educational and Social Support Experiences Of Young People Aged 13–14 Years in Long-Term Foster Care.* Dublin: Children's Research Centre, Trinity College.

Demir, M., Özen, A., Doğan, A., Bilyk, N. A., and Tyrell, F. A. (2011) I Matter to My Friend, Therefore I Am Happy: Friendship, Mattering, and Happiness. *Journal of Happiness Studies, 12*(6), 983–1005.

Department for Education. (2018) *The Designated Teacher for Looked After and Previously Looked-After Children: Statutory Guidance on Their Roles and Responsibilities.* London: Crown Copyright.

Department for Education. (2019a) *Outcomes for Children Looked After By Local Authorities in England, 31 March 2018.* Crown Copyright. https://www.gov.uk/government/statistics/outcomes-for-children-looked-after-by-las-31-march-2018

Department for Education. (2019b) *Children Looked After in England (Including Adoption), Year Ending 31st March 2019.* UK: National Statistics https://assets.publishing.service.gov.uk/government/uploads/system/uploads/attachment_data/file/850306/Children_looked_after_in_England_2019_Text.pdf

Department for Education. (2020) *Children Looked After in England (Including Adoption), Year Ending 31st March 2020.* UK: National Statistics https://explore-education-statistics.service.gov.uk/find-statistics/children-looked-after-in-england-including-adoptions/2020

Emond, R. (2014) Longing to Belong: Children in Residential Care and Their Experiences of Peer Relationships at School and in the Children's Home. *Child and Family Social Work, 19*(2), 194–202.

Ford, T., Vostanis, P., Meltzer, H., and Goodman, R. (2007) Psychiatric Disorder Among British Children Looked After by Local Authorities: Comparison with Children Living in Private Households. *The British Journal of Psychiatry, 190*(4), 319–325.

Geddes, H. (2006) *Attachment in the Classroom: The Links Between Children's Early Experience, Emotional Wellbeing and Performance in School.* London: Worth Publishing.

Gilligan, R. (2009) *Promoting Resilience: A Resource Guide on Working with Children in the Care System,* 2nd ed. London: British Agencies for Adoption and Fostering.

Hertfordshire County Council. (2007) *Working with Looked After or Adopted Children in School.* Hertfordshire: Children, Schools and Families.

Isle of Wight Council. (2021) https://www.iow.gov.uk/Residents/care-and-Support/Childrens-Services/Looked-After-Children/What-is-a-Looked-After-Child

Jackson, S. (Ed.) (2001) *Nobody Ever Told Us School Mattered: Raising the Educational Attainments of Children in Care.* London: British Agencies for Adoption and Fostering.

McMahon, C., and Curtin, C. (2013) The Social Networks of Young People in Ireland with Experience of Long-Term Foster Care: Some Lessons for Policy and Practice. *Child and Family Social Work, 18*(3), 329–340.

Meltzer, H., Gatward, R., Corbin, T., Goodman, R., and Ford, T. (2003) *The Mental Health of Young People Looked After by Local Authorities in England.* London: The Stationery Office.

OfSTED. (2007) *Looked After Children – Good Practice in Schools.* London: Crown Copyright.

Ofsted. (2012) *Children's' Care Monitor 2011: Children on the State of Social Care in England.* London: Crown Copyright.

Rees, A. (2015) *The Virtual School Handbook*. Oxford: Rees Centre.

Ridge, T., and Millar, J. (2000) Excluding Children: Autonomy, Friendship and the Experience of the Care System. *Social Policy and Administration, 34*(2), 160–175.

Rogers, J. (2017) 'Different' and 'Devalued': Managing the Stigma of Foster-Care with the Benefit of Peer Support. *British Journal of Social Work, 47*(4), 1078–1093.

Selwyn, J., Saunders, H., and Farmer, E. (2010) The Views of Children and Young People on Being Cared for by an Independent Foster-Care Provider. *British Journal of Social Work, 40*, 696–713.

Sharp, S., and Thompson, D. (1992) Sources of Stress: A Contrast Between Pupil Perspective and Pastoral Teachers' Perceptions. *School Psychology International, 13*(3), 229–242.

Siegel, J. P. (2013) Breaking the Links in Intergenerational Violence: An Emotional Regulation Perspective. *Family Process, 52*(2), 163–178.

Smith, M. C. (1995) A Preliminary Description of Non-School-Based Friendship in Young High-Risk Children. *Child Abuse and Neglect, 19*(12), 1497–1511.

Turkel, S. B., and Eth, S. (1990) *Psychopathological Response to Stress: Adjustment Disorder and Post-Traumatic Stress Disorder in Children and Adolescents. Childhood stress.* New York: John Wiley.

Van Harmelen, A. L., Kievit, R. A., Ioannidis, K., Neufeld, S., Jones, P. B., Bullmore, E.,... and NSPN Consortium. (2017) Adolescent Friendships Predict Later Resilient Functioning Across Psychosocial Domains in a Healthy Community Cohort. *Psychological Medicine, 47*(13), 2312–2322.

Wilson, K., Sinclair, I., Taylor, C., Pithouse, A., and Sellick, C. (2004) *Fostering success: An Exploration of the Research Literature in Foster Care.* London: Social Care Institute for Excellence

Zarrella, I., Lonigro, A., Perrella, R., Caviglia, G., and Laghi, F. (2018) Social Behaviour, Socio-Cognitive Skills and Attachment Style in School-Aged Children: What Is the Relation With Academic Outcomes? *Early Child Development and Care, 188*(10), 1442–1453.

Pedagogies of Welcome: Simple Yet Profound Acts to Support Refugee Pupils' Mental Wellbeing

Caroline Bagelman

Synopsis

Schools are a key access point in the resettlement of 'new arrivals' (which includes asylum seekers and refugees) and as such, teachers tend to largely shoulder this great challenge and honour. This chapter begins by considering mental health interventions at school to respond to trauma experienced by new arrivals, and then suggests that thinking beyond trauma and towards a more 'ecological approach' is also necessary to support mental wellbeing of new arrivals (Rutter, 2006). It will suggest how community, or 'cross-sector', approaches can provide new arrival pupils and their families more robust welcome and support than schools and teachers alone, which can mitigate some of the difficult psychological impacts of resettlement. It will look at the Schools of Sanctuary (SOS) movement which reveals the power of teacher solidarity in supporting mental wellbeing. Turning an eye to specific teaching approaches, this chapter suggests that in the initial stages of their resettlement, new arrivals require a focus on 'form' (e.g. what routines and practices are in place). This means that teachers must be able to identify and reveal elements of the 'hidden curriculum' for new arrivals in order to provide them vital access to school culture, norms, and expectations and support their mental wellbeing (Lynch & Lynch, 1989). Lastly, it will offer guidance on celebrating the 'funds of knowledge' new arrivals bring with them, and how this seeks to build self-esteem and positive relationships linked to mental wellbeing (Moll et al, 1992).

Background

The United Kingdom's Home Office names and classifies forcibly displaced peoples according to their legal status: asylum seeker, indicating that one is making a claim to obtain refugee status to live in a host country, and refugee, indicating that one has gained legal status to live in the host country) (UNHCR, 2021a). Confusingly,

DOI: 10.4324/9781003160526-11

the common usage of the term Refugee, for instance, 'refugee camps', generally indicates anyone who has been forcibly displaced from their homes, and not their legal status. It is the contention of critical migration scholars and activists that no one is illegal, and that categorising people according to status is dehumanising:

> People cannot be illegal, only acts can. Furthermore, the word 'illegal' implies a juridical conclusion, without giving the individual migrant the benefit of pleading his or her case.
>
> (Pace & Severance, 2016, p. 69)

With this in mind, I will be using the term 'new arrival' in this chapter where possible to identify forcibly displaced peoples.

One of the most powerful ways for a teacher to support their new arrival pupils is to develop an awareness of forced migration and resettlement (or: a forced migration acumen) and from there, to create a culture of awareness in their school (Hope, 2008). Understanding the push factors, nature of migration, nature of resettlement, and practicalities of navigating a new host country can inform pedagogy and practice in important ways and better enable teachers to support the mental wellness of their new arrival pupils. In this spirit, I will aim to briefly outline some of these factors in this chapter and provide some further reading to deepen an awareness of forced migration.

What we know is that this year, the UNHCR reports that over 70 million people are displaced from their homes, and more than half are children (UNHCR, 2021b). There is also a wealth of research to show that many new arrivals have endured traumas associated with displacement and family separations, deaths in the family, the violence and insecurity of war, poverty, loss of structure, community, friendships, and homes (see below). In addition to firstly sketching some of this background information, I will second make use of Jill Rutter's (1999) work which encourages educators to see refugees through a more nuanced lens beyond trauma. As I will note, she advocates for an ecological view of new arrival children. I will end this section with a discussion on some of the realities of resettlement that new arrivals face.

Trauma and forced migration

The cause of the forced migration (what is often referred to as 'push factors' that require one to leave their home) can of course impact the mental health and wellbeing of new arrivals in serious ways. If a refugee has fled from war and has witnessed the violent death of friends and family, their scores on measures of Post-Traumatic Stress Disorder (PTSD) experiences are unsurprisingly high (Heptinstall, Senthna & Taylor, 2004). What might be more surprising, to those less familiar with the resettlement process, is that new arrivals' PTSD-like experiences are not only affected by their migration circumstance, but they are also linked to post-migration experiences. This includes life events like insecurity linked to precarious asylum status, financial difficulties, and food insecurity (considering each new arrival in England currently survives on between £35.39 and £37.75 each week, depending on the status of the asylum claim; Gov.uk, 2021). This precarious status means initially living in large, cramped, hostels for an undeclared period, facing scrutiny at regular visits to the home office, the threat of deportation, the inability to enrol children in schools while waiting for family housing, challenges in accessing essential services, randomised relocation (or 'dispersal') to new UK cities with very little notice, and so on (Heptinstall, Senthna & Taylor, 2004). Throughout their resettlement, these pupils can experience not only this post-migration trauma associated with precarious status, but also post-migration 'acculturation stress'. This involves feelings of conflicting identities (being torn between adopting new cultures and preserving their heritage cultures), alienation, and depression linked to feeling disconnected from their home of origin and new home. This acculturation stress also grows from the adult roles new arrival children are often asked to fill. As the ones in school, and thus receiving the most consistent English as an Additional Language (EAL) learning in the family and most consistent access to local culture, children often unwittingly take on the role of translator or cultural ambassador for parents and guardians, while also encountering possible loss of their first languages as they resettle into the host country (referred to as heritage language loss; Pumariega, 2010). To add to this, new arrivals can face discrimination in their new places of resettlement 'affecting socioemotional adjustment' and wellbeing (Benner, 2009). The trauma of various push factors, precarity experienced upon arriving to a host country, and specific forms of acculturation stress refugees face shines some light on the findings that refugees experience heightened levels of depression and other mental illness compared to immigrants (Pernice & Brook, 1994).

Schools and responding to trauma

Fazel (2012) finds that a stable source of social support in the host country has "a positive effect on the child's psychological functioning", and further research suggests that schools are the most important point of access for such support (Suarez-Orozco, 2001; Thommessen & Todd, 2018). Schools are the places where children spend most of their waking hours, make contact with locals, have opportunities to learn language authentically through dialogue, and receive services to ease the asylum-seeking or resettlement process. New arrival families tend to underutilise mental health services, according to Rousseau and Guzder (2008), and therefore "schools have a key mediation role in helping refugee children adapt to their host country and may become the main access point to prevention and treatment services for mental health problems" (Rousseau & Guzder, 2008). It has been found that "culturally informed, evidence-based treatment and preventive interventions that meet the mental health and cultural needs of [..]migrant children and families have the potential to minimise this higher risk of adverse mental health consequences" (Pumariega, 2010). Examples of such school interventions to support new arrivals' mental health include creative expression workshops (Rousseau et al., 2005), drama therapy workshops (Rousseau et al., 2007), music therapy workshops (Baker & Jones, 2006), and sand play programmes to name a few (Rousseau et al., 2009). Many schools offer Cognitive Behavioural Therapy (Ehntholt et al., 2005) and other counselling services provided by mental health key workers such as those who practice individual therapy and family work (Fazel et al., 2012). Such interventions seek to "develop a sense of stability, safety and trust, as well as to [assist pupils to] regain a sense of control over their lives" (Ehntholt & Yule, 2006, p. 202).

When schools and other institutions "incorporated aspects of culture and placed emphasis on adapting or developing new intervention programmes to meet the specific needs and backgrounds of refugee groups", pupil's mental wellbeing is positively impacted. Schools can develop this cultural responsiveness, as Murray, Davidson, and Schweitzer suggest, through collaborating with relevant communities to develop interventions together, or asking for feedback or audits of educational programmes from members of relevant communities (2008, p. 580). As the latter sections of this chapter will explore, teachers can also support their new arrivals' mental wellbeing not simply through therapeutic interventions but through thoughtful induction practices, connecting pupils with other community services, and cultivating a multilingual classroom.

Beyond trauma

Jill Rutter's (1999) ecological approach, which takes into account the wide range of pre-migration and post-migration experiences refugees might have, resists oversimplifying and pathologising refugees and their experiences. What Rutter observes is common within discussions of new arrivals is the 'traumatisation' of refugee lives has dominated discussions and research to the extent that "it has presumed a homogeneity amongst refugee children", which is "an assumption which needs to be broken down" (Rutter, 2006, p. 5). Refugee children's experiences are unique and wide-ranging, meaning that one cannot simply assume that traumatisation has occurred, or what trauma might look like. Rather than viewing all refugee children as traumatised and in need of therapeutic interventions, Rutter's ecological view considers diverse experiences of new arrivals, and how they operate within a web of relations including community, family, language, and country. What these children may need, Rutter contends, may not be 'English and therapy' but opportunities for connection in learning environments which invite them to bring their valued knowledge and experience to the table (Rutter, 1999).

Indeed, in my own work I have found the available language to speak and write about new arrivals ('vulnerable' on one end, and 'resilient' on the other) fails us. Troublingly, the language of resilience suggests that wellbeing is down to the strength of the new arrival's spirit when it is, in actuality, a reflection of socio-political circumstances and the ability to access necessary supports that are very often beyond an individual's control. In focusing on an individual's mental fortitude, societies fail to take responsibility for the systems and circumstances that generate vulnerability such as the UK migration infostructures forming what Teresa May unapologetically termed the 'hostile environment', under which fears of deportation, dispersal at any given moment, and a lack of dignified housing and schooling animate the lives of new arrivals (Brittle, 2019). In working alongside new arrival children and their parents or guardians through a council-funded Initial Accommodation (IA) provision while they await housing and school enrolment, I made the sad discovery that though most young children had not acquired the English words for toys or play, they were fluent in "home office", "hostel", and "Aspen card". They are not vulnerable people, but rather, I would suggest, made vulnerable or: 'vulnerablised'.

The focus on trauma and vulnerability also distracts educators from taking accountability for the ways in which many aspects of schooling underserves, and even disadvantages, new arrival pupils. Rutter's exhaustive work outlines some of the key reasons for underperformance of refugee pupils: little understanding of educators on new arrivals' circumstances, a tendency to put them in bottom sets, inappropriate pedagogy, and a tendency to view them as traumatised and in need of mostly 'English and therapy' (Rutter, 1999). It is important, in this sense, for educators to focus their attention not on the 'attainment gap', but rather the provision gap. In the final sections of this chapter, I will discuss some approaches that can be taken to serve new arrival pupils in a fulsome way.

New arrivals and schooling

> It is six months into the academic year when I first visit the Glasgow primary school serving the largest number of new arrival pupils in the city to conduct a study. As the research team introduces a project relating to forced migration, year 4 Scottish boy who has been sharing a work table all term with his recently-resettled Libyan classmate interjects: 'I've never met a refugee!'
>
> (Author's reflection)

Once children and families scaled these serious obstacles to simply access schools in the United Kingdom, there are often challenges with new arrivals becoming full members of a school community once they do enter mainstream school. In the perennial shuffle of completing prescribed learning outcomes, EAL lessons and assessments, the experiences of these children are often rendered invisible in classrooms, and opportunities for deeper learning and understanding between pupils are missed as the opening vignette from a Scottish classroom illustrates (Arizpe et al., 2014). Despite the changing nature of our cities and the fact that schooling is a child's primary access point for resettlement support, United Kingdom's Department for Education (DfE) has not made new arrival resettlement support (like induction packages) or learning on migrations statutory – nor have they offered practical resources (Suarez-Orozco, 2001; Thommessen & Todd, 2018).

The government also stipulates in Section 115 of the 1999 Immigration and Asylum Act that new arrivals have 'no recourse to public funds', which means free school meals are not available to these pupils (unless schools make under-the-table exceptions), which is highly problematic because these pupils are some of the most food insecure in the country (Farmer, 2017). Since they have no access to public funds, and most schools depend on per-pupil funding, schools generally do not get funding for new arrival pupils. Consequently, there is a sort of resourcing or institutional burden on the school involved in welcoming new arrival pupils, which sometimes means that schools might resist ushering a lot of new arrivals through their doors. These issues again illustrate the ways in which the governmental systems around asylum, and its attendant institutions, vulnerablise new arrivals.

In response to the growing new arrival populations in the United Kingdom, and the lack of DfE and other systemic supports, the SOS movement was born. SOS is a grassroots initiative coming out of the 'Cities of Sanctuary' movement which first started in Sheffield in 2005 to build infrastructures to welcome new arrivals. This comprises various streams: arts, faith, maternity, health, schools). There are currently hundreds of SOS in the United Kingdom at different levels from early years to post-secondary, and they gain this 'status' through meeting three principles which include:

1. *Learning what it means to seek sanctuary*. This involves both staff and pupils developing awareness of refugee experience, causes for forced migration, and other issues associated with displacement.

2. *Taking positive action to embed concepts of welcome safety and inclusion within the school and wider community*. This involves induction practices for new arrivals and curriculum being tailored to relate to themes of forced migration, identity, and displacement. It also takes the form of projects and events oriented towards diversity, cultures, languages, and welcome.

3. *Sharing the SOS vision and achievements*. This means disseminating curricular resources, guidelines, induction packages, reflective notes, videos, and other media related to work being done in the school with other institutions so that they might draw from those experiences to become SOS themselves.

Importantly, the SOS movement makes visible the experiences, and needs of new arrivals within school cultures and curriculum. In reviewing some applications for SOS in Liverpool, I have been moved by the range and creativity of the resources being developed within SOS to create a culture of welcome. For example, text-to-speech pens and the use of pictures and flash cards worn around an 'induction buddy's' neck on a lanyard were used to ensure that new arrivals' needs were being heard and addressed. I have reviewed primary school curriculum examining labour exploitation vs fair trade, which intelligently linked to existing learning outcomes. This was a springboard into conversation with pupils on global poverty, what role the West plays in generating this poverty, and how it can result in the displacement and migration of people (Illich, 1997). It is also heartening to see how SOS provides pupils opportunities to present their work on forced migration in the wider community alongside local poets and authors. Pupil work has been disseminated in libraries and other public spaces to be celebrated and raise awareness. This visibility improves new arrivals' self-esteem, and the awareness of native pupils in SOS on forced migration helps to tackle xenophobia, which can impact negatively on the mental wellbeing of new arrivals (Arizpe et al., 2014; Kastrup, 2016).

What can teachers do?

Reveal and rework the 'hidden curriculum'

When new arrival pupils enter a classroom anew in the host country, it might be the case that this is the first classroom they have ever attended. It is almost definitely the case that this classroom will look different from the one that they attended before. This difference could be in the form of the built environment and organisation of space: what types of resources are available, what is the layout of the learning environment, how are particular? The difference might also appear in terms of elements of the hidden curriculum such as routine: how to respond to bells, when to raise a hand or playfully shout an answer, how subjects are paced through the day, what is the accepted way to transition between those subjects (such as putting books away and accessing supplies)?

In the first months of joining a school, new arrivals therefore often require a focus on 'form' (how the classroom functions, what routines are in place, what is the nature of learning and play in this school). Understanding how schooling operates in their new context is the foundational knowledge which will enable them to build curricular knowledge in the future (Bourdieu & Moishe, 1993). This awareness of social codes, routines, and approaches in schools reduces the alienation, uncertainty, and acculturation stress new arrival children can experience during resettlement, which can have a serious impact on wellbeing (Block et al., 2014; Pernice & Brook, 1994). The ability for new arrivals to thrive in their environment will largely depend on making space for this specific type of induction, which can include: modelling classroom behaviour through role-playing exercises, pictorial schedules identifying some of the more granular aspects of schooling discussed at the top of this section, employing the use of pupil ambassadors or buddies to give 'pupil view' tours of the school, mapping exercises of the school with annotations, and reflective journaling on resettlement in the school.

In Bourdieusian terms, echoed by many scholars and researchers: "education-related capital must be accessible to promote academic achievement. The effectiveness of schools becomes limited when these forms of capital are unequally distributed" (Barani et al., 2011; Giroux & Penna, 1979; Gordon et al., 2005). This means that teachers must be able to identify and reveal elements of the hidden curriculum for new arrivals in order to provide them vital access to school culture, norms, and expectations (Lynch & Lynch, 1989). As with citizens in relation to their legal systems, all pupils have the basic "pedagogic right" to know what standards (however archaic and biased) they are being held to (Davies et al., 2004). Where this hidden curriculum is seen to disadvantage new arrival pupils, which will not be uncommon, teachers can take steps to challenge and make changes to such practices, and not simply expect these pupils to assimilate, (which often results in poor mental health outcomes) or to face the consequences (d'Abreu, Castro-Olivo & Ura, 2019).

Guo Fang Li's work 'Culturally Contested Pedagogies' illustrates the importance of form in educating migrant children. Often, migrant communities come to their new homes with their own received and internalised hidden curricula, and particular conceptions of 'good education' from their home contexts. This might mean that certain subjects are considered more valuable to cognitive development than others (for instance, Li notes that maths and sciences are often afforded greater value in Chinese communities) (Li, 2012). In my own experience in teaching internationally, I noticed that play was occasionally interpreted as frivolous and reckless whereas my North American training regarded play as a form of powerful engaged pedagogy. According to Li, these culturally contested pedagogies should be explicitly recognised and navigated with both pupil and parent or guardian. Teachers should show a willingness in these discussions to introduce their pedagogy, explain the rationale for it, and find opportunities to adapt it in the spirit of culturally relevant teaching. The importance of culturally relevant approaches in supporting new arrivals' wellbeing is echoed in research on effective mental health interventions (Murray, Davidson & Schweitzer, 2010). It is noted that when practitioners are mindful of pupils' cultural backgrounds, belief systems, and values, and consult with members of that community on effective ways to support children in keeping with these beliefs and values, the benefits are greater.

Cast the net out

While schools often focus single-mindedly on the importance of teacher-to-pupil relationship for providing support and welcome, this can be a limiting and overwhelming approach. Especially when it comes to supporting the complex needs and gifts of new arrival pupils, the often neglected but vital teacher-to-community relationship deserves more attention. Community or 'cross-sector' approaches can provide new arrival pupils and their families more robust welcome and support than schools and teachers alone (Hesse, Kreutzer & Diehl, 2019). Within education, cross-sector approaches mean schools must become knowledgeable about refugee or community services on offer, and work to forge connections with them as schools have traditionally done with social work systems (Fehsenfeld, & Levinsen,

2019). This becomes an essential part of a teacher's forced migration acumen: an understanding not just of circumstances causing refugees to flee, and the nature of their migration and resettlement, but also the practicalities of navigating a new host country. The value of such cross-sector approaches is not only in providing access to goods and services, but the impact such goods and services have on the new arrivals' mental wellbeing. In providing pupils opportunities for connection, community, and support outside of the classroom, teachers help to mitigate levels of alienation and stress connected to poor mental health (Block et al., 2014).

Knowledge of official services and signposting these for families is vital, but so too is a knowledge of the informal community spaces that can support and welcome new arrivals, such as community gardens and cultural associations or societies. Supporting new arrivals in making these connections can also be facilitated in active ways that move beyond simple referrals. In IA, we took pupils on a field trip to a local community garden with interested parents and guardians, and then to the community farm shop and kitchen linked to the garden which offers free cookery classes, free lunches, space to sit and meet with others, and hosts regular community gatherings. This was not only an immersive EAL lesson where the pupils learned garden and food vocabulary and practised ordering food, it was also, more importantly, a way of opening up the city.

Where site visits are not possible, it is also beneficial to invite speakers from both official and community organisations to speak to classrooms about their roles and ways in which they promote resettlement. This will mean pupils and their guardians will have a better awareness of what is on offer, but equally, it will mean the schools have forged (hopefully lasting) cross-sector connections which they can continue to build to best support new arrivals (Fehsenfeld & Levinsen, 2019). This is symbiotic. The services and organisations benefit in their mental health provisioning and other supports from knowing what schools provide, what gaps exist, and why they are not reaching certain new arrivals. Working across sectors in this way helps to ease the overwhelming feeling that teachers often experience that they cannot do enough. This is a simple and effective way to build bridges between different forms of care, and the result is often that the teachers themselves feel supported in supporting their pupils – that they do not need to shoulder the demands alone (Fehsenfeld & Levinsen, 2019).

Move beyond tokenism: meaningful engagement with 'funds of knowledge'

When welcoming new arrivals into schools and educating native pupils on migration, it is common even within many SOS classrooms for teachers to unintentionally engage with new arrival pupils in a tokenistic manner. Many SOS will have hallway displays of flags to represent their pupils' origins, or words like 'hello' written in the different languages represented in the school. New arrivals might be asked to recite facts about their home country for the classroom, and talk about national dishes, clothing, and traditions (Dachyshyn & Kirova, 2008). While some new arrivals might be very keen to engage this way, and it may be a way of bringing pupils' experience into the classroom, it is beneficial to use this only as a stepping-stone (if at all) to move into more meaningful terrain.

Asking pupils to act as representatives of their home countries may be complicated for the new arrival in a number of ways. Some may feel at odds with their home country's practices and mainstream cultures (for instance, Iranian families may flee due to religious persecution as non-Muslims, and feel disconnected from national norms like mandatory headscarves for women). These new arrivals are also in the midst of forming new, hybrid identities combining their home cultures and languages with host cultures and languages (Chao, 2019). Expecting pupils to represent their home countries may have the deleterious effect of making new arrivals feel cemented in the position of outsider, rather than being free to craft their new, complex identities (Bahbha, 2015).

Providing space for to connect to peers in a non-tokenistic way, but helps local pupils understand identities that go deeper than the tip of the 'cultural iceberg' (Hall, 1976). This tip of the iceberg comprises the visible aspects of culture (such as dress and cuisine) and says little of the more meaningful belief systems, values, and knowledge beneath the surface that informs those visible practices (Hall, 1976). Employing visual methods such as using picturebooks, illustration, photography, and comic book making have been found to be highly effective for this self-representation and expression of new arrivals specifically (Arizpe et al., 2014). This is partly the case because visual methods support pupils who are EAL, as images can serve to enrich and explain the associated written texts to help build comprehension and confidence, and partly because they often require further elaboration, making visual methods especially generative of discussion, personal story-telling, and empathy building (Goodwin, 2009).

Also, in the spirit of supporting hybrid identities, it is beneficial to temper the drive to teach English with some explicit attention paid to heritage languages. Heritage language loss is common considering the pressures to quickly assimilate into home countries (where being EAL is often viewed as a deficit). This language loss can have the knock-on effect of creating a chasm between the child's home cultures, family, and friends who use the language(s) which add(s) to acculturation stress and interpersonal conflict associated with poor mental health outcomes (Crawford, 1992; Murillo & Smith, 2011; Wright, Taylor & Macarthur, 2000). It can mean not merely a loss of vocabulary, but a disconnect from the knowledge that is embedded in first languages too (Cho, 2000). Providing ongoing opportunities in school for multilingualism (beyond the tokenistic 'hello' in different languages) has been found to increase pupil engagement, self-esteem, and self-image (Lucas & Katz, 1994; Murillo & Smith, 2011; Sheets, 2009). In addition to these psychological benefits, this approach is also tied to greater academic outcomes (Lee, 1996).

Trans-languaging teaching strategies, which can be as simple as promoting multilingual texts in the classroom and using them to engage in meaningful translation activities with English-speaking classmates can serve to build a climate of multilingualism. Such a trans-languaging strategy places new arrivals in the empowering position of 'language broker' rather than the disempowering one of 'non-fluent' English speaker (Hélot & Laoire, 2011). Importantly, what these strategies do is legitimise the new arrival's languages within the school environment and host country and underscore that these languages are not barriers to their 'acculturation' (as some schools' EAL approaches might suggest to new arrivals) but rather: wonderful assets (Hélot & Laoire, 2011).

The funds of knowledge approach focuses on "the skills and knowledge that have been historically and culturally developed to enable an individual or household to function within a given culture" (Moll et al., 1992). Moll et al. suggest that putting these funds of knowledge at the heart of classroom activities, discussion, and ethos "creates a richer and more-highly scaffolded learning experience for pupils" (Moll et al., 1992). As noted above, Li emphasises the ways in which pedagogy is culturally informed, so a significant way to embrace funds of knowledge is not only to make space for expression within the present system, but to work thoughtfully towards developing a 'culturally relevant pedagogy' (Berumen & Silva, 2014).

The question of language in the classroom and pedagogical approaches used with culturally diverse pupils is not only vital to promote welcoming pupils, but is directly linked to pupils' mental wellbeing. Murillo and Smith (2011) emphasise that heritage language maintenance in schools "does have lasting implications for children's emotional well-being and academic development, as well as their access to higher education, healthy relationships, and meaningful employment" (Murillo & Smith, 2011, p. 147). Further, when teaching is mindful of and adjusted to pupils' cultural backgrounds, which can make one feel valued and included on their terms, this makes for more successful educational interventions that can positively impact on mental health (Murray, Davidson & Schweitzer, 2010).

Takeaway points

■ To best support new arrival pupils' mental and overall wellbeing, developing a forced migration acumen that involves an awareness of what forced displacement and resettlement looks like for young people is key.

■ With this awareness, we are able to both begin to understand trauma, and also look beyond it towards more complex ecological views of new arrivals and forced migration. For instance, through this lens, we can see their needs may not be chiefly 'English and therapy', but importantly: fair conditions in host countries that enable full access to education, and opportunities for meaningful connection with peers, teachers, and communities.

▨ Ways to generate these fair conditions and connections, as suggested in this chapter, can include:

● Easing access to services through cross-sector approaches.

● Revealing and reworking hidden curriculum through reflexive praxis and culturally relevant pedagogy.

● Celebrating funds of knowledge through supporting creative self-representation, and through using trans-languaging approaches.

Further Reading

City of Sanctuary. Schools of Sanctuary. 2021. <https://schools.cityofsanctuary.org/>

Hélot, C. and Laoire, M.Ó. eds., (2011). *Language policy for the multilingual classroom: Pedagogy of the possible*. Multilingual Matters.

Rutter, J., (2006). *Refugee children in the UK*. McGraw-Hill Education (UK).

Thommessen, S. & Todd, B., (2018). How do refugee children experience their new situation in England and Denmark? Implications for educational policy and practice. *Children and Youth Services Review*, 85, 228–238. doi: 10.1016/j.childyouth.2017.12.025

References

d'Abreu, A., Castro-Olivo, S. & Ura, S.K., (2019). Understanding the role of acculturative stress on refugee youth mental health: A systematic review and ecological approach to assessment and intervention. *School Psychology International*, 40(2), 107–127.

Apple, M.W. & King, N.R., (1977). What do schools teach? *Curriculum Inquiry*, 6(4), 341–358.

Baker, F. & Jones, C., (2006). The effect of music therapy services on classroom behaviours of newly arrived refugee pupils in Australia—A pilot study. *Emotional and Behavioural Difficulties*, 11(4), 249–260.

Barani, G., Azma, F. & Seyyedrezai, S.H., (2011). Quality indicators of hidden curriculum in centers of higher education. *Procedia-Social and Behavioral Sciences*, 30, 1657–1661.

Benner, K., (2009). Experiences of discrimination among Chinese American adolescents and the consequences for socioemotional and academic development. *Developmental Psychology*, 45(6), 1682–1694.

Berumen, F.C. & Silva, C., (2014). A journey with a refugee family: Raising culturally relevant teaching awareness. *New Directions for Teaching and Learning*, 140, 51–67.

Brittle, R., (2019). A hostile environment for children? The rights and best interests of the refugee child in the United Kingdom's asylum law. *Human Rights Law Review*, 19(4), 753–785.

Block, K., Cross, S., Riggs, E. & Gibbs, L., (2014). Supporting schools to create an inclusive environment for refugee pupils. *International Journal of Inclusive Education*, 18(12), 1337–1355.

Chao, X., (2019). 'What defines me is what I have been through': Bhutanese refugee youth identity in the United States. *British Journal of Sociology of Education*, 40(6), 809–825.

Cho, G., (2000). The role of heritage language in social interactions and relationships: Reflections from a language minority group. *Bilingual Research Journal*, 24(4), 369–384.

Crawford, J., (1992). *Language loyalties: A source book on the official English controversy.* The University of Chicago Press.

Dachyshyn, D.M. & Kirova, A., (2008). Understanding childhoods in-between: Sudanese refugee children's transition from home to preschool. *Research in Comparative and International Education,* 3(3), 281–294.

Davies, B., Morais, A. & Muller, J. eds., (2004). *Reading Bernstein, Researching Bernstein.* Routledge.

Department for Education, (2010). 'Pupil Guidance' Available at https://webarchive.nationalarchives.gov.uk/20120106191112/https://www.education.gov.uk/publications[accessed May 1, 2021].

Ehntholt, K.A., Smith, P.A. & Yule, W., (2005). School-based cognitive-behavioural therapy group intervention for refugee children who have experienced war-related trauma. *Clinical Child Psychology and Psychiatry,* 10(2), 235–250.

Ehntholt, K.A. & Yule, W., (2006). Practitioner Review: Assessment and treatment of refugee children and adolescents who have experienced war-related trauma. *Journal of Child Psychology and Psychiatry,* 47(12), 1197–1210.

Farmer, N.J., (2017). 'No Recourse to Public Funds', insecure immigration status and destitution: The role of social work? *Critical and Radical Social Work,* 5(3), 357–367.

Fazel, R., (2012). Mental health of displaced and refugee children resettled in high-income countries: Risk and protective factors. *The Lancet* (British edition), 379 (9812), 266–282.

Fehsenfeld, M. & Levinsen, K., (2019). Taking care of the refugees: Exploring advocacy and cross-sector collaboration in service provision for refugees. *Voluntas: International Journal of Voluntary and Nonprofit Organizations,* 30(2), 422–435.

Giroux, H.A. & Penna, A.N., (1979). Social education in the classroom: The dynamics of the hidden curriculum. *Theory & Research in Social Education,* 7(1), 21–42.

Goodwin, P., (2009). Developing understanding of narrative, empathy and inference through picturebooks. *Talking beyond the page: Reading and responding to picturebooks* (pp. 152–167), Routledge.

Gordon, E.W., Bridglall, B.L. & Meroe, A.S., (2005). *Supplementary education: The hidden curriculum of high academic achievement.* Rowman & Littlefield.

Hélot, C. & Laoire, M.Ó. eds., (2011). *Language policy for the multilingual classroom: Pedagogy of the possible.* Multilingual Matters.

Heptinstall, E., Sethna, V. & Taylor, E., (2004). PTSD and depression in refugee children. *European child & adolescent psychiatry,* 13(6), 373–380.

Hope, J., (2008). "One day we had to run": The development of the refugee identity in children's literature and its function in education. *Children's Literature in Education,* 39(4), 295–304.

Hesse, A., Kreutzer, K. & Diehl, M.R., (2019). Dynamics of institutional logics in a cross-sector social partnership: The case of refugee integration in Germany. *Journal of Business Ethics,* 159(3), 679–704.

Illich, I., (1997). Development as planned poverty. *The post-development reader,* 94–102.

Kastrup, M., (2016). The impact of racism and discrimination on mental health of refugees and asylum seekers. *European Psychiatry,* 33(S1), S43–S43.

Lee, P., (1996). Cognitive development in bilingual children: A case for bilingual instruction in early childhood education. *The Bilingual Research Journal,* 20(3/4), 499–522.

Li, G., (2012). *Culturally contested pedagogy: Battles of literacy and schooling between mainstream teachers and Asian immigrant parents.* SUNY Press.

Lucas, T. & Katz, A., (1994). Reframing the debate: The role of native languages in English only programs for language minority pupils. *TESOL Quarterly*, 28(3), 537–561.

Lynch, K. & Lynch, K.R., (1989). *The hidden curriculum: Reproduction in education, a reappraisal*. Psychology Press.

Moll, L.C., Amanti, C., Neff, D. and Gonzalez, N. (1992). Funds of knowledge for teaching: Using a qualitative approach to connect homes and classrooms. *Theory into practice*, *31*(2), 132–141.

Murray, K., Davidson, G. & Schweitzer, R., (2008). Psychological wellbeing of refugees resettling in Australia: A literature review prepared for the Australian Psychological Society. Australian Psychological Society. https://eprints.qut.edu.au/59164/

Murillo, L.A. & Smith, P.H., (2011). "I will never forget that": Lasting effects of language discrimination on language-minority children in Colombia and on the US-Mexico border. *Childhood Education*, 87(3), 147–153.

Pace, P. & Severance, K., (2016). Migration terminology matters. *Forced Migration Review*, 51, 69.

Pernice, R. & Brook, J., (1994). Relationship of migrant status (refugee or immigrant) to mental health. *International Journal of Social Psychiatry,* 40, 177–188.

Pumariega, R., (2010). Leaving no children or families outside: The challenges of immigration. *American Journal of Orthopsychiatry*. [Online] 80(4), 505–515.

Rousseau, C., Benoit, M., Gauthier, M.F., Lacroix, L., Alain, N., Viger Rojas, M., Moran, A. & Bourassa, D., (2007). Classroom drama therapy program for immigrant and refugee adolescents: A pilot study. *Clinical Child Psychology and Psychiatry*, 12(3), 451–465.

Rousseau, C., Drapeau, A., Lacroix, L., Bagilishya, D. & Heusch, N., (2005). Evaluation of a classroom program of creative expression workshops for refugee and immigrant children. *Journal of Child Psychology and Psychiatry*, 46(2), 180–185.

Rousseau, C., Benoit, M., Lacroix, L. & Gauthier, M.F., (2009). Evaluation of a sandplay program for preschoolers in a multiethnic neighborhood. *Journal of Child Psychology and Psychiatry*, 50(6), 743–750.

Rousseau, C. & Guzder, J., (2008). School-based prevention programs for refugee children. *Child and Adolescent Psychiatric Clinics of North America*, 17(3), 533–549.

Rutter, J., (2006). *Refugee children in the UK*. McGraw-Hill Education (UK).

Sheets, R.H., (2009). What is diversity pedagogy? *Multicultural Education*, 16(3), 11–17.

Suarez-Orozco, M., (2001). Globalization, immigration, and education: The research agenda. *Harvard Educational Review*, 71(3), 345–366.

Thommessen, S. & Todd, B., (2018). How do refugee children experience their new situation in England and Denmark? Implications for educational policy and practice. *Children and Youth Services Review*, 85, 228–238. doi: 10.1016/j.childyouth.2017.12.025

UK Government, 2021. What you'll get. Gov.uk. Jan 2, 2021. https://www.gov.uk/asylum-support/what-youll-get

UNHCR (United Nations High Commissioner for Refugees), 2021a. *Global trends: Forced displacement in 2017*. Geneva: UNHCR.

UNHCR (United Nations High Commissioner for Refugees), 2021b. *Turn the tide: Refugee education in crisis*. Geneva: UNHCR.

Wright, S.C., Taylor, D.M. & Macarthur, J., (2000). Subtractive bilingualism and the survival of the Inuit language: Heritage- versus second-language education. *Journal of Educational Psychology*, 92(1), 63–84. doi: 10.1037//0011–0663.92.1.63

Mental Wellbeing Challenges of Muslim Pupils in UK Schools

Sania Shakoor, Muthanna Samara, and Hisham M. Abu-Rayya

Synopsis

Islamic identity is a way of life which guides and determines various aspects of behaviours and interactions amongst Muslim populations. Islamic norms, values, and practices can present unique challenges and conflicting discourse for Muslim adolescents living in the United Kingdom. The presence of acculturative pressures to maintain and negotiate traditional, cultural, and religious identities, in addition to exposure to violence in the form of increasing Islamophobic narratives (including bullying in schools), highlights this population as having unique needs when maintaining mental wellbeing. This chapter presents a discussion of the wellbeing of Muslim adolescents attending British schools within the context of bullying and cultural diversity and identity.

Background

For Muslim adolescents, Islam is considered as a guide which determines their behaviours and interactions. Islamic teachings shape emotional responses, cognitive processing of life experiences, development of interpersonal relationships, and health-seeking behaviours. Religious identity should thus be taken into consideration when supporting the mental health of Muslim populations (Koenig & Al Shohaib, 2019).

Islamic norms, values, and some practices can present unique challenges and conflicting discourse for Muslim adolescents, in particular, amongst those who live in non-Muslim majority countries (Shah, 2006). Furthermore, experiences are often complicated by the presence of multiple social identities based, for instance, on ethnicity (e.g., South Asian), race (e.g., Somali Muslims), and gender. In non-majority Muslim countries, Muslim adolescents have reported feeling acculturative pressures from family, same ethno-religious peers, and the wider Muslim

DOI: 10.4324/9781003160526-12

community to maintain and negotiate their traditional, cultural, and religious practices (Bigelow, 2008; Davies, 2019). Furthermore, vulnerabilities for mental health difficulties may be heightened amongst Muslim adolescents due to their exposure to violence in the form of increasing Islamophobic narratives (e.g., faith-based bullying in school contexts; Mirza, 2015; Sian, 2015), and exposure to trauma in the form of ethnic cleansing, political and civil wars, and natural disasters resulting in displacement and migration to non-majority Muslim countries (Ahmed & Hashem, 2016; Samara et al., 2020b, 2020c).

Traditionally, causes and treatments of mental health amongst minority groups have been framed around ethnicity, nationality, and race. Evidence to date illustrates the heterogeneity in mental health problems and service use amongst ethnic minorities (Goodman, Patel & Leon, 2008). However, literature exploring the mental health of Muslim adolescents and adult populations suggests religion as an additional point of interest (Cinnirella & Loewenthal, 1999), yet seldom are Muslim adolescents understood and treated as a unique group when supporting their mental health. With approximately 8% of all school-age children (5–15 years of age) in the United Kingdom being identified as Muslim and estimates of approximately 300,000 Muslim teenagers having lived in the United Kingdom in 2021 (Office of National Statistics, 2017), Muslim adolescents represent a substantial proportion of the population who may go on to need mental health service provisions. For Muslim children, issues of acculturation and prejudice become complicated as they transition into adolescence and young adulthood, where they often struggle with issues such as bullying and increasing Islamophobia which views Muslims as suspects (Mirza, 2015; Sian, 2015). It is during this key developmental period that they develop their identity, independence, peer relationships, and support systems (Erikson, 1968). Gaining a better understanding of their current mental health and associated aetiological profiles is thus pertinent to those working within the education and public health sectors. This chapter presents a discussion on the wellbeing of Muslim adolescents attending British schools within the context of bullying and cultural diversity and identity.

Mental wellbeing amongst Muslim adolescents

Literature exploring the mental wellbeing amongst Muslim populations has predominantly come from outside of the United Kingdom, including the USA, Australia, Netherlands, and some Muslim-majority countries, such as Turkey, Iran, and Malaysia. Albeit mixed, studies have found that identifying as a Muslim has been considered either as a risk or as a protective factor against the development of mental health difficulties (Altalib, Elzamzamy, Fattah, Ali & Awaad, 2019). For example, studies from the Middle East have reported significant negative correlations between religiosity, depression, and anxiety (Abdel-Khalek & Eid, 2011; Baroun, 2006). Furthermore, a number of studies have reported significant relationships between discrimination experienced by Muslims from a variety of backgrounds and psychological distress (e.g., depressive symptoms, anger, and anxiety, see Samari, Alcalá & Sharif, 2018). However, literature within the United Kingdom is limited. The majority of studies explored differences amongst ethnic minority groups, which include majority Muslim ethnicity groups, such as those of Pakistani and Bangladeshi descent (Goodman et al., 2008). Ethnic minority adolescents, in this regard, have reported better mental health wellbeing in comparison to their White counterparts (Terhaag, Fitzsimons, Daraganova & Patalay, 2021). Longitudinal data suggest that after accounting for individual, family, and neighbourhood characteristics, the mental health of White British adolescents was poorer than that of their ethnic minority peers (Jonsson, Vartanova & Södergren, 2018; Knowles et al., 2021). Furthermore, in a study amongst 38,000 children aged 10-12Y from 16 countries, researchers observed that Muslim children reported higher levels of subjective wellbeing. This included satisfaction with life as a whole, as well as family, friends, and the self in comparison to Hindu and Asian-Christian/Buddhist children (Kosher & Ben-Arieh, 2017). Similarly, cross-sectional data from British school-aged cohorts suggest that Muslim adolescents (aged 14-16Y) have lower levels of psychological distress as measured by symptoms of depression, anxiety, and behavioural problems (Dabbagh, Johnson, King & Blizard, 2012). It is proposed that belonging to a minority Muslim group may act as a protective factor as this encourages social cohesion, structure, and support, and thus promotes mental wellbeing. Although data from these studies give us an indication of the mental health landscape amongst British Muslim adolescents, it is important to note that religion and ethnicity are not synonyms of one another, thus highlighting the need for more scientifically vigorous studies exploring the mental health conditions of Muslim adolescents in the UK.

Despite the heightened mental wellbeing, there is still a greater unmet need for mental health services amongst Pakistani and Bangladeshi adolescents, a majority of whom identify as Muslim (Goodman et al., 2008; see Chapter 3 where this topic is covered in more detail). In a study of South Asian adolescents, 65–66% reported that they, or their friends and family, would not seek help from a mental healthcare clinic for their difficulties. However, adolescents of South Asian descent did have a similar level of awareness of services as other ethnic groups (Randhawa & Stein, 2007). In contrast, in a study exploring Pakistani young people's views on barriers to accessing mental health services, respondents reported limited knowledge about the types of therapies available (i.e., cognitive behavioural therapy and family therapy). Understanding mental health provisions primarily centred around counselling (Ali, McLachlan, Kanwar & Randhawa, 2017). Therefore, most children with mental health problems probably go undetected and do not access treatment promptly. To address this, it is essential to identify barriers to healthcare use, and improve screening, detection, and practitioners' knowledge of adolescent mental health problems and needs, including minorities and Muslim communities' needs (Danese, McLaughlin, Samara & Stover, 2020). Some of these barriers may be related to cultural mistrust, not wanting to disclose personal information, poor mental health literacy, stigma around mental illness, and structural barriers (e.g., access or transportation; see Danese et al.,

2020), which contribute towards a lack of engagement with mental health services and provisions (Ali et al., 2017; Amri & Bemak, 2013). Therefore, firstly, there is a great need for improving knowledge amongst Muslim adolescents and families on detecting mental health problems, emphasising the necessity of intervening to prevent long-term negative consequences, and secondly, improve training amongst healthcare practitioners who are working amongst ethnic and religious minorities towards adolescent mental health needs and causes (Danese et al., 2020).

Bullying and discrimination: the role of religion and ethnicity as risk factors

Research has shown that Muslims in Britain experience racial as well as religiously motivated discrimination (Meer & Modood, 2012). Muslim victims of faith-based violence report multiple and repeated acts of cyber and 'real world' victimisation, including verbal and physical attacks (Awan & Zempi, 2015). Amongst Muslim adolescents, this may present itself as a form of bias-based bullying, where bullying is directed towards a minority population based on discrimination or prejudice (Walton, 2018). Individuals are bullied because they are considered to not fit in (Nadeem & Graham, 2005), and identifying with a minority group contributes towards a power imbalance. Thus, it is possible that faith-based violence may be occurring in educational environments in the form of bullying.

However, studies' findings differ depending on what factors are considered and the relationships between minority and majority groups and subgroups. Some studies from the UK have shown no significant difference in the prevalence of bullying directed against children from ethnic minority groups compared to White Caucasian children (Durkin et al., 2012; Tippett, Wolke & Platt, 2013). This, however, largely comes from small sample groups, and evidence suggests that ethnic minority children are more likely to attribute their bullying victimisation to race or culture (Monks, Ortega-Ruiz & Rodríguez-Hidalgo, 2008) rather than religious identity. A study by Green, Collingwood, and Ross (2010) revealed that young people from minority ethnic groups were less likely to report being bullied than white young people at all ages. Furthermore, they found little relationship between bullying and the importance of religion, with the exception of name-calling. Young people who placed more importance on their religion were more likely to report being bullied by name-calling at all ages, which may indicate that this type of bullying was targeted directly towards their religion. Similarly, another report also indicated that in 2012–2013, 1,400 Muslim adolescents (aged 12-15Y) had experienced racist bullying, a 69% increase compared with 2011–2012 figures with the most common being verbal bullying (e.g., being called terrorist, bomber, go back to where you came from; NSPCC/Childline, 2013). Archer (2003, 2012) reported that specifically British Muslim boys were exposed to various verbal and physical racism attacks during their commute to school. Most common reasons for these attacks are people's responses to change and arrival of unknown others. Furthermore, Archer (2003) described the form of racism experienced by British Muslim boys within the school environment as physical bullying and colour-based racism through name-calling. Some events (e.g., Brexit) or UK government initiatives on counter-terrorism (Prevent) are believed to have made Muslim students more vulnerable to verbal and physical assaults as reported in the media. A study of Muslim and non-Muslim focus groups revealed that counter-terrorism measures are contributing to a wider sense among Muslims of being treated as a 'suspect community' and targeted by authorities simply because of their religion. Many participants felt that counter-terrorism law and policy generally was contributing towards hostility to Muslims by treating Muslims as a 'suspect group' and creating a climate of fear and suspicion towards them. These measures were also seen to add to perceptions of racial and religious profiling and discrimination (Choudhury & Fenwick, 2011). The study reported on how schools have been impacted by terrorism incidents and the policy responses to it. For instance, following the 7/7 bombings, schools were monitoring for a potential backlash against Muslim pupils and with the introduction of the Prevent programme, Muslim youth were viewed as both 'risky and at risk' (Thomas, 2016). These led some schools to amend their incident report forms to include Islamophobia as one of the categories for reporting. In addition, schools had to consider how to address issues arising out of wider discussions around these topics. The aim of these was for non-Muslim students to understand the views and feelings of Muslim students. The report revealed that schools should encourage discussions within the classrooms by providing an opportunity for pupils to externalise their feelings and to say what they think or perceive to be happening (Choudhury & Fenwick, 2011).

Research has indicated that bullying is also likely to happen among ethnic groups. Eslea and Mukhtar (2000) investigated bullying amongst Asian schoolchildren in Britain from Hindu, Indian Muslim, and Pakistani backgrounds. They revealed that bullying was at least as likely to be by other Asian children of a different ethnic group as it was by white children, and it was likely to relate to cultural differences (e.g., clothing, food, language spoken). In the study, for instance, Indian Muslims and Pakistanis were most frequently bullied by Hindus, while Pakistani boys were also frequently bullied by Indian Muslims. Archer (2003) also referred to more subtle forms of racism where white boys would be friendly with them at school but would ignore them in public when they were with their friends and families. The same was reported about teachers, where Muslim boys reported that their teachers are racist by ignoring or talking over them (Archer, 2003). In addition, Bowlby and Lloyd-Evans (2012) reported that Muslim boys experienced low expectations from teachers, negatively affecting the aspirations and attainment of Muslim adolescents. Young male and female Muslims also reported that some teachers had a stereotypical image of 'young Muslim women' as submissive, uninterested in work and prevented by family or community pressures from pursuing a career (Bowlby & Lloyd-Evans, 2012). In addition, it was reported that some Muslim girls were bullied in schools because they wore a headscarf (NSPC, 2016).

A more recent study by Francis and McKenna (2018) amongst 335 (13-15Y) Muslim students from England, Northern Ireland, Scotland, and Wales demonstrated that one in four Muslim students (25%) reported being bullied. In addition, it was found that psychological (specifically neuroticism personality) and religious (worship attendance) factors predicted vulnerability to victimisation among Muslim students. It is those Muslim students who are seen to take their religious faith seriously through participation in worship attendance who experience higher levels of victimisation and bullying. The study by Francis and McKenna (2018) utilised a victimisation questionnaire that illustrated specific reasons of victimisation related to minorities, including race, religion, language, clothes, name, country origin, and friends. Thus, studies investigating bullying and victimisation amongst minorities should be comprehensive to capture the real reasons and motives of these behaviours rather than ask about general bullying and/or victimisation (Samara et al., 2019). Vulnerability and victimisation can be taken to be closely associated with reasons due to religion, race, food, and language rather than to be operating independently.

As discussed, to date, empirical evidence exploring the impact of bullying amongst Muslim adolescents is limited; thus, in its absence, it is important to learn from existing large nationally representative cohort studies, which mostly include Muslims. Involvement in bullying as victims and/or bullies is associated with various mental and physical health and behavioural problems (Arseneault, Bowes & Shakoor, 2010; Copeland et al., 2013; Shakoor et al., 2015). For example, externalising problems such as hyperactivity and conduct disorder have been typically reported among bullies, whereas internalising problems, such as anxiety and mood disorders, have been mainly observed among victims (e.g., Shakoor et al., 2011), while a combination of both internalising and externalising problems are observed amongst bully/victims (Copeland et al., 2013; Wolke & Samara, 2004). These in turn reduce students' school engagement leading to lower academic achievement (Samara et al., 2021), specifically amongst victims (Nakamoto & Schwartz, 2010; Strøm, Thoresen, Wentzel-Larsen & Dyb, 2013), with this effect persisting over time (Wang et al., 2014). In addition, children who are victimised by their peers tend to have negative attitudes towards the school (Rueger et al., 2010), negative perceptions of school climate (Wang et al., 2014), and difficulties concentrating on school work (Li et al., 2010). Involvement in bullying victimisation is thus believed to reduce bullied Muslim students' motivations, aspirations (Shukla, Konold & Cornell, 2016), school relatedness (Huang & Vidourek, 2019), and academic competence (Young-Jones, Fursa, Byrket & Sly, 2014), and these, in turn, negatively affect academic achievement in comparison to their non-bullied peers (Samara et al., 2021). These outcomes can also be manifested in the long term when they enter university (Goodboy, Martin & Goldman, 2016).

Bullying and victimisation can also be moderated by the ethnic composition of the class (living in a more multicultural or less multicultural area) and being from a majority or minority population (Tolsma, van Deurzen, Stark & Veenstra, 2013; Vervoort, Scholte, & Overbeek, 2010). Moreover, different ethnic groups might value high academic achievement differently, which may also affect individual academic achievement. Hence, governmental reports revealed high academic achievement for some Muslim minority groups (Department of Education, 2021).

Cultural diversity: cultural identity, acculturation, and adaptation

In the ever-increasing culturally diverse world we live in, social-cultural psychologists and policy-makers have been concerned with prompting wellbeing, social cohesion, and acceptance of all cultural groups as major goals. The UK society is no exception. Yet, various studies have indicated a rise in anti-Muslim sentiments in the UK. For instance, the HM Government's Hate Crime report (2019) recorded a general 10% increase in hate crimes (i.e., 'criminal offences motivated by race-based hostility or prejudice') between the years 2017/2018 (94,121 offences) and 2018/2019 (103,379 offences). Hate crimes directed at Muslims comprised 47% of the total 2018/2019 recorded cases.

Various meta-analytic studies have demonstrated the adverse effects of hate crimes, racism, and discrimination on mental health of minorities (e.g., Paradies et al., 2015; Schmitt, Branscombe, Postmes & Garcia, 2014). This is also true for Muslim minorities in Western societies. A recent systematic review summarising the results of studies on the relationship between discrimination and psychological distress (e.g., depressive symptoms, anger, and anxiety) among Muslims supported a consistent pattern of negative effects of discrimination on mental health (Samari, Alcalá & Sharif, 2018). Muslim adolescents living in a context where hate crimes, racism, and ethno-religious prejudice prevail are thus at risk of experiencing psychological instability and poorer mental health, factors that might in turn undermine their academic achievement. Since hate crimes, racism, and prejudice occur in the context connected to Muslim adolescents' conceptualisation of their own cultural identity (e.g., Wang, Raja & Azhar, 2020) and acting toward combating such negative experiences (e.g., Abu-Rayya et al., 2016), it is vital to introduce schoolteachers to the concepts of cultural identity and acculturation and their role in shaping Muslim adolescents' functioning in response to racism and discrimination.

At its core, acquiring a cultural identity means sharing with other in-group members a set of cultural values, norms, modes of perception, cultural skills and knowledge, ways of formulating experience, and senses of community and self. Once heritage cultural identity is achieved, it provides a frame of reference within which individuals develop their out-group judgements, perceptions, and attitudes (e.g., Phinney & Kohatsu, 1997; Segall, Dasen, Berry & Poortinga, 1999). As contended by Arce (1981) "for [cultural] minority group members, identification with others who share their origins and traditions is critical in developing both a positive [cultural] identity and feelings of self-esteem and efficacy rather than self-blame and powerlessness" (p. 82).

Similarly, other experts in the field maintain that heritage cultural identity denotes an important aspect of cultural minority individuals' sense of self, and it has been hypothesised as psychologically crucial to the development and establishment of their self-meaning (e.g., Abu-Rayya et al., 2016; Berry, Phinney, Sam, & Vedder, 2006). Cultural identity can be a vital protective factor for Muslim adolescents, buffering the negative effects of prejudice and discrimination stressors, they might experience in interactions with majority members, on their mental health (e.g., Abu-Rayya et al., 2016; El Bouhaddani, van Domburgh, Schaefer, Doreleijers & Veling, 2019; Sheldon, Oliver & Balaghi, 2015). While heritage cultural identity starts to develop in childhood, it is during adolescence that it becomes more vital; the attainment of cognitive maturity that accompanies this period enables cultural minority individuals to actively engage in the development of their own cultural membership (Berry et al., 2006; Ryckman, 2000).

The psychological benefits of heritage cultural identity achievement for the psychological functioning of cultural minority adolescents (Muslims and non-Muslims) are well established. In the face of prejudice, racism, and discrimination, some minority individuals may, consciously or unconsciously, distance themselves from their cultural identity, and downplay or even hide aspects of their cultural identity to avoid hostility, harming further their mental health and social well-being (Sadek, 2017). A plethora of research evidence on cultural minorities have shown that diffused cultural identification is associated with lower levels of academic achievement, and self-esteem, and accounts for deteriorated mental health measured by parameters of delinquency, substance abuse, suicidal episodes, and depression (e.g., Abu-Rayya et al., 2016; Tineo, Lowe, Reyes-Portillo & Fuentes, 2021; Williams, Clark & Lewycka, 2018).

On the contrary, an extensive body of research has indicated that cultural minority individuals who internalise confident and secure heritage cultural identities demonstrate better psychological, social, and school adaptation; they show a higher level of academic performance, perceived self-efficacy, self-esteem and confidence, purpose in life and optimism, and lower incidences of behavioural problems (e.g., Abu-Rayya et al., 2016; Heim, Hunter & Jones, 2011; Tineo et al., 2021; Williams et al., 2018). Additionally, research indicated that cultural minority Muslim adolescents' connection with their heritage culture mitigates the negative effects their experiences with prejudice, racism, and discrimination have on their mental health and functioning (Abu-Rayya et al., 2016; Tineo et al., 2021). Besides, minority Muslims' attachment to their Muslim identity, which shapes their common identity beyond their ethnic heterogeneity, associates with better self-acceptance, satisfaction with life, and school adjustment, and less school and community problems (e.g., Abu-Rayya et al., 2016). Minority Muslim adolescents' involvement in both their heritage culture and religion will likely provide the social and community support needed for protective social interactions and emotional care and instil in Muslim adolescents positive self-views and faith- and culture-based norms that assist in their psychological and social functioning (Abu-Rayya et al., 2016; Tineo et al., 2021).

Beyond the evidence-based psychosocial benefits Muslim adolescents would experience out of developing and maintaining a positive view of their cultural identity, how they acculturate to the national identity and values of their larger society (i.e., White British) seems also important to their psychological functioning. Acculturation as a broad construct is defined as modifications in values, identities, and behaviours that cultural minority individuals experience due to contact with the larger mainstream society (Berry, 2017). The acculturation view asserts that more beneficial psychological outcomes for cultural minority adolescents will ideally be achieved when they pursue *integration*, i.e., cultural engagement with both their heritage culture (e.g., British Muslim) and the culture of the mainstream society (e.g., White British) (Abu-Rayya & Brown, 2021; Berry, 2017).

A plethora of research has documented the mental health, wellbeing, and school adjustment benefits of endorsing integration among various cultural minority groups (e.g., Abu-Rayya et al., 2016; Berry, 2017; Berry et al., 2006; Ward & Kus, 2012). For instance, in their meta-analysis of 83 studies totalling 23,197 participants, Nguyen and Benet-Martínez (2013) reported significant evidence of a positive link between integration (bicultural identity) and a range of psychological, social, and cultural indicators of adaptation. Abu-Rayya and Sam's (2017) meta-analytic study supported the consistency of this conclusion, even when the effects of participants' reported level of perceived discrimination, across various contexts, on their adaptation was controlled for in the analyses (Abu-Rayya & Sam, 2017). Although available research suggests that cultural minorities, including Muslims, tend generally to prefer integration (over other modes of acculturation as assimilation; Brown & Zagefka, 2011), it should be noted that anti-Muslim sentiments and behaviours may lead to the development of social segregation among Muslim adolescents in the UK, hamper the development of their British identity, and result in intense tensions with White Britons (e.g., Abu-Rayya & Brown, 2021; Abu-Rayya et al., 2016; Berry, 2017).

The abovementioned findings suggest that policies and practices that emphasise and promote equity for cultural minority Muslim adolescents, and eliminate prejudices and discrimination can make a difference to adolescents' identity development, mental health, wellbeing, and academic achievement. In addition, such practices would also facilitate Muslim adolescents' endorsement of integration (bicultural) style of identity and enjoy the benefits this carries for their development, wellbeing, and quality of relationships with White Britons.

British Muslim adolescents spend a significant amount of their development in school, suggesting that schools are an important setting to intervene and provide positive experiences that facilitate their healthy development. Indeed, research has shown that schools can have a significant impact on shaping the values, identity, and aspirations of pupils (White & Abu-Rayya, 2012).

What can teachers do?

There are various pedagogical methods that British schoolteachers and educators can implement to strengthen Muslim pupils' (and hopefully also other cultural minorities') sense of cultural identity, engage them in the teaching materials, promote inclusivity and equity in the classroom, encourage critical thinking, and improve academic results. We chose to focus our discussion here on co-production of toolkits, offsetting bullying, and culturally responsive/relevant teaching (e.g.,

Brown-Jeffy & Cooper, 2011; Gardner, 2001; Villegas & Lucas, 2002) and make suggestions for its implementation in schools.

Co-production of toolkits

As schools are safe and familiar environments for adolescents, they have the potential to be influential in providing information and support with regard to mental health wellbeing, services, and provisions. Schools need to be aware of the barriers and vulnerabilities some minority groups may have (Goodman et al., 2008). In particular, as Muslim adolescents and their families report profound feelings of peer pressure to conform to popular social norms, and as they struggle with reconciling pressures and conflicts with their religious and cultural values (Bradby et al., 2007; Hodge, 2002; Islam, Multani, Hynie, Shakya & McKenzie, 2017; Khan, Khan, Soyege, Maklad & Center, 2019), the importance of schools to adopt culturally appropriate strategies and interventions for promoting and supporting mental wellbeing is ever more critical (Hodge, 2002). One strategic way to do this would be to invite parents, community, and religious leaders to co-produce toolkits with schools that can be used on educational and community levels. Schools can further foster mental wellbeing and constrain risk trajectories of poor mental wellbeing amongst their Muslim pupils by recognising their varying composition and particular needs. This integrative approach is important to encourage dialogue and develop positive narratives to help Muslim parents and the wider community be a part of this therapeutic journey, whilst feeling supported and understanding that their values and religious practices are being considered.

Offsetting bullying

Collectively, the literature to date suggests that the experiences and detrimental effects of bullying warrant particular attention within the context of identity and religion. Gaining a better understanding about such experiences and their consequent impact on wellbeing and mental health amongst Muslim adolescents would be an important addition for anti-bullying and anti-Islamophobia-based policies (Smith et al., 2012). Tikly et al. (2004) identified certain strategies adopted by schools that made all their pupils, including those from minority backgrounds, perform well. These strategies created a positive culture within the school environment, which contributed to making the students feel valued; reduced marginalisation made Muslim pupils feel they were part of an inclusive school environment; reduced bullying, tackled attitudes of Islamophobia and underachievement among pupils, and increased their achievements (Samara et al., 2020a). These strategies include (1) an emphasis on common values of respect and tolerance; (2) effective systems in place for recording racist incidents and bullying and for responding to these; (3) incident report forms should include faith-based bullying as one of the categories for reporting; (4) schools to encourage discussions within the classrooms by providing an opportunity for pupils to externalise their feelings; (5) high levels of communication and openness between the school staff, parents, and adolescents; (6) visible presence of minority ethnic staff, mentors, and members of the local community in schools; (7) diversity is highly valued and reflected in the curriculum, in wall displays, in assemblies, etc.

Culturally responsive/relevant teaching

This method refers to a type of pedagogy grounded in teachers' cultural competence, and it recognises the importance of integrating pupils' cultural backgrounds into the classroom's learning environment and in the teaching curriculum. Richards, Brown, and Forde (2006) denote culturally responsive pedagogy at the institutional (i.e., values and ethos reflected in the school policies and practices), personal (i.e., teachers' mindset), and instructional (i.e., teaching and classroom practices) dimensions. Culturally responsive teaching explicitly acknowledges, respects, and understands cultural differences, and builds on these issues to facilitate pupils' learning and develop their cultural competence and critical cultural consciousness (Brown-Jeffy & Cooper, 2011; Villegas & Lucas, 2002).

There are various translations of these notions to practical steps and suggestions. For instance, as far as the institutional (school) level is concerned, British schools might need to (1) acknowledge anti-Muslim bias as a form of racism; (2) include lessons on what constitutes Islamophobia and ways to combat it; (3) provide cultural sensitivity training sessions to teachers and administrators; (4) make sure that educational materials pertaining to Muslims and Islam are free of bias; (5) endorsing a formal statement emphasising the values and practices that clearly promote peace and intercultural understanding; (6) emphasise respect for the rights of Muslims and understanding the multicultural make-up of UK society; and (7) endorse the principles that encourage pupils' participation in building a prosperous, harmonious, and safe Britain to all.

At the personal (teacher) and instructional levels, for instance, teachers may

- Affirm differences and emphasise also commonalities;

- Initiate learning about their Muslim pupils' cultural background and their hobbies;

- Create an emotionally supportive and positive classroom;

- Emphasise cooperative learning involving Muslim and White British pupils and pupils from other cultural backgrounds;

- Promote positive peer interactions in the classroom and encourage perspective taking in culturally relevant discussions;

- Encourage substantive dialogue and the building of respectful relationships between Muslim and British pupils;

- Taking the class on a journey into the community;

- Evaluate teaching materials for bias and acknowledge and adjust the delivery of the materials accordingly;

- Bring Muslim guest speakers to add context to a lesson;

- Incorporate media that positively depict Muslim cultures;

- Involve the pupils' parents in the learning process; and

- Acknowledge Muslim holidays in the classroom.

For more detailed practical guides, refer to work by Fristwell, Lovett, Reed, Turner, and Ponder (2013) and Shermer and Fenner (2018).

As noted, British schools and teachers can play a significant role in providing a positive British context for minority Muslim adolescents. It is also hoped that adopting, implementing, and tailoring culturally responsive teaching in British schools to cater for Muslim pupils' needs do not only contribute to the cultivation of their cultural identity, wellbeing, mental health, and academic achievement, but also consolidate Muslim adolescents' British belongingness and endorsement of integration. This will further enhance Muslim adolescents' psychosocial functioning and beyond that also improve the quality of their relationships with and attitudes towards White Britons and culture. This idea is supported by the findings of Abu-Rayya and Brown's (2021) recent experimentally designed study on British Muslim adolescents, which showed that Muslim adolescents' endorsement of integration reduced their negative emotions and intergroup anxiety, increased their inclusion of others in the self and positive emotions, ameliorated Muslim adolescents' attitudes towards White Britons, and increased their behavioural intentions and willingness to culturally engage with the majority culture in the future. Importantly, the respondents of this study were required to read and reflect on a set of short stories depicting a positive intercultural contact between British Muslim and White British adolescents. All intergroup attitude benefits of this activity followed from only one brief intercultural interaction session. Such types of activities can easily be implemented in culturally responsive teaching programmes in British schools.

Takeaway points

- Muslim adolescents are a heterogeneous (diverse and varied) group, and their cultural and religious identities are vital to their psychological functioning and mental health.

- They experience acculturative pressures to maintain and negotiate their traditional, cultural, and religious identities and practices. They also face the challenge of adapting to British norms and values.

- They possess heightened vulnerabilities to mental health risks due to their exposure to violence in the form of increasing Islamophobic narratives (including bullying), and exposure to trauma in the form of ethnic cleansing, political and civil wars, and natural disasters, resulting in displacement and migration to non-majority Muslim countries.

- Psychological outcomes for cultural minority adolescents will ideally be achieved when they pursue integration, cultural engagement with both their heritage culture (e.g., British Muslim), and the culture of the mainstream society (e.g., White British).

- Enhancing friendship quality and peer support in schools can help Muslim pupils overcome some of their mental health problems and enhance their wellbeing.

- Schools should develop clear policies on dealing with any form of racism, Islamophobia, or bullying and emphasise common values of respect and tolerance.

- Introduce schoolteachers to the concepts of cultural identity and acculturation and their role in shaping Muslim adolescents' functioning in response to racism and discrimination.

- School policies and practices that emphasise and promote equity for cultural minority Muslim adolescents, and eliminate prejudices and discrimination are needed to support the development of identity, mental health, wellbeing, and academic achievement.

Further reading

Abu-Rayya, H.M., & Brown, R. (2021). Living together: An integrated acculturation-contact strategy to promote ethnic harmony between young British Muslims and Anglo-Britons. *Group Processes & Intergroup Relations.* 1(1), 1–20. Doi: 10.1177/13684302211019471

Altalib, H., Elzamzamy, K., Fattah, M., Ali, S., & Awaad, R. (2019). Mapping global Muslim mental health research: Analysis of trends in the English literature from 2000 to 2015. *Global Mental Health, 6.*

Berry, J. W. (2017). Theories and models of acculturation. In S. J. Schwartz & J. Unger (Eds.), *The Oxford handbook of acculturation and health* (online). Oxford: Oxford University Press.

Samari, G., Alcalá, H. E., & Sharif, M. Z. (2018). Islamophobia, health, and public health: A systematic literature review. *American Journal of Public Health, 108*, e1–e9.

References

Abdel-Khalek, A. M., & Eid, G. K. (2011). Religiosity and its association with subjective well-being and depression among Kuwaiti and Palestinian Muslim children and adolescents. *Mental Health, Religion & Culture, 14*(2), 117–127. doi:10.1080/13674670903540951

Abu-Rayya, H.M., & Brown, R. (2021). Living together: An integrated acculturation-contact strategy to promote ethnic harmony between young British Muslims and Anglo-Britons. *Group Processes & Intergroup Relations.* 1(1), 1–20. doi: 10.1177/13684302211019471

Abu-Rayya, H. M., & Sam, D. L. (2017). Is integration the best way to acculturate? A re-examination of the bicultural-adaptation relationship in the "ICSEY-Data Set" using the bilineal method. *Journal of Cross-cultural Psychology, 48,* 287–293.

Abu-Rayya, M. H., Walker, R., White, F. A., & Abu-Rayya, H. M. (2016). Cultural identification and religiosity contribute differentially to the adaptation of Australian adolescent Muslims. *International Journal of Intercultural Relations, 54,* 21–33.

Ahmed, S., & Hashem, H. (2016). A decade of Muslim youth: Global trends in Research. *Journal of Muslim Mental Health, 10*(1), 25–49.

Ali, N., McLachlan, N., Kanwar, S., & Randhawa, G. (2017). Pakistani young people's views on barriers to accessing mental health services. *International Journal of Culture and Mental Health, 10*(1), 33–43. doi:10.1080/17542863.2016.1248456

Altalib, H., Elzamzamy, K., Fattah, M., Ali, S., & Awaad, R. (2019). Mapping global Muslim mental health research: Analysis of trends in the English literature from 2000 to 2015. *Global Mental Health, 6,* 1–10.

Amri, S., & Bemak, F. (2013). Mental health help-seeking behaviors of Muslim immigrants in the United States: Overcoming social stigma and cultural mistrust. *Journal of Muslim Mental Health, 7*(1), 43–63.

Archer, L. (2003). *Race, masculinity and schooling: Muslim boys and education.* Maidenhead: Open University Press.

Archer, L. (2012). Race, 'face' and masculinity: The identities and local geographies of Muslim boys. In P. Hopkins & R. Gale (Eds.), *Muslims in Britain: Race place and identities* (pp. 74–91). Edinburgh: Edinburgh University Press.

Arseneault, L., Bowes, L., & Shakoor, S. (2010). Bullying victimization in youths and mental health problems: 'Much ado about nothing?'. *Psychological Medicine, 40*(5), 717–729. doi:10.1017/S0033291709991383

Awan, I., & Zempi, I. (2015). *We fear for our lives: Offline and online experiences of anti-Muslim hostility.*

Baroun, K. A. (2006). Relations among religiosity, health, happiness, and anxiety for Kuwaiti adolescents. *Psychological Reports, 99*(3), 717–722.

Berry, J. W. (2017). Theories and models of acculturation. In S. J. Schwartz & J. Unger (Eds.), *The Oxford handbook of acculturation and health* (online). Oxford: Oxford University Press.

Berry, J. W., Phinney, J. S., Sam, D. L., & Vedder, P. (2006). Immigrant youth: Acculturation, identity, and adaptation. *Applied Psychology: An International Review, 55,* 303–332.

Bowlby, S., & Lloyd-Evans, S. (2012). 'You seem very westernised to me': Place, identity and othering of Muslim workers in the UK labour market. In P. Hopkins & R. Gale (Eds.), *Muslims in Britain: Race place and identities* (pp. 37–54). Edinburgh: Edinburgh University Press.

Brown, R., & Zagefka, H. (2011). The dynamics of acculturation: An intergroup perspective. *Advances in Experimental Social Psychology, 44,* 129–184.

Brown-Jeffy, S., & Cooper, J. E. (2011). Toward a conceptual framework of culturally relevant pedagogy: An overview of the conceptual and theoretical literature. *Teacher Education Quarterly, 38,* 65–84.

Bigelow, M. (2008). Somali adolescents' negotiation of religious and racial bias in and out of school. *Theory into Practice, 47*(1), 27–34.

Bradby, H., Varyani, M., Oglethorpe, R., Raine, W., White, I., & Helen, M. (2007). British Asian families and the use of child and adolescent mental health services: A qualitative study of a hard to reach group. *Social Science & Medicine, 65*(12), 2413–2424.

Choudhury, T., & Fenwick, H. (2011). *The impact of counter-terrorism measures on Muslim communities*. Equality and Human Rights Commission Research Report series. ISBN 978 1 84206 383 5.

Cinnirella, M., & Loewenthal, K. M. (1999). Religious and ethnic group influences on beliefs about mental illness: A qualitative interview study. *British Journal of Medical Psychology, 72*(4), 505–524.

Copeland, W. E., Wolke, D., Angold, A., & Costello, E. J. (2013). Adult Psychiatric Outcomes of Bullying and Being Bullied by Peers in Childhood and Adolescence. *JAMA Psychiatry, 70*(4), 419–426. https://doi.org/10.1001/jamapsychiatry.2013.504

Dabbagh, N., Johnson, S., King, M., & Blizard, R. (2012). Muslim adolescent mental health in the UK: An exploratory cross-sectional school survey. *International Journal of Culture and Mental Health, 5*(3), 202–218. doi:10.1080/17542863.2011.594246

Danese, A., McLaughlin, K. A., Samara, M., & Stover, C. S. (2020). Psychopathology in children exposed to trauma: Detection and intervention needed to reduce downstream burden. *BMJ, 371*, m3073. https://doi.org/10.1136/bmj.m3073

Davies, A. (2019). Tradition and transformation: Pakistani-heritage young people explore the influences upon their educational progress. *Race Ethnicity and Education, 22*(5), 683–702.

Department of Education. (2021). *GCSE English and Maths results. Retrieved on 27 June 2021: https://www.ethnicity-facts-figures.service.gov.uk/education-skills-and-training/11-to-16-years-old/a-to-c-in-english-and-maths-gcse-attainment-for-children-aged-14-to-16-key-stage-4/latest#download-the-data.*

Durkin, K., Hunter, S., Levin, K. A., Bergin, D., Heim, D., & Howe, C. (2012). Discriminatory peer aggression among children as a function of minority status and group proportion in school context. *European Journal of Social Psychology, 42*(2), 243–251.

El Bouhaddani, S., van Domburgh, L., Schaefer, B., Doreleijers, T. A., & Veling, W. (2019). Psychotic experiences among ethnic majority and minority adolescents and the role of discrimination and ethnic identity. *Social Psychiatry and Psychiatric Epidemiology, 54*, 343–353.

Erikson, E. (1968). *Identity: Youth and crisis*. Oxford: Norton & Co.

Eslea, M., & Mukhtar, K. (2000). Bullying and racism among Asian schoolchildren in Britain. *Educational Research, 42*(2), 207–217.

Francis, L. J., & McKenna, U. (2018). The experience of victimisation among Muslim adolescents in the UK: The effect of psychological and religious factors. *Religions, 9*(8), 243. https://www.mdpi.com/2077-1444/9/8/243

Fristwell, T., Lovett, K., Reed, M., Turner, C., & Ponder, K. (2013). *Practical recommendations and interventions: Culturally diverse students*. School of Education, Delaware University, USA. https://www.education.udel.edu/wp-content/uploads/2013/01/CulturallyDiverseStudents.pdf

Gardner, P. (2001). *Teaching and learning in the multicultural classroom*. London: David Fulton Publishing.

Goodboy, A. K., Martin, M. M., & Goldman, Z. W. (2016). Students' experiences of bullying in high school and their adjustment and motivation during the first semester of college. *Western Journal of Communication, 80*(1), 60–78. https://doi.org/10.1080/10570314.2015.1078494

Goodman, A., Patel, V., & Leon, D. A. (2008). Child mental health differences amongst ethnic groups in Britain: A systematic review. *BMC Public Health, 8*(1), 1–11.

Green, R., Collingwood, A., & Ross, A. (2010). *Characteristics of bullying victims in schools.* London: Department for Education.

Heim, D., Hunter, S. C., & Jones, R. (2011). Perceived discrimination, identification, social capital, and well-being: Relationships with physical health and psychological distress in a U.K. minority ethnic community sample. *Journal of Cross-Cultural Psychology, 42,* 1145–1164.

HM Government. (2019). *Integrated communities strategy green paper: Summary of consultation responses and government response.* London: HM Government. Available at https://www.gov.uk/government/consultations/integrated-communities-strategy-green-paper

Hodge, D. R. (2002). Working with Muslim youths: Understanding the values and beliefs of Islamic discourse. *Children & Schools, 24*(1), 6–20.

Huang, S.-T., & Vidourek, R. A. (2019). Bullying victimization among Asian-American youth: A review of the literature. *International Journal of Bullying Prevention, 1*(3), 187–204. https://doi.org/10.1007/s42380-019-00029-3

Islam, F., Multani, A., Hynie, M., Shakya, Y., & McKenzie, K. (2017). Mental health of South Asian youth in Peel Region, Toronto, Canada: A qualitative study of determinants, coping strategies and service access. *BMJ Open, 7*(11), e018265.

Jonsson, K. R., Vartanova, I., & Södergren, M. (2018). Ethnic variations in mental health among 10–15-year-olds living in England and Wales: The impact of neighbourhood characteristics and parental behaviour. *Health & Place, 51,* 189–199.

Khan, F., Khan, M., Soyege, H. O., Maklad, S., & Center, K. (2019). Evaluation of factors affecting attitudes of Muslim Americans toward seeking and using formal mental health services. *Journal of Muslim Mental Health, 13*(2), 5–21.

Knowles, G., Gayer-Anderson, C., Beards, S., Blakey, R., Davis, S., Lowis, K., … Pinfold, V. (2021). Mental distress among young people in inner cities: The Resilience, Ethnicity and AdolesCent Mental Health (REACH) study. *Journal of Epidemiology Community Health, 75*(6), 515–522.

Koenig, H.G., & Al Shohaib, S.S. (2019). Religiosity and Mental Health in Islam. In: Moffic H., Peteet J., Hankir A., & Awaad R. (eds). *Islamophobia and Psychiatry.* Switzerland: Springer.

Kosher, H., & Ben-Arieh, A. (2017). Religion and subjective well-being among children: A comparison of six religion groups. *Children and Youth Services Review, 80,* 63–77.

Li, L., Chen, X. and Li, H., 2020. Bullying victimization, school belonging, academic engagement and achievement in adolescents in rural China: A serial mediation model. Children and youth services review, *113*(1), 104946.

Meer, N., & Modood, T. (2012). For "Jewish" read "Muslim"? Islamophobia as a form of racialisation of ethno-religious groups in Britain today. *Islamophobia Studies Journal, 1*(1), 34–53.

Mirza, H. S. (2015). Dangerous Muslim girls? Race, gender and Islamophobia in British schools. In Alexander, C., Weekes-Bernard, D., & Arday, J. (eds). *The Runnymede School Report: Race, Education and Inequality in Contemporary Britain.* London: Runnymede.

Monks, C. P., Ortega-Ruiz, R., & Rodríguez-Hidalgo, A. J. (2008). Peer victimization in multicultural schools in Spain and England. *European Journal of Developmental Psychology, 5*(4), 507–535.

Nadeem, E., & Graham, S. (2005). Early puberty, peer victimization, and internalizing symptoms in ethnic minority adolescents. *The Journal of Early Adolescence, 25*(2), 197–222.

Nakamoto, J., & Schwartz, D. (2010). Is peer victimization associated with academic achievement? A meta-analytic review. *Social Development, 19*(2), 221–242. https://doi.org/10.1111/j.1467-9507.2009.00539.x

Nguyen, A.D., & Benet-Martínez, V. (2013). Biculturalism and adjustment: A meta-analysis. *Journal of Cross-Cultural Psychology, 44*, 122–159.

NSPCC/Childline. (2013). *Can I tell you something? What's affecting children in 2013. Childline review of 2012/13.*

Office of National Statistics. (2017). *Office for National Statistics; National Records of Scotland; Northern Ireland Statistics and Research Agency 2011 Census aggregate data. UK Data Service (Edition: February 2017).*

Paradies, Y., Ben, J., Denson, N., Elias, A., Priest, N., Pieterse, A., … & Gee, G. (2015). Racism as a determinant of health: A systematic review and meta-analysis. *PLoS One, 10*, e0138511.

Phinney, J. S., & Kohatsu, E. (1997). Ethnic and racial identity development and mental health. In J. Schulenberg, J. Maggs, & K. Hurrelman (Eds.), *Health risks and developmental transitions in adolescence* (pp. 420–443). New York: Cambridge University Press.

Randhawa, G., & Stein, S. (2007). An exploratory study examining attitudes toward mental health and mental health services among young south Asians in the United Kingdom. *Journal of Muslim Mental Health, 2*(1), 21–37. doi:10.1080/15564900701238518

Richards, H.V., Brown, A., & Forde, T.B. (2006). *Addressing diversity in schools: Culturally responsive pedagogy.* Denver: Buffalo State College.

Ryckman, R. M. (2000). *Theories of personality.* Belmont, CA: Wadsworth.

Sadek, N. (2017). Islamophobia, shame, and the collapse of Muslim identities. International *Journal of Applied Psychoanalytic Studies, 14*, 200–221.

Samara, M., Da Silva Nascimento, B., El-Asam, A., Hammuda, S., & Khattab, N. (2021). How can bullying victimisation lead to lower academic achievement? A systematic review and meta-analysis of the mediating role of cognitive-motivational factors. *International Journal of Environmental Research and Public Health, 18*(5). Retrieved 2021/02/ from http://europepmc.org/abstract/MED/33668095, https://doi.org/10.3390/ijerph18052209

Samara, M., Da Silva Nascimento, B., El Asam, A., Smith, P., Hammuda, S., Morsi, H., & Al-Muhannadi, H. (2020a). Practitioners' perceptions, attitudes, and challenges around bullying and cyberbullying. *International Journal of Emotional Education, 12*(2), 8–25.

Samara, M., El Asam, A., Khadaroo, A., & Hammuda, S. (2020b). Examining the psychological well-being of refugee children and the role of friendship and bullying. *British Journal of Educational Psychology, 90*(2), 301–329. https://doi.org/10.1111/bjep.12282

Samara, M., Foody, M., Göbel, K., Altawil, M., & Scheithauer, H. (2019). Do cross-national and ethnic group bullying comparisons represent reality? Testing instruments for structural equivalence and structural isomorphism. *Frontiers in Psychology, 10*(1621). https://doi.org/10.3389/fpsyg.2019.01621

Samara, M., Hammuda, S., Vostanis, P., El-Khodary, B., & Al-Dewik, N. (2020c). Children's prolonged exposure to the toxic stress of war trauma in the Middle East. *BMJ, 371*, m3155. https://doi.org/10.1136/bmj.m3155

Samara, M., & Smith, P. (2020). School design, climate and safety: Strategies for anti-bullying interventions and inclusiveness. *International Journal of Emotional Education, 12*(2), 2–7.

Samari, G., Alcalá, H. E., & Sharif, M. Z. (2018). Islamophobia, health, and public health: A systematic literature review. *American Journal of Public Health, 108*(6), e1–e9.

Schmitt, M. T., Branscombe, N. R., Postmes, T., & Garcia, A. (2014). The consequences of perceived discrimination for psychological well-being: A meta-analytic review. *Psychological Bulletin*, 140, 921–948.

Segall, M. H., Dasen, P. R., Berry, J. W., & Poortinga, Y. H. (1999). *Human behaviour in global perspective*. Boston: Allyn & Bacon.

Shah, S. (2006). Leading multiethnic schools: A new understanding of Muslim youth identity. *Educational Management Administration & Leadership, 34*(2), 215–237.

Shakoor, S., Jaffee, S. R., Andreou, P., Bowes, L., Ambler, A. P., Caspi, A., … Arseneault, L. (2011). Mothers and children as informants of bullying victimization: Results from an epidemiological cohort of children. *Journal of Abnormal Child Psychology*, 39(3), 379–387. doi:10.1007/s10802-010-9463-5

Shakoor, S., McGuire, P., Cardno, A. G., Freeman, D., Plomin, R., & Ronald, A. (2015). A shared genetic propensity underlies experiences of bullying victimization in late childhood and self-rated paranoid thinking in adolescence. *Schizophrenia Bulletin, 41*(3), 754–763. doi:10.1093/schbul/sbu142

Sheldon, J. P., Oliver, D. G., & Balaghi, D. (2015). Arab American emerging adults' ethnic identity and its relation to psychological well-being. *Emerging Adulthood, 3*, 340–352.

Shermer, N. K., & Fenner, D. (2018). *Bridging cultures: Issues and strategies, a guide for schools*. Washington, USA: Middle East Centre: University of Washington.

Shukla, K., Konold, T., & Cornell, D. (2016). Profiles of student perceptions of school climate: Relations with risk behaviors and academic outcomes. *American Journal of Community Psychology, 57*(3–4), 291–307. https://doi.org/10.1002/ajcp.12044

Sian, K. P. (2015). Spies, surveillance and stakeouts: Monitoring Muslim moves in British state schools. *Race Ethnicity and Education, 18*(2), 183–201.

Smith, P. K., Kupferberg, A., Mora-Merchan, J. A., Samara, M., Bosley, S., & Osborn, R. (2012). A content analysis of school anti-bullying policies: A follow-up after six years. *Educational Psychology in Practice, 28*(1), 47–70. https://doi.org/10.1080/02667363.2011.639344

Strøm, I. F., Thoresen, S., Wentzel-Larsen, T., & Dyb, G. (2013). Violence, bullying and academic achievement: A study of 15-year-old adolescents and their school environment. *Child Abuse & Neglect, 37*(4), 243–251. https://doi.org/10.1016/j.chiabu.2012.10.010

Terhaag, S., Fitzsimons, E., Daraganova, G., & Patalay, P. (2021). Sex, ethnic and socioeconomic inequalities and trajectories in child and adolescent mental health in Australia and the UK: Findings from national prospective longitudinal studies. *Journal of Child Psychology and Psychiatry, 62*(10), 1255–1267.

Thomas, P. (2016). Youth, terrorism and education: Britain's Prevent programme. *International Journal of Lifelong Education, 35*(2), 171–187. DOI: 10.1080/02601370.2016.1164469.

Tikly, L., Caballero, C., Haynes, J., Hill, J. (2004). *Understanding the educational needs of mixed heritage pupils*. London: Department for Education and Skills.

Tineo, P., Lowe, S. R., Reyes-Portillo, J. A., & Fuentes, M. A. (2021). Impact of perceived discrimination on depression and anxiety among Muslim college students: The role of acculturative stress, religious support, and Muslim identity. *American Journal of Orthopsychiatry*. Advance online publication, *91*(4), 454–463.

Tippett, N., Wolke, D., & Platt, L. (2013). Ethnicity and bullying involvement in a national UK youth sample. *Journal of Adolescence, 36*(4), 639–649.

Tolsma, J., van Deurzen, I., Stark, T. H., & Veenstra, R. (2013). Who is bullying whom in ethnically diverse primary schools? Exploring links between bullying, ethnicity, and ethnic diversity in Dutch primary schools. *Social Networks, 35*(1), 51–61. https://doi.org/10.1016/j.socnet.2012.12.002

Vervoort, M. H. M., Scholte, R. H. J., & Overbeek, G. (2008). Bullying and victimization among adolescents: The role of ethnicity and ethnic composition of school class. *Journal of Youth and Adolescence, 39*(1), 1. https://doi.org/10.1007/s10964-008-9355-y

Villegas, A.M., & Lucas, T. (2002). Preparing culturally responsive teachers: Rethinking the curriculum. *Journal of Teacher Education, 53*, 20–32.

Walton, L. M. (2018). The effects of "Bias Based Bullying" (BBB) on health, education, and cognitive–social–emotional outcomes in children with minority backgrounds: Proposed comprehensive public health intervention solutions. *Journal of Immigrant and Minority Health, 20*(2), 492–496.

Wang, S. C., Raja, A. H., & Azhar, S. (2020). "A lot of us have a very difficult time reconciling what being Muslim is": A phenomenological study on the meaning of being Muslim American. *Cultural Diversity and Ethnic Minority Psychology, 26*, 338–346.

Wang, W., Vaillancourt, T., Brittain, H. L., McDougall, P., Krygsman, A., Smith, D., Cunningham, C. E., Haltigan, J. D., & Hymel, S. (2014). School climate, peer victimization, and academic achievement: Results from a multi-informant study. *School Psychology Quarterly, 29*(3), 360–377. https://doi.org/10.1037/spq0000084

Ward, C., & Kus, L. (2012). Back to and beyond Berry's basics: The conceptualisation, operationalisation and classification of acculturation. *International Journal of Intercultural Relations, 36*, 472–485.

Wolke, D., & Samara, M. M. (2004). Bullied by siblings: Association with peer victimisation and behaviour problems in Israeli lower secondary school children. *Journal of Child Psychology and Psychiatry, 45*(5), 1015–1029.

White, F. A., & Abu-Rayya, H. M. (2012). A dual identity-electronic contact (DIEC) experiment promoting short- and long-term intergroup harmony. *Journal of Experimental Social Psychology, 48*, 597–608.

Williams, A. D., Clark, T. C., & Lewycka, S. (2018). The associations between cultural identity and mental health outcomes for indigenous Māori youth in New Zealand. *Frontiers in Public Health, 6*, 319. doi.org/10.3389/fpubh.2018.00319

Young-Jones, A., Fursa, S., Byrket, J. S., & Sly, J. S. (2015). Bullying affects more than feelings: The long-term implications of victimization on academic motivation in higher education. *Social Psychology of Education, 18*(1), 185–200. https://doi.org/10.1007/s11218-014-9287-1

Accommodating King Saul: Jewish Pupils and Mental Health

Maxim G. M. Samson

Synopsis

This chapter explores some of the challenges faced by Jewish pupils pertaining to mental health – specifically regarding questions of identity, antisemitism, and educational pressure – and presents some strategies for teachers to cater to their distinctive needs. In particular, the chapter encourages teachers to familiarise themselves with some of the (often overlooked) diversity of the British Jewish community in order to help recognise their assorted experiences and concerns. Indeed, by remaining attentive to the various potential causes of distress among Jewish pupils, teachers can play an important role in enabling them to negotiate their highs and lows and ultimately feel part of inclusive classrooms.

Background

Three thousand years ago, King Saul, the first King of Israel, became probably the first reported example of a Jewish figure to be afflicted by a mental health issue. According to the Book of Samuel, Saul, a great warrior and popular leader, starts to experience various symptoms of mental distress late in his life. In one incident, Saul, suffering from the stress of waiting a week for Samuel to arrive with advice for confronting the much larger Philistine army, crumbles, undertaking a ritual that is forbidden to him. This stimulates Samuel to admonish the king, triggering recognisable signs of depression (Huisman, 2003). Although the music of his armour-bearer David seems to provide Saul temporary respite, the king also frequently manifests clear delusional signs of jealousy and psychotic hatred towards him, in two separate episodes even attempting to murder him (see Ben-Noun, 2003). The men eventually reconcile, but due to his earlier disobedience, Saul is abandoned by God and his kingdom is offered to David. Following the ill-fated

Battle of Gilboa, Saul commits suicide, providing a tragic end to what in many ways had been a fruitful life.

Why is this story important to a chapter on the potential mental health challenges faced by Jewish pupils? Despite his military achievements and role as his people's first king, Saul's status in Jewish history is somewhat downplayed, certainly compared to his successor David, in large part due to his increasingly erratic behaviour, which Ben-Noun (2003) suggests may have been diagnosable as bipolar disorder I. Mental health scarcely appears in the Jewish tradition beyond the story of Saul. Did Saul's afflictions provide some sort of justification for his ousting and for his eventual overshadowing by the more popular David? It is essential that educators identify the signs of psychological distress and integrate rather than disregard pupils in need of support. This chapter explores some of the distinctive challenges faced by many Jewish children and teenagers at school and provides some recommendations for teachers so that they can accommodate their mental health needs as seamlessly as possible. First, it highlights three broad areas in which Jewish children and adolescents may feel that their mental health is being compromised: Jewish identity; educational pressure; and antisemitism. Subsequently, the chapter offers some strategies to support Jewish pupils.

Jewish identity

First, it should be acknowledged that the question of 'Who is a Jew?' forms one of the longest-running debates within the Jewish community. There is not the space here to consider this debate in detail, but a few key elements should be acknowledged by teachers unfamiliar with Jewish identity.

Crucially, there is no single way of defining one's Jewishness, and so teachers should not draw any assumptions about their pupils' ways of self-identifying. Despite Judaism often being described as a religion, for instance, many Jews do not consider themselves religious, but secular. A substantial proportion of Jews do not attend a synagogue or other Jewish community institution on a regular basis, if at all. Furthermore, many Jewish pupils especially today are the children of parents of different faiths, who may themselves self-identify in a wide range of ways. Other distinctions pertain to nationality, ethnicity (in the UK, primarily Ashkenazi Jews with origins in Central and Eastern Europe, and Sephardic Jews with roots in the Mediterranean region) and race.

Complicating the issue further is the fact that, for centuries, there has been considerable disagreement among Jews about who may even be considered 'Jewish'. Historically, a Jew was regarded as such if they had a Jewish maternal line; Orthodox Jews still generally adhere to this principle. By contrast, Liberal and Reform Judaism both now regard a Jewish paternal line as sufficient to being considered Jewish. Masorti or Conservative Judaism is often deemed as falling between these two broad camps, combining traditional beliefs and practices with modern science and scholarship. Importantly, though, these are just official positions which are not accepted by all. Teachers must also recognise that the categories presented here are themselves fairly vague: for instance, Orthodox Judaism is itself a conspicuously diverse category, ranging from 'strict' strands such as Haredi and Hasidic Jews, who tend to send their children to generally private schools where their children can be immersed in their beliefs, largely or entirely separate from other forms of identity, to mainstream (often called 'modern' or 'central') branches, like the United Synagogue (US), which are more open to broader society (Staetsky & Boyd, 2016; Valins, 2003). In short, teachers must acknowledge that there is more than one way of understanding and practising Judaism.

Given these variations, quite unsurprisingly the British Jewish community – if one can even describe something so broad in such a way – has in recent decades seen fierce debates over who may be considered Jewish. Importantly, these discussions often centre on schools. Probably the most controversial case was what has been colloquially termed the Jewish Free School (JFS) case,[1] involving the rejection of a self-identifying Jewish boy by the JFS in North London because his mother had converted into Judaism through a non-Orthodox synagogue. The Supreme Court ruled in 2009 that selection based on matrilineal descent is racially discriminatory, thereby preventing all state-funded Jewish day schools from defining Jewishness in such a way for admission purposes. The case has had numerous implications, one of which is the unprecedented possibility for pupils who identify as Jewish in a wide range of ways to attend these educational institutions (Samson, 2019a). Accompanied by the (separate) growth in state-funded Jewish schools in the past 20 years, today around two-thirds of all Jewish school-age children in the UK are enrolled in such institutions (Staetsky & Boyd, 2016). Teachers should thus be aware that unless they are working in a Jewish school, most of which are located in North or Northwest London or Southwest Hertfordshire (Hart et al., 2007; Staetsky & Boyd, 2016), Jewish pupils are likely to constitute a small proportion of their classes, especially in the state sector.

Given such disputes over Jewishness as well as the growing likelihood that where they attend non-Jewish schools, they will be in the minority, Jewish pupils may be sensitive to how they are perceived by others. In particular, and just like many other children and teenagers, Jewish pupils often disavow labels and do not want to be seen as different from others, even if they feel proudly Jewish. If they follow any Jewish traditions, they may not perceive this as information that their peers need to know, perhaps because they are worried about attracting antisemitism, as the following section will explore further. Jewish pupils may also feel protective of their distinctive form of Jewish identity; hence, any assumption that all Jews are religiously Orthodox and ethnically Ashkenazi (for instance) is likely to be met with consternation. Where they are aware of them, many Jewish pupils also internalise the above-mentioned debates about who may be considered Jewish and may even have experience of being 'denied' as a Jew by others (Samson, 2019b). Coupled with experiences of antisemitism, the topic of the following subsection, it is unsurprising that many Jewish pupils experience doubts about their identity at some point.

Antisemitism

The second area considered here is the most insidious and often the most impactful: antisemitism. There is not the space here to provide an in-depth history of antisemitism, a virulent issue that has shifted and adapted to societal changes over time. Nevertheless, a very brief summary is in order. Antisemitism in medieval Europe largely emphasised Jews' religious differences from Christianity and in particular focused on erroneous beliefs that they had killed Jesus and would murder Christian children to use their blood for rituals like making *matzah*[2] (Johnson, 2012; Matteoni, 2008). Following the Enlightenment and the general secularisation of society, antisemitic tropes shifted to economic themes, with Jews simultaneously blamed for the worst elements of both communism and capitalism as well as being portrayed as self-interested puppet-masters of society (Arad, 2000; Goldstein, 2006). Most recently, antisemitism has become tangled in anti-Zionism and anti-Israel sentiment, resulting in fierce conversations about how the two can be fully differentiated, if this is even possible (Herf, 2007; Kaplan & Small, 2006; Staetsky, 2017). Sadly, Jews may still experience versions of all three, requiring that teachers be familiar with them.

Common to these three broad antisemitic tropes, as in any form of scapegoating, is the notion that Jews are a clearly distinguishable group from the rest of society. The belief of Jewish 'foreignness' has a long history and has never been far from the three types mentioned here: It was used as 'justification' for medieval expulsions and subsequent edicts about where Jews could and could not live, was central to Hitler's 'Jewish question', and is today seen in charges that Jewish families, many of which have lived in countries such as the UK for decades and even centuries, are more loyal to Israel and should 'go back there' (see Anti-Defamation League, 2019; Brenner, 2010; Hammerschlag, 2010; Kaplan & Small, 2006). Although recent research suggests that antisemitism in the UK remains relatively low compared to other European countries (Anti-Defamation League, 2019; Staetsky, 2017), one must not assume that it does not exist at all, or that Jews should not be fearful, as such prejudice is regarded by many British Jews as a severe and growing problem (Staetsky, 2017). Furthermore, as is common to most forms of discrimination, Jews' distinctions are often expressed in physical terms, most notably as 'looking Jewish' (or not) (Gilman, 1991; Glenn, 2010), despite the fact that Jews come from diverse ethnic and racial backgrounds. And of course, such sentiments are often highly offensive: even as recently as the 1990s, some plastic surgery texts described the 'Jewish nose' as a standard physical deformity in need of correction, for example (see Preminger, 2001).

Crucially, antisemitism may also be found in schools. For instance, Gross and Rutland (2014) have revealed diverse forms of antisemitic teasing in Australian schools, whether pertaining to political (e.g. the Israeli–Palestinian conflict), religious (e.g. kosher food laws and circumcision), or classical racial themes (e.g. the avarice stereotype, accompanied by coin-throwing and swastika graffiti). Several pupils even felt compelled to change schools and damningly some headteachers refused to even entertain the suggestion that antisemitism existed in their schools (Gross & Rutland, 2014). In the UK, Moulin (2016) has highlighted how for many Jewish pupils, attending a non-Jewish secondary school is a potentially alienating experience, characterised by undesired and uncomfortable curiosity (including antisemitic remarks), or awkward attempts to explain their identity, while Ipgrave (2016) has illustrated Jewish pupils' familiarity with antisemitic stereotypes such as 'all Jews have long noses' and 'all Jews are rich'.

How do Jewish pupils respond to antisemitism? Cutler (2006) uses the terms 'invisible' and 'hypervisible' to describe how many Jews experience their Jewishness in places where they are in the minority. In order to manage their feelings of being simultaneously conspicuous as a distinct group and inconspicuous as a group that often has the potential to 'pass' as something else, Cutler demonstrates how Jews may conceal public displays of Jewishness, educate others, or utilise humour to deflect attacks on their identity. In the case of schools specifically, Jewish pupils may adopt various coping strategies; they may choose to conceal their Jewishness in public entirely, such as by refusing to wear 'markers' such as *kippot*,[3] or by denying that they have a Jewish background (Gross & Rutland, 2014; Moulin, 2015). Alternatively, they may seek a 'safe space' within the school where they can discuss their identity with trusted figures (Gross & Rutland, 2014, 2016). Still other pupils may proudly outwardly identify as Jewish, attend Jewish societies and clubs, and happily teach others about their identity (Moulin, 2016). Unfortunately, there is also the risk that they will internalise antisemitic stereotypes over time and choose to deny their Jewishness in order to avoid being labelled in a derogatory way (Gilman, 1986; Klein, 1976; MacDonald-Dennis, 2006). It must be remembered that for most, adolescence is a period marked by personal insecurity and finding one's place in the world, and so where individuals are subjected to prejudice, the outcomes can be particularly distressing. In the case of Jewish pupils, antisemitic harassment has the potential to stimulate fear, anxiety, and a feeling of not fitting in (Dubow et al., 2000; Schlossberger & Hecker, 1998). Coupled with educational pressures, as the following subsection explores, the result can be damaging for Jewish pupils' mental health.

Learning needs or needing to learn?

Education has long been a central value in Judaism. Formal Jewish schooling can be traced back to at least the 5th century BCE, albeit mainly for the purpose of training priests and scribes (Aberbach, 2009), and arguably the faith's most important prayer, the *Shema*, instructs Jewish parents to teach their children to love God. Today, Jewish families often place considerable emphasis on the importance of academic achievement (Rosen & Weltman, 1996; Schlossberger & Hecker, 1998; Teller, 2010), reflected in Jewish pupils' disproportionate levels of enrolment at Russell Group universities and attainment of first or upper-second class degrees (Advance HE, 2020). Previous research has also identified secular academic standards as the main criterion used by Jewish parents to select a specific school for their children (Miller et al., 2015; Samson, 2020), encapsulating their general interest in educational achievement.

However, the flipside is that many Jewish pupils feel a great deal of pressure (whether from the family, or communally in general) to attain high grades and to be among or *the* highest achievers in their class (Goldberg & O'Brien, 2005; Schlossberger & Hecker, 1998). And of course, not all Jewish pupils do as well as their parents expect or demand. Although causation is unclear, affective disorders such as depression appear to be especially common among Jews (see Goldberg & O'Brien, 2005; McCullough & Larson, 1999), with academic stress seemingly representing a significant influence, as pupils come to internalise their families' substantial expectations (Teller, 2010). Other factors behind Jews' apparent susceptibility to depression may be related to perceptions of not fitting in with one's cultural surroundings and experiences of discrimination (McCullough & Larson, 1999; Sanua, 1992) as well as many individuals' predisposition to undergo psychotherapy (Sanua, 1989, 1992; Schlossberger & Hecker, 1998), at least outside of strictly Orthodox communities, which by contrast tend to stigmatise mental health issues and avoid seeking clinical diagnoses (Baruch et al., 2014; Greenberg, 1991; Schnall, 2011). Indeed, reflecting the general diversity of the Jewish community described above, variations within these broad mental health trends appear to exist by factors such as religious observance, neighbourhood, income, and ethnicity (see e.g. Rahav et al., 1986; Rosmarin et al., 2009a, 2009b; Sanua, 1992).

Specific learning needs present an additional challenge. Although some Jewish schools cater specifically to needs such as autism, in part reflecting the fact that Ashkenazi Jews appear disproportionally likely to have this condition (see Goodman, 1994; Sanua, 1983), and parents may be proactive in educating themselves about their child's condition and helping them to make progress (Bass, 2012), there is the possibility that some Jewish children will not be diagnosed or will not have the same access to special educational resources, while at the same time being subjected to considerable academic pressure. Again, factors such as religious beliefs appear to be significant in influencing parents' understandings and perceptions of developmental disorders (Manor-Binyamini, 2012) and teachers need to be sensitive to these distinctions in their work.

Given these three broad themes with the potential to compromise Jewish pupils' mental health, some specific strategies for teachers may prove valuable. These will be explained in the following section.

What can teachers do?

Sensitivity

The first set of strategies may in principle seem the easiest to implement: be sensitive. However, as current debates over microaggressions ("brief, everyday exchanges that send denigrating messages to certain individuals because of their group membership"; Sue, 2010, p. 24) illustrate, much remains to be done to build truly egalitarian societies. Microaggressions are often very subtle and may be committed unconsciously or unintentionally, but they have the potential to cause considerable damage both psychologically (depression, anxiety, paranoia) and physically (e.g. by causing sleeping difficulties, with implications for productivity), especially as they accumulate over time (Nadal et al., 2010, 2014; Sue, 2010). Common microaggressions committed against Jewish individuals include accusations of being 'cheap' (Nadal et al., 2010), dismissing Jewish holidays (Johnson et al., 2018) – including by organising important activities on them (Altman et al., 2010; Kahn-Harris, 2009), or asking about one's participation in Christian rituals (Cutler, 2006) – and downplaying antisemitism and Jewish people's engagement in anti-racist and diversity programmes (MacDonald-Dennis, 2006). Moreover, statements like 'You're the first Jew I've ever met' or 'I didn't know there were Jews in Britain' only serve to make many Jewish people feel undesirably conspicuous and can be a source of considerable embarrassment through reducing their identities to a single label. Again, the possible negative outcome of these microaggressions is that Jewish pupils will feel both hypervisible (as a group that is somehow 'different') and invisible (in that their needs are overlooked).

As this chapter has emphasised, it is important to avoid generalising Jewish pupils, as doing so has the effect of stereotyping them in a way that may be deemed irrelevant and even offensive. Many, perhaps even most, British Jewish pupils do not meet a number of Jewish stereotypes or undertake traditional religious or cultural practices, such as keeping kosher or attending synagogue each week (see Samson, 2018, 2019c; Scholefield, 2004). Although many Orthodox Jewish boys wear *kippot*, a large number do not, in certain cases in order to avoid being marked out from their peers (Moulin, 2015). Some pupils simply do not regard their Jewish background as important to them. Consequently, in order to let them identify as they desire, teachers are advised to avoid labelling pupils as Jewish or raising the subject of Jewish practice.

As noted above, particular sensitivity is advised regarding Jewish holidays, especially the High Holidays of Rosh Hashanah and Yom Kippur, which tend to fall in September or early October. Some Jewish parents will withdraw their children from school for both these days and possibly more, at a time of year when teachers are still in the early stages of building relationships with their classes. Consequently, teachers should ensure that Jewish pupils are not made to feel like an inconvenience, especially given that many will not be given a choice by their parents about whether to be absent. Teachers should demonstrate understanding and commit to aiding their Jewish pupils catch up on missed work, helping to build a more inclusive school culture as a result.

Another area in which sensitivity is required is prayer and hymns. For instance, community, foundation, and voluntary schools in England and Wales must legally include a daily act of worship that is 'wholly, or mainly of a broadly Christian nature'.[4] Although many Jewish pupils agree to this regulation, others (and their parents) may perceive it as restrictive of alternative faiths and/or as compelling them to participate in a practice that is irrelevant to them.[5] Furthermore, even though parents are legally able to have their child excused from worship in such schools,[6] many fear that doing so would mark their child out as different from their class-mates (Humanists UK, 2020; Richardson et al., 2013), or that they would be simply required to sit in a room and do homework, akin to detention (Dupper et al., 2014). Therefore, in order to show greater respect for minority faiths, teachers should seek to develop more creative and less stigmatising options for pupils whose parents might want them to opt out of Christian worship.

Clamping down on antisemitism

As mentioned earlier, antisemitism still exists in British society, and schools provide a microcosm of this broader dynamic. Teachers have the wonderful job of role-modelling behaviours that future generations will adopt, but some schools are more vigilant than others in identifying and challenging antisemitism. Just like with any other type of racism, it is necessary to make clear that such behaviour and attitudes are inappropriate and offensive.

History and English teachers may be required to cover the Holocaust, a challenging topic, not only due to the sombre subject matter, but because it provides the potential for inappropriate comments to arise. Again, sensitivity is encouraged. One issue identified by Ellison (2017) is that the Holocaust can be abstracted as a general tragedy with general causes, such as stereotyping and intolerance, which may lead to the specific ways in which Jews were hunted and murdered being forgotten or underplayed. It may thus be preferable to teach the Holocaust as an event in which Jews and other minority groups were intentionally targeted, rather than risking its significance being minimised. Another challenge is posed by the existence of Holocaust denial (the claim that the event was a hoax) is engaging with it may be interpreted as giving it credibility (Lindquist, 2010), but rejecting it may be construed as marginalising some pupils' perspectives. Nevertheless, given the considerable anxiety Holocaust denial has created for Jews, the latter strategy is advisable, accompanied by a presentation of the facts (Brabham, 1997; Miller, 1995) and a prescription such as "it is our firm belief that the discussion of denial has no place in the classroom during a study of the Holocaust" (Totten et al., 2001, p. 20). Teachers should not shy away from allowing their pupils to express their personal ties to the Holocaust, but should also ensure that this is not mandatory and be vigilant for signs of anxiety, as the subject matter can be frightening and cause some pupils to feel that as Jews, they are always potential victims (Lindquist, 2010). Finally, educators in a position to choose whether or not to teach the Holocaust should think carefully not only about what aspects to cover, but also *why* they want to teach about the event in the first place, as doing so will enable them to pre-empt potential problems like those mentioned above (see also Lindquist, 2010).

The Israeli–Palestinian conflict presents another dilemma. It should be mentioned that many British Jews are sceptical of large aspects of Israel's politics, even though most feel that the country plays a 'central' or 'important' role in their

Jewish identities (Graham & Boyd, 2010; Miller et al., 2015). Furthermore, one recent study of young Jewish Europeans revealed that "seven in ten…believe that when a non-Jew criticises Israel, they are either probably or definitely not being antisemitic" (Boyd, 2019, p. 19–20). However, the investigation also revealed the prevalence of concerns regarding antisemitism, identifying the boundary defining where anti-Israel criticism starts to be perceived as antisemitism in the degree of hostility expressed towards the country: 70% claimed that boycotts of Israel or Israelis are either 'definitely' or probably 'antisemitic', and 80% regarded the claim that 'Israelis behave "like Nazis" towards the Palestinians' as antisemitic (Boyd, 2019). Moreover, a study of British Jews found that criticism of Israel is widely regarded as a 'cover' for antisemitism and as reflecting an application of double standards with respect to military actions, especially among the various Orthodox communities (Miller et al., 2015). Crucially, Jewish pupils may feel that their own lives are affected by events in Israel. In Boyd's (2019) study, 90% claimed that the Arab–Israel conflict affects their feelings of safety at least a little and 37% 'a great deal', while 85% claimed that they feel blamed as Jews by their compatriots for anything done by the Israeli government; further, in Graham and Boyd's (2010) investigation into British Jews' attitudes towards Israel, 56% felt that antisemitic incidents in the UK are 'probably' or 'definitely' related to the abuser/assailant's views on Israel. In these ways, the country (and the war) is far from an irrelevance to many Jewish pupils' lives.

Therefore, teachers must remain aware that Jewish pupils may have their own misgivings about Israeli politics, but that they can still feel attached to the one Jewish-majority country in the world, with an attack on it by a non-Jew potentially being perceived as an attack on Jews as a whole. When teaching about Israel, teachers should be conscious that any clear stance against the country is likely to make Jewish pupils feel uncomfortable, and also gives licence for their peers to criticise it as well, compounding the issue. A major concern held by many Jews pertains to the recent growth of anti-Zionist rhetoric in a number of schools and universities (most clearly exemplified in boycotts of Israel and abuse targeted at Israelis) in part because antisemitic tropes are sometimes adopted by participants and counter-arguments may be silenced, delegitimising them in the process (Klaff, 2010). Instead, recognising and demonstrating that the conflict is highly nuanced is crucial. Teachers are thus well-advised to provide opportunities for meaningful discussion and to direct conversations away from a one-sided perspective, in order to ensure that all pupils, Jewish pupils included, feel safe to express an opinion.

Finally, with social media providing a space for many people to disseminate a range of antisemitic theories, and Boyd (2019) has even found that the Internet is now regarded by young Jewish Europeans as the primary context for antisemitism, teachers are encouraged to familiarise themselves not only with common antisemitic tropes, but also with their school's cyberbullying policies. Boyd's (2019) research participants were particularly sensitive to tropes pertaining to Holocaust denial or trivialisation, nefarious uses of power by Jews and equations of Israelis with Nazis, hence these represent fruitful areas to start.

All of these strategies can be used to help Jewish pupils feel safe to express themselves as they desire and enable the development of inclusive classrooms that minimise pupils' risks of suffering from mental health afflictions like King Saul.

Takeaway points

■ Be aware that there are multiple ways of 'being Jewish' and so Jewish pupils should not be generalised.

■ Avoid labelling pupils or marking them out as somehow different from others, and instead let them self-identify as they desire.

■ Remain conscious that many Jewish families have high educational expectations and that this can affect pupils' confidence and mental health.

■ If relevant, consider how your teaching of weighty subjects like the Holocaust and the Israel–Palestine conflict will look from your pupils' perspective.

■ Be attentive to antisemitism (including in the form of microaggressions) and challenge it.

Notes

1 *R* (on the application of E) *v Governing Body of JFS and the Admissions Appeal Panel of JFS and others* [2009] UKSC 15.
2 Unleavened bread, traditionally eaten at Passover.
3 Singular: *kippah*. A brimless skullcap, also known as a *koppel* or *yarmulke*.
4 School Standards and Framework Act, 1998, Schedule 20, S.3(2).
5 Collective worship is also a requirement in Northern Ireland's controlled, grant-maintained, and voluntary schools (The Education and Libraries (Northern Ireland) Order 96, Part III, Article 21). In Scotland, public schools are able to provide religious instruction to pupils whose parents do not object (Education (Scotland) Act 1980, c. 44, Part I, Section 8(1)).
6 For England and Wales, see the School Standards and Framework Act, 1998, Section 71; for Scotland, see Education (Scotland) Act 1980, c. 44, Part I, Section 9; for Northern Ireland, see the Education and Libraries (Northern Ireland) Order 1986, Part III, Article 21(5).

Further reading

Dubow, E. F., Pargament, K. I., Boxer, P. & Tarakeshwar, N., (2000) Initial investigation of Jewish early adolescents' ethnic identity, stress, and coping. *Journal of Early Adolescence*, vol. 20, no. 4, pp. 418–441.

Gross, Z. & Rutland, S. D., (2014) Combatting antisemitism in the school playground: An Australian case study. *Patterns of Prejudice*, vol. 48, no. 3, 309–330.

McCullough, M. E. & Larson, D. B., (1999) Religion and depression: A review of the literature. *Twin Research*, vol. 2, pp. 126–136.

Moulin, D., (2016) Reported schooling experiences of adolescent Jews attending non-Jewish secondary schools in England. *Race Ethnicity and Education*, vol. 19, no. 4, pp. 683–705.

Schlossberger, E. S. & Hecker, L. L., (1998) Reflections on Jewishness and its implications for family therapy. *The American Journal of Family Therapy*, vol. 26, no. 2, pp. 129–146.

References

Aberbach, M., (2009) *Jewish education and history: Continuity, crisis and change.* Abingdon: Routledge.

Advance HE, (2020) *Religion and belief in UK higher education* [Online]. Available from: https://www.advance-he.ac.uk/knowledge-hub/research-insight-religion-and-belief-uk-higher-education

Altman, A. N., Inman, A. G., Fine, S. G., Ritter, H. A. & Howard, E. H., (2010) Exploration of Jewish ethnic identity. *Journal of Counseling & Development*, vol. 88, no. 2, pp. 163–173.

Anti-Defamation League (ADL), (2019) *United Kingdom* [Online]. Available from: https://global100.adl.org/country/united-kingdom/2019

Arad, G. N., (2000) *America, its Jews, and the rise of Nazism.* Bloomington: Indiana University Press.

Baruch, D. E., Kanter, J. W., Pirutinsky, S., Murphy, J. & Rosmarin, D. H., (2014) Depression stigma and treatment preferences among Orthodox and non-Orthodox Jews. *The Journal of Nervous and Mental Disease*, vol. 202, no. 7, pp. 556–561.

Bass, R., (2012) *The experiences of orthodox Jewish parents of children with autism spectrum disorder and attention deficit/hyperactivity disorder.* Undergraduate thesis. University of Salford.

Ben-Noun, L., (2003) What was the mental disease that afflicted King Saul? *Clinical Case Studies*, vol. 2, no. 4, pp. 270–282.

Boyd, J., (2019) *Young Jewish Europeans: Perceptions and experiences of antisemitism.* Vienna: European Union Agency for Fundamental Rights (FRA).

Brabham, E. G., (1997) Holocaust education: Legislation, practices, and literature for middle-school students. *Social Studies*, vol. 88, no. 3, pp. 139–142.

Brenner, M., (2010) *A short history of the Jews.* Princeton: Princeton University Press.

Cutler, M., (2006) Minority group, majority space: Negotiating Jewish identity in a Southern Christian context. *Journal of Contemporary Ethnography*, vol. 35, no. 6, pp. 696–728.

Dubow, E. F., Pargament, K. I., Boxer, P. & Tarakeshwar, N., (2000) Initial investigation of Jewish early adolescents' ethnic identity, stress, and coping. *Journal of Early Adolescence*, vol. 20, no. 4, pp. 418–441.

Dupper, D. R., Forrest-Bank, S. & Lowry-Carussilo, A., (2014) Experiences of religious minorities in public school settings: Findings from focus groups involving Muslim, Jewish, Catholic, and Unitarian Universalist youths. *Children and Schools*, vol. 37, no. 1, pp. 37–45.

Ellison, J. A., (2017) How they teach the Holocaust in Jewish day schools. *Cogent Education*, vol. 4, no. 1, pp. 1–14.

Gilman, S. L., (1986) *Jewish self-hatred: Anti-Semitism and the hidden language of the Jews.* Baltimore: The John Hopkins University Press.

Gilman, S. L., (1991) *The Jew's body.* New York: Routledge.

Glenn, S. A., (2010) "Funny, you don't look Jewish". Visual stereotypes and the making of modern Jewish identity. In: S. A. Glenn and N. B. Sokoloff, eds., *Boundaries of Jewish identity*. Seattle: University of Washington Press, pp. 64–90.

Goldberg, J. L. & O'Brien, K. M., (2005) Jewish women's psychological well-being: The role of attachment, separation, and Jewish identity. *Psychology of Women Quarterly*, vol. 29, pp. 197–206.

Goldstein, E. L., (2006) *The price of whiteness: Jews, race, and American identity*. Princeton: Princeton University Press.

Goodman, A. B., (1994) A family history study of schizophrenia spectrum disorders suggests new candidate genes in schizophrenia and autism. *Psychiatric Quarterly*, vol. 65, no. 4, pp. 287–297.

Graham, D. & Boyd, J., (2010) *Committed, concerned and conciliatory: The attitudes of Jews in Britain towards Israel*. London: Institute for Jewish Policy Research (JPR).

Greenberg, D., (1991) Is psychotherapy possible with unbelievers?: The care of the ultra-Orthodox community. *Israel Journal of Psychiatry and Related Sciences*, vol. 28, no. 4, pp. 19–30.

Gross, Z. & Rutland, S. D., (2014) Combatting antisemitism in the school playground: An Australian case study. *Patterns of Prejudice*, vol. 48, no. 3, pp. 309–330.

Gross, Z. & Rutland, S. D., (2016) Creating a safe place: SRE teaching as an act of security and identity formation in government schools in Australia. *British Journal of Religious Education*, vol. 38, no. 1, pp. 30–46.

Hammerschlag, S., (2010) *The figural Jew: Politics and identity in postwar French thought*. Chicago: The University of Chicago Press.

Hart, R., Schmool, M. & Cohen, F., (2007) Jewish day schools in Britain 1992/3 to 2003/4. *Contemporary Jewry*, vol. 27, no. 1, pp. 137–156.

Herf, J., ed. (2007) *Anti-Semitism and anti-Zionism in historical perspective: Convergence and divergence*. New York: Routledge.

Huisman, M., (2003) King Saul, work-related stress and depression. *BMJ*, vol. 61, no. 10, p. 890.

Humanists UK, (2020) *Collective worship and school assemblies: Your rights* [Online]. Available from: https://humanism.org.uk/education/parents/collective-worship-and-school-assemblies-your-rights/

Ipgrave, J., (2016) Identity and inter religious understanding in Jewish schools in England. *British Journal of Religious Education*, vol. 38, no. 1, pp. 47–63.

Johnson, H. R., (2012) *Blood libel: The ritual murder accusation at the limit of Jewish history*. Ann Arbor: The University of Michigan Press.

Johnson, K. A., Johnson, W. M., Thomas, J. M. & Green, J. J., (2018) *Microaggressions at the University of Mississippi: A report from the UM Race Diary Project* [Online]. Available from: https://socanth.wp2.olemiss.edu/wp-content/uploads/sites/154/2018/10/Microaggressions-report-10-9-18.pdf

Kahn-Harris, K., (2009) *Communities in conversation: Jewish involvement in inter faith activities in the UK*. London: The Board of Deputies of British Jews and the Department for Communities and Local Government (DCLG).

Kaplan, E. H. & Small, C. A., (2006) Anti-Israel sentiment predicts anti-Semitism in Europe. *Journal of Conflict Resolution*, vol. 50, no. 4, pp. 548–561.

Klaff, L., (2010) Anti-Zionist expression on the UK campus: Free speech or hate speech? *Jewish Political Studies Review*, vol. 22, no. 3/4, pp. 87–109.

Klein, J. W., (1976) Ethnotherapy with Jews. *International Journal of Mental Health*, vol. 5, no. 2, pp. 26–38.

Lindquist, D. H., (2010) Complicating issues in Holocaust education. *The Journal of Social Studies Research*, vol. 34, no. 1, pp. 77–93.

MacDonald-Dennis, C., (2006) Understanding anti-Semitism and its impact: A new framework for conceptualizing Jewish identity. *Equity & Excellence in Education*, vol. 39, no. 3, pp. 267–278.

Manor-Binyamini, I., (2012) Parental coping with developmental disorders in adolescents within the ultraorthodox Jewish community in Israel. *Journal of Autism and Developmental Disorders*, vol. 42, no. 5, pp. 815–826.

Matteoni, F., (2008) The Jew, the blood and the body in late medieval and early modern Europe. *Folklore*, vol. 119, pp. 182–200.

McCullough, M. E., & Larson, D. B., (1999) Religion and depression: A review of the literature. *Twin Research*, vol. 2, pp. 126–136.

Miller, S., (1995) Denial of the Holocaust. *Social Education*, vol. 59, no. 6, pp. 342–345.

Miller, S., Harris, M. & Shindler, C., (2015) *The attitudes of British Jews towards Israel.* London: School of Arts and Social Sciences.

Moulin, D., (2015) Religious identity choices in English secondary schools. *British Educational Research Journal*, vol. 41, no. 3, pp. 489–504.

Moulin, D., (2016) Reported schooling experiences of adolescent Jews attending non-Jewish secondary schools in England. *Race Ethnicity and Education*, vol. 19, no. 4, pp. 683–705.

Nadal, K. L., Griffin, K. E., Wong, Y., Hamit, S. & Rasmus, M., (2014) The impact of racial microaggressions on mental health: Counseling implications for clients of color. *Journal of Counseling & Development*, vol. 92, no. 1, pp. 57–66.

Nadal, K. L., Issa, M.-A., Griffin, K. E., Hamit, S. & Lyons, O. B., (2010) Religious microaggressions in the United States: Mental health implications for religious minority groups. In: D. W. Sue (ed.), *Microaggressions and marginality: Manifestation, dynamics, and impact.* Hoboken: John Wiley & Sons, Inc, pp. 287–310.

Preminger, B., (2001) The "Jewish nose" and plastic surgery: Origins and implications. *The Journal of the American Medical Association (JAMA)*, vol. 286, no. 17, p. 2161.

Rahav, M., Goodman, A. B., Popper, M. & Lin, S. P., (1986) Distribution of treated mental illness in the neighborhoods of Jerusalem. *American Journal of Psychiatry*, vol. 143, no. 10, pp. 1249–1254.

Richardson, N., Niens, U., Mawhinney, A. & Chiba, Y., (2013) Opting out or opting in? Conscience clauses, minority belief communities and the possibility of inclusive religious education in Northern Ireland. *British Journal of Religious Education*, vol. 35, no. 3, pp. 236–250.

Rosen, E. J. & Weltman, S. F., (1996) Jewish families: An overview. In M. McGoldrick, J. K. Pearce & J. Giordano, eds., *Ethnicity and family therapy.* 2nd ed. New York: Guilford Press, pp. 611–630.

Rosmarin, D. H., Krumrei, E. J. & Andersson, G., (2009a). Religion as a predictor of psychological distress in two religious communities. *Cognitive Behaviour Therapy*, vol. 38, no. 1, pp. 54–64.

Rosmarin, D. H., Pirutinsky, S., Pargament, K. I. & Krumrei, E. J., (2009b) Are religious beliefs relevant to mental health among Jews? *Psychology of Religion and Spirituality*, vol. 1, no. 3, pp. 180–190.

Samson, M. G. M., (2018) Competition or cooperation? Jewish day schools, synagogues, and the (re)construction of young people's Jewish identities in England. *Children's Geographies*, vol. 16, no. 3, pp. 225–238.

Samson, M. G. M., (2019a) Jewish schools and the challenges of denominationalism in England. *Contemporary Jewry*, vol. 39, no. 2, pp. 245–271.

Samson, M. G. M., (2019b) Krav maga and chicken soup: Symbolic Jewish identities within and beyond the Jewish school. *British Journal of Sociology of Education*, vol. 40, no. 6, pp. 742–758.

Samson, M. G. M., (2019c) 'Marching at the speed of the slowest man': The facilitation and regulation of student autonomy in a pluralist Jewish day school. *Journal of Jewish Education*, vol. 85, no. 3, pp. 268–292.

Samson, M. G. M., (2020) Jewish schools rather than Jewish education? School choice and community dynamics in multicultural society. *Social & Cultural Geography*, vol. 21, no. 2, pp. 222–244.

Sanua, V. D., (1983) Infantile autism and childhood schizophrenia: Review of the issues from the sociocultural point of view. *Social Science and Medicine*, vol. 17, no. 21, pp. 1633–1651.

Sanua, V. D., (1989) Studies in mental illness and other psychiatric deviances among contemporary Jewry: A review of the literature. *Israel Journal of Psychiatry and Related Sciences*, vol. 26, no. 4, pp. 187–211.

Sanua, V. D., (1992) Mental illness and other forms of psychiatric deviance among contemporary Jewry. *Transcultural Psychiatric Research Review*, vol. 29, pp. 197–233.

Schlossberger, E. S. & Hecker, L. L., (1998) Reflections on Jewishness and its implications for family therapy. *The American Journal of Family Therapy*, vol. 26, no. 2, pp. 129–146.

Schnall, E., (2011) Multicultural counseling and the Orthodox Jew. *Journal of Counseling & Development*, vol. 84, no. 3, pp. 276–282.

Scholefield, L., (2004) Bagels, schnitzel and McDonald's—'fuzzy frontiers' of Jewish identity in an English Jewish secondary school'. *British Journal of Religious Education*, vol. 26, no. 3, pp. 237–248.

Staetsky, L. D., (2017) *Antisemitism in contemporary Great Britain: A study of attitudes towards Jews and Israel*. London: Institute for Jewish Policy Research (JPR).

Staetsky, L. D. & Boyd, J., (2016) *The rise and rise of Jewish schools in the United Kingdom: Numbers, trends and policy issues*. London: Institute for Jewish Policy Research (JPR).

Sue, D. W., (2010) *Microaggressions in everyday life: Race, gender, and sexual orientation*. Hoboken: John Wiley & Sons, Inc.

Teller, L. T., (2010) *The effects of Jewish religious identity and age on levels of perceived academic stress*. PhD thesis. Walden University.

Totten, S., Feinberg, S. & Fernekes, W., (2001) The significance of rationale statements in developing a sound Holocaust education program. In S. Totten & S. Feinberg, eds., *Teaching and studying the Holocaust*. Boston: Allyn and Bacon, pp. 1–23.

Valins, O., (2003) Defending identities or segregating communities? Faith-based schooling and the UK Jewish community. *Geoforum*, vol. 34, no. 2, pp. 235–247.

14 Children with Physical or Intellectual Impairments and Mental Wellbeing

Sian E. Jones, Clare Uytman,
Leanne Ali, Laura Dalnoki, Alicia Kaliff,
Daphne Lola-Luz, Morvern Mackintosh,
Amanda McCune, William Muir, and
Kiia Uusitalo

Synopsis

With increasing inclusive practice in UK schooling, school staff and children are now more likely to encounter people with differing abilities. There is growing literature on good practice to promote the wellbeing of children with dis/abilities in the classroom. Here, we review that literature. This chapter first reviews the different frameworks that are used to understand the meaning of dis/ability, and how children themselves conceive dis/ability. Then, we look at the evidence linking disability-based bullying, and responses to it, to wellbeing. We then look at research on what "wellbeing" means to children with dis/abilities and how they would like to see their wellbeing supported. Finally, we consider wider issues around classroom participation and the representation of children with dis/abilities. We consider the actions that may be taken with these in mind to bolster the wellbeing of children with dis/abilities.

Background

Who are we talking about?

On a global scale, UNICEF estimates that 93 million (5%) of children aged 14 years or younger are disabled (UNICEF, 2013). Using a definition in line with the Equality Act Section 6 (Equality Act 2010), this means that in the UK there are 14.1

DOI: 10.4324/9781003160526-14

million disabled people of whom around 900 000 are disabled children under 18 years (in other words, around 8% of the UK child population; Department for Work and Pensions, Family Resources Survey, 2020). It is worth noting that experiences of disability vary by sex, with girls less likely than boys to have problems with memory, physical coordination, or concentration (Blackburn et al., 2010). It is also worth remembering that Blackburn et al. (2010) determined that disabled children in the UK were more likely to live in poverty than non-disabled children and that childhood disability was correlated with single parenthood and parental disability. Despite the considerable number of children affected by disability, Foley et al. (2012) note that there is a real paucity of studies that have investigated the views of children with disabilities. What follows then is a review of the literature that does exist.

What matters here more perhaps, is the extent to which children themselves consider that they have a disability or understand that other children have a disability. In this regard, research indicates that children start to become conscious of disability as a concept around the age of four and that their grasp of that concept becomes more nuanced with age (e.g., Diamond, 1993). In one study, Diamond (1993) asked 28 four year olds about their peers. Children easily recognised children with physical disabilities, but not their peers with intellectual disabilities. In a similar vein, Conant and Budoff (1983) showed that in school-aged children, physical disabilities were more easily understood than social or intellectual disabilities, even though children are more likely to meet a child with a social or intellectual impairment.

What are we talking about?

Over the past 20 years, there has been a major shift in the language used to describe disability and impairment, and in the frameworks that are used to understand them. Since 2001, the World Health Organization (WHO) has been using a bio-psycho-social model to construe health and disability. This model brings together two different understandings of disability (UN Convention on the Rights of Persons with Disabilities, 2007): First, the biomedical model, which attributes bodily impairment as the primary reason for any disability or disadvantage; second, the social model, which in contrast to the biomedical model, highlights the roles played by physical obstacles and people's attitudes in giving rise to the limits on participation in community life faced by people with disabilities (Shakespeare, 2013). These two models have implications for the ways in which disability may be viewed in the classroom, so it is worth pausing here to consider them. In the case of the biomedical model, solutions should be determined within the health system, to "correct" the bodily impairment as far as possible. Viewing disability from the perspective of the social model means that solutions are found through social and political change, as well as in the removal of social attitudinal barriers. More latterly disability activists have framed a cultural model of disability. The cultural model of disability (Waldschmidt, 2018) contends that "dis/ability" is not a distinct and meaningful category, but one whose content can only be understood with reference to how one conceives of "ability". Thinking about these models in schools, it can be seen how important it is to validate how children with impairments self-identify, and to recognise the dynamic way in which dis/ability may be apparent in different contexts. Children, too, understand disability within the frame of the models outlined above. In this regard, Meloni et al. (2015) showed that children, aged six to eight-years-old conceive people with disabilities as 'ill'. This early conception of disability is in line with the biomedical model of disability mentioned above and was unrelated to children's parents' accounts of disability. Older children (aged 9–11 years) knew more about disability, and had tended to share their parents' explanations, which were also broadly similar to a biomedical model of disability. However, it should be noted that current academic literature is moving away from the notion that disability is purely a medical issue which requires treatment, as this has negative connotations (Patel & Brown, 2017). Instead, it could be argued that we should focus on overcoming the socially constructed barriers which prohibit individuals with a physical impairment from functioning fully within society as stated by the social model of disability (Feeley, 2016). Recent evidence has not only found biomedical model beliefs to be associated with negative attitudes towards physical disabilities and social model beliefs to be associated with positive attitudes, but has also shown that educational interventions focusing on the social model are effective in reducing these negative attitudes (Bogart et al., 2020) With this in mind, one might argue that it is the understandings of the social and cultural models of disability that are worth working towards, and helping children to work towards, because they forefront the weight of context in empowering children and represent something that we hold in our collective power, to change. Furthermore, in the past, children with a disability have been grouped together – or even described as "a group" or "outgroup" (e.g., Cameron, 2007). However, current research acknowledges that this is not always helpful as not everyone with an intellectual or physical impairment shares the same life experiences, has the same disability, or sees themselves as similar to other people with a disability (Jones et al., 2020). After taking the above points into account, this chapter will take a social/cultural standpoint. The remainder of this chapter looks at links between physical or intellectual impairment in children and mental wellbeing before outlining strategies aimed at promoting wellbeing for these children of children.

Links between children's disability and mental wellbeing

As noted at the outset of this chapter, there is little research that asks children with impairments about their mental wellbeing; instead, most research relies on data collected from parents or teachers. One study of parents, considering wellbeing among children with physical impairments, was conducted by Davis et al. (2017).

These researchers focused on cerebral palsy aiming to identify the things that brought quality of life for their participants. Eighteen parents of children with cerebral palsy took part in qualitative semi-structured interviews. The aspects that were identified here as being important to quality of life included access to nature and outdoors, independence, social connectedness, freedom of emotional expression, communication, and physical activity. Di Marino et al. (2018) found links between children's participation at preschool and their social connectedness. They looked at children with disabilities younger than six-years-old, and through a survey of parents, examined their participation at home, at preschool, and in the community. Children's impairments were only directly related to one aspect of participation: their level of involvement in preschool. Di Marino et al. (2018) suggest that this might be accounted for by the type of activities typically done in preschools, underpinned by structured group learning, that may depend upon social aptitude (with the most common activity reported in the study being socialising with friends). Since participation is linked with mental wellbeing, this study suggests that in the early years, practitioners need to be particularly mindful of including children with impairments in their daily activities.

One study examining wellbeing through the voices of children themselves was conducted by Foley et al. (2012). This was a focus group study of 20 children (in five focus groups) with diagnoses of cerebral palsy, autism, Down syndrome, intellectual disability, and visual impairment. The children were interviewed about their understanding of wellbeing. From the participants' perspective, "wellbeing" included feeling supported (participants valued their friends and family for encouragement and help – and that this help may be reciprocal), of being included and respected ("of feeling belonged" with concerns around bullying), of being seen as valued and capable (having something to strive for and not being underestimated), and of having a sense of self-respect and self-esteem (feeling good about oneself, one's body image, and behaviour). Interestingly, for a conversation about wellbeing, there was little discussion on hospital visits, medical conditions, or therapy. Rather, these factors were not mentioned by the children and did not seem to matter to them when it came to their views on wellbeing. Instead, Foley et al. (2012) highlighted the value that young children placed on participation in their wellbeing, which was referred to across different contexts and by children regardless of their disability. They argue that affirming these children's sense of belonging is critical to their wellbeing. Similar to Davis et al. (2017) and to Di Marino et al. (2018), Foley et al. (2012) also highlighted some of the occasions when physical barriers get in the way of participation (e.g., the size of the ball during sports). Given the findings of these studies, it is critical to consider how far school environments enable children's participation in school life and how this might impact their mental wellbeing.

Picking up on Foley et al.'s (2012) finding around capability and self-esteem, McCoy et al. (2016) looked at the influence of expectations on the wellbeing of children with disabilities. They examined the extent to which parental academic expectations affected educational progress and self-concept among nine 13-year-old children, with a range of disabilities, taking part in the Growing Up in Ireland Study. It was found that children with any disability were less likely to have a positive view of themselves than those with no disability. Among children with a disability, those who had less self-confidence at 13-years-old often had parents with lower expectations of them. This highlights the need for parents and educators to promote positive expectations and school engagement for all children, and particularly for those with a physical disability.

Another factor that is known to contribute to the wellbeing of pupils with disabilities is the nature of the pupil-teacher relationship. One study by Mu et al. (2017) conducted on Chinese pupils showed that actively seeking out resources for their pupils helped teachers foster the resilience of pupils with disabilities, and, in turn, to enhance their wellbeing. As in the studies above, this study found that the wellbeing of pupils with disabilities was lower than that of their non-disabled counterparts. These researchers also showed that those teachers who purposefully seek help for their pupils in and beyond school indirectly strengthen the resilience of pupils with disabilities and promote their wellbeing. That is, where resources are scarce, the work of teachers to seek support on behalf of their pupils matters to these pupils: there were direct positive links between teachers' help seeking and pupils' sense of wellbeing.

A focus on social connectedness

Whilst participation, expectations, and the nature of the pupil-teacher relationship contribute to pupils' wellbeing, for children with disabilities, social connectedness and a sense of belonging are high on the list of contributing factors. By virtue of having a concept of "disability", young children may discriminate against people with disabilities (Nota et al., 2018). One review found that children without disabilities had a marked preference for playing with other children without disabilities (Nowicki & Sandieson, 2010). Another study showed that children who themselves had a physical disability, rated the academic and physical skills of children with disabilities higher than did non-disabled children (Trepanier-Street et al., 2011). The consensus in the literature is that disabled children are on the receiving end of peer rejection more than their peers and are at increased risk of isolation and bullying (Koster et al., 2010). This is particularly true of contexts where the disability might "get in the way", such as when it is perceived to be a barrier to participation in activities. One study demonstrated that children tended not to anticipate the inclusion of peers with disabilities in athletic or academic scenarios, including social activities (e.g., eating lunch; Gasser et al., 2014). What is important here is considering the voices of children with disabilities: Spencer-Cavaliere and Watkinson (2010) asked Canadian 8–12-year-olds with a range of physical disabilities about their peers, finding that they all felt at some point that they had "not being included" and that this was due to their disability. Being on the receiving end of negative attitudes has been linked with problems for targets of this type of discrimination (arising from a group membership) when it comes to their ability to take part in social activities, their academic progress, and behaviour in class (e.g., Aluede, et al., 2008).

On the other hand, young children can show empathy towards children with disabilities. In one study, children were told stories about a child with an intellectual disability and reported their emotional reactions (Nowicki, Brown & Stepien, 2014). It was found that negative emotions were driven by perceptions of difference between the participants and children with disabilities, but that acts of social exclusion were attributed to "other children in the class" rather than to the participants. The authors therefore recommend that teachers model inclusive interactions with children with an intellectual disability. Other children have reported a moral impetus to help peers with disabilities (Beaulieu-Bergeron & Morin, 2016). For example, 15-year-olds in Japan were more eager than 11 year olds to report their willingness to support a classmate with a physical disability, but they did not empathise with that peer to the same extent as 11 year olds did (Crystal et al., 1999). Similarly, US and Canadian high-school pupils felt that children with disabilities should not be excluded (Shalev et al., 2016). The authors recommend that in order to embody this, peer-mediated interventions be used. This allows peers with and without severe disabilities to work cooperatively on tasks. The benefits of this are twofold as peers with severe disabilities are included and children without a disability witness the skills of their peers, and their positive attitudes are enhanced (for more on peer-mediated interventions, see Carter et al., 2016). Children's moral reactions towards peers with disabilities might then be one way of helping pupils feel supported and connected in the classroom – if one also bears in mind the finding from Foley et al. (2012) that rather than being paternalistic – children with disabilities themselves want the avenues of support to run in both directions.

What can teachers do?

Representation

From a practical perspective, research has shown that representation can help foster positive attitudes towards school-age children with disabilities. A first step here is to consider the pedagogical materials in classrooms, given that positive representation in books and other media lend children higher self-esteem, a sense of belonging, and more positive attitudes towards others (e.g., Cameron et al., 2011). Beyond this, Kim et al. (2016) highlight how integrating diversity into the literacy curriculum can encourage the acquisition of specific information, and socio-emotional skills, such as social awareness, empathy with others, and building positive relationships. Such diversity might be brought into the classroom through books that have characters with a range of backgrounds, including representation of children with disabilities. Unfortunately, the depiction of people with disabilities in children's literature and media has been largely absent or unhelpful (think Captain Hook as the villain in Peter Pan) or imbued with a "recovery" narrative reminiscent of the biomedical model of disability (think Clara in Heidi or Colin in The Secret Garden). Along these lines, Hintz and Tribunella (2019) explore the notion of a recovery narrative within the context of children's fairy tales. The structure of these stories frequently exalts the main character by presenting them as able-bodied whilst promoting stereotypes that depict a fulfilled longing for the disabled antagonist to be freed from the apparent restrictions of their physical form by means of a magical miracle. Consequently, portrayals such as this reinforce a thoughtless message to children and young people as if to say strive to change, discouraging their appreciation for the qualities making them who they are. In a comparative study conducted by Hodkinson et al. (2016), the authors look at how classroom materials can assist in developing an understanding of issues associated with disability for pupils with limited prior knowledge and experience. However, this stresses the importance of conveying representation appropriately. Presenting disability by highlighting existing differences also poses the risk of reinforcing a social divide and further ostracism for children with a disability. Wilkins et al. (2016) examined children's perceptions of fictional characters with disabilities over a range of 12 books. Findings showed that both the influence of the teacher and the depiction of the character shaped children's responses to them. Moreover, in another study, Monoyiou and Symeonidou (2016) analysed 50 texts finding that the character representing diversity actually was not representative of people sharing their identity, and commonly only gained approval of other story characters through the intervention of someone else. These pieces of research place emphasis on the need to remain conscious of the content of diversity resources. Similarly, they highlight the adult's responsibility to encourage social reflection whilst deterring stereotype formation. Hayden and Prince (2020) argue that conveying disabled fictional characters in an empowering light helps tackle outdated impressions and leads to positive counter effects. This is achieved not only by promoting self-worth for disabled children but also by reaffirming their true capabilities to surrounding peers.

Beyond children's literature, teachers may consider representation in the classroom more generally. In one study, Favazza and colleagues (2017) looked at the proportional representation of disabled people in school resources in 32 infant classrooms. They found that 2 classrooms had some representation, 22 classrooms had low representation, and 8 classrooms had no representation of disabled people. In a similar vein, Ellis (2015) investigated the representation of disabled people in the products of the toy industry. As Ellis reports, when Barbie was manufactured in a wheelchair in 1996, the figure could not fit into the Barbie Dream House and was discontinued. Representation of people with disabilities is evolving in toys. Two new Barbie figures, one wheelchair user and another with a prosthetic limb, have recently been added to Mattel's collection (McNamara, 2019). The existence of representative books and toys in classrooms matters, to allow children to see disabled people as part of a diverse society and to imagine interactions with them in their play.

Inclusive practice

In England, the changes in educational policy over the years have presented challenges for promoting the inclusion of children with disabilities. An act in 1981 encouraged the inclusion of children with disabilities in mainstream schools, challenged the routine practice of the 1970s to educate physically disabled separately, and resulted in improvements in the training of teachers, higher student-to-teacher ratios, and improved resources in mainstream schools (Selfe, 2021). However, the 1988 Education Reform Act took steps back by making schools competitive by attempting to raise their academic standards (Department for Education and Employment, 1997). As children with special needs were seen as unlikely to improve a school's academic results, their position in the new system became unclear. Unfortunately, education of children with disabilities is still recovering from this ideology, as local education authorities in England are underfunded and pressured to make use of existing special school provision, decreasing the number of disabled pupils in mainstream schools. Yet, inclusive education is seen as a critical part of disabled children's broader right to social inclusion. In comparison, Scotland aims to better integrate the additional support needs of children with disabilities into the national curriculum and celebrate their achievements. Indeed, strides are being made in improving funding for training, increasing the roll out of school counsellors, as well as a providing mental health services more widely (Scottish Government, Additional Support for Learning Act, 2017). Thus, policy and practice are headed in the right direction in the UK.

However, there are vast differences regarding the practice of social inclusion globally, for children with disabilities. Kutnick et al. (2007) compared inclusive practice in England, Finland, Greece, Italy, Spain, and Sweden. When it came to pupil to teacher ratios, England had one member of school staff and one Learning Support Assistant working with a large class of children, while Sweden had multiple members of school staff working with 10–15 children at a time. In Finland, but not in other countries, school staff had received sufficient social-inclusion-specific training. This shows that currently the biggest systematic obstacles to creating inclusive education are rooted in resourcing issues as not only is the number of teachers and assistants low for the number of pupils in the classroom in some countries, but there is also a difference between regions in training about how to equally support all children.

Nonetheless, on closer examination, social inclusion is a complicated and subjective social construct (Le Boutillier & Croucher, 2010) and it is worth stopping for a moment to reflect, as a reader, what you understand by it. It is often seen as the antithesis to social exclusion (the oppression of certain people based on group memberships, such as race, gender, or disability). Does that mean that social inclusion is simply the absence of social exclusion? We have already seen, linked to wellbeing above, something of what social inclusion might mean for children with disabilities. The research reviewed thus far has highlighted physical, social, and environmental barriers to wellbeing – to making friends, to leisure-time and play, and to academic progress. Social inclusion, therefore, and inclusive practice, could be seen as the umbrella that underpins the wellbeing of children with disabilities (Mâsse et al., 2012).

In this regard, one factor that is strongly linked with pupils' meaningful inclusion is teachers' beliefs and attitudes. Teachers' beliefs about inclusion are strongly related to their level of experience (e.g., van der Veen et al., 2010), regardless of the setting in which they work. In Japan, in line with the findings of Mu et al. (2017), education reform has seen teachers being given greater responsibility for liaising with parents to support children with disabilities, and, in turn, teachers' attitudes have become more inclusive (Kayama et al., 2016). Indeed, children with disabilities attach great weight to the attitudes of their teachers since teachers can bring unhelpful attitudes to their schools or try to overprotect them (Rheams & Bain, 2005). Teachers' attitudes can, in turn, affect how classmates respond to peers with disabilities, in line with either a biomedical or social (or cultural) model of disability. Happily, most teachers from both specialist and inclusive settings assert that all children should be included. However, whilst evidence demonstrates the influence of teachers' attitudes on enabling social inclusion, little research has paid attention to teachers' reflections about how social inclusion can be enacted. So, at the time of writing, we do not know much about how teachers perform social inclusion for these children. We do know that highly structured activities organised in class-time lead to a higher sense of social inclusion. For example, children engaging in games which involved a shared set of rules, either in a sport or fantasy play setting, led to moderate or high inclusion (Carvalho et al., 2014). This follows a suggestion that the presence of structure and rules makes it easier for all children to feel included, because there is less of a reliance on social competence or ability, as may be the case in more free-play scenarios (McConkey et al., 2013). We also know that pedagogy that directly encourages cooperation between pupils can facilitate social relationships in the classroom, for example, using peer tutoring and other cooperative teaching strategies (Gibb et al., 2007), and that adaptations to classroom design are often needed to cultivate a sense of inclusion (Rheams & Bain, 2005). That said, given the importance of friendships and the potential for bullying, little research attention has been paid to whether teachers believe they have any role in helping children with disabilities to establish friendships (Koller et al., 2018).

A recent review by Maciver and colleagues (2018) also focuses on the role of schoolteachers in supporting children with disabilities and highlights further aspects of inclusive practice that schools may consider adopting. In particular, and similar to research highlighted above, Maciver et al. highlight the role of boosting teachers' confidence around increased participation in achieving inclusion, and, in turn, pupils' wellbeing. This review suggests that inclusion may be enacted through focusing on children's perceptions of themselves and their roles, and through helping them to build routines. Further studies reviewed by Maciver and colleagues underline the role of individual coaching and mentoring to support pupil wellbeing. But, as these authors argue, such interventions will only be effective to the extent that they consider pupils' interactions with others, and schools are at a disadvantage when the league tables speak to achievement rather than to participation goals. They also note a decided lack of detail in the literature regarding specific intervention strategies and critique a focus on diagnoses in the intervention literature: different programmes targeted to different diagnoses being potentially overwhelming for school staff, making choosing between them difficult. Given earlier reflections on variation in teachers' own attitudes, understanding of disability, and the importance of considering the wider impact of inclusion on children's wellbeing, this review underlines that teachers should be supported to consider the core elements highlighted in the literature and select interventions which allow them to target these issues in an achievable way. For example, thinking about the language that is used around the classroom and the school which moves away from a medicalised understanding of disability and towards inclusion. Similarly, introducing a more diverse and inclusive range of books and toys to the school environment, in order that differing abilities are normalised in a day-to-day manner, fosters an inclusive environment for all rather than as a targeted, but often temporary, project.

A considerable number of children in the UK are affected by disability with approximately 8% of the UK child population reported to have a disability (Department for Work and Pensions, Family Resources Survey, 2020). However, as discussed above, despite these figures, research investigating the wellbeing of children with disabilities is limited. Foley et al. (2012) found that, rather than physical health, children's sense of their wellbeing was reflected in being supported (by both friends and family) and supporting others, by not being excluded from activities (feeling like they belonged in the group), being respected, and valued as members of a group and developing a sense of self-respect and worth through being seen as capable and valued members of a group. Other research suggests that teachers' attitudes towards inclusion of a child with a physical or intellectual impairment strongly links with a child's experience of wellbeing in an educational setting (e.g., van der Veen et al., 2010). Alongside this, carefully structured activities in the classroom can facilitate children's peer relationships and, in turn, their wellbeing (Gibb et al., 2007). The pupil-teacher relationship is also a contributory factor to the overall wellbeing of a child (Mu et al., 2017). Studies have shown that generally the wellbeing of pupils with impairments is lower than those without. Teachers who proactively encourage these pupils and seek solutions to the challenges facing them can not only make these pupils more resilient in the face of any adversity they may face, but also strengthen their wellbeing. The practical steps that teachers can take in light of this research evidence are reviewed below.

Takeaway points

- There are multiple views on how "best" to frame dis/ability. There is a relative paucity of research on what social inclusion means to disabled children or to school staff and on how it is practised. Talk with young people and their carers (as appropriate) about what suits them in the language that you use and how to help them to feel (more) included.

■ Children with disabilities are more likely than their peers to be the targets of bias-based bullying. Be alert to this and create opportunities in your class-time for cooperative work.

■ Social inclusion and a sense of belonging underpin the wellbeing of many children with impairments of school age. In particular, children with disabilities like to see that the rivers of help, support, and encouragement run bidirectionally between themselves and their peers: think about how children with disabilities may give support as well as receive it.

■ Participation matters: how accessible is your school, its resources, for children with an impairment to be able to participate in school life?

■ Representation matters: look at your school and your classroom. Are children with impairments represented in your library? In your welcome materials? In classroom displays?

Further reading

Encarnação, P., Ray-Kaeser, S., & Bianquin, N. (2018) *Guidelines for supporting children with disabilities' play: Methodologies, tools, and contexts.* Warsaw: Sciendo.

Garces-Bacsal, R. M. (2020) Diverse books for diverse children: Building an early childhood diverse booklist for social and emotional learning. *Journal of Early Childhood Literacy.* https://doi.org/10.1177/1468798420901856

Selfe, L. (2021) Changing ideologies and the role of the educational psychologist. *The Psychologist*, 34, 44-47.

References

Aluede, O., Adeleke, F., Omoike, D. & Afen-Akpaida, J. (2008) A review of the extent, nature, characteristics and effects of bullying behaviour in schools. *Journal of Instructional Psychology*, 35(2), 151–158.

Beaulieu-Bergeron, R. & Morin, D. (2016) A qualitative investigation of fifth- and sixth-grade pupils' attitudes towards intellectual disability. *International Journal of Disability, Development and Education*, 63(5), 514–528. doi: 10.1080/1034912X.2016.1144874

Blackburn, C. M., Spencer, N. J. & Read, J. M. (2010) Prevalence of childhood disability and the characteristics and circumstances of disabled children in the UK: Secondary analysis of the Family Resources Survey. *BMC Pediatrics*, 10, 21. https://doi.org/10.1186/1471-2431-10-21

Bogart, K. R., Bonnett, A. K., Logan, S. W. & Kallem, C. (2020) Intervening on disability attitudes through disability models and contact in psychology education. *Scholarship of Teaching and Learning in Psychology*. Advance online publication. https://doi.org/10.1037/stl0000194

Cameron, C. (2007) Whose problem? Disability narratives and available identities. *Community Development Journal*, 42(4), 501–511.

Cameron, L., Rutland, A., Turner, R., Holman-Nicolas, R. & Powell, C. (2011) Changing attitudes with a little imagination: Imagined contact effects on young children's intergroup bias. *Anales de Psicologia*, 27(3), 708–717.

Carvalho, M., Perry, A., Bebko, J. & Minnes, P. (2014) Brief report: Social inclusion of Ontario children with developmental disabilities in community settings. *Journal on Developmental Disabilities*, 20(3), 88.

Conant, S. & Budoff, M. (1983) Patterns of awareness in children's understanding of disabilities. *Mental Retardation*, 21(3), 119–125.

Crystal, D. S., Watanabe, H. & Chen, R. (1999) Children's reactions to physical disability: A cross-national and developmental study. *International Journal of Behavioral Development*, 23, 91–111. https://doi.org/10.1080/016502599384017

Davis, E., Reddihough, D., Murphy, N., Epstein, A., Reid, S. M., Whitehouse, A., Williams, K., Leonard, H. & Downs, J. (2017) Exploring quality of life of children with cerebral palsy and intellectual disability: What are the important domains of life? *Child: Care, Health and Development*, 43, 854–860. https://doi.org/10.1111/cch.12501

Department for Education and Employment. (1997) Excellence for all children, meeting special educational needs. Available at https://www.achieveability.org.uk/files/1270740065/dfes-excellence-for-all-children-2001.pdf [Accessed 05–21–2021]

Department for Work and Pensions. (2020) Family Resources Survey: Financial year 2018/19 [Blog post]. Available at https://www.gov.uk/government/statistics/family-resources-survey-financial-year-201819 [Accessed 05–21–2021].

Di Marino, E., Tremblay, S., Khetani, M. & Anaby, D. (2018) The effect of child, family and environmental factors on the participation of young children with disabilities. *Disability and Health Journal*, 11(1), 36–42. https://doi.org/10.1016/j.dhjo.2017.05.005

Diamond, K. E. (1993) Preschool children's concepts of disability in their peers. *Early Education and Development*, 4, 123–129.

Ellis, K. (2015) One moment in time: The transitory and concrete value of disability toys. In K. Ellis (ed.), *Disability and Popular Culture: Focusing Passion, Creating Community and Expressing Defiance* (pp. 15–34). Burlington: Ashgate.

Favazza, P. C., Ostrosky, M. M., Meyer, L. E., Yu, S. & Mouzourou, C. (2017) Limited representation of individuals with disabilities in early childhood classes: Alarming or status quo? *International Journal of Inclusive Education*, 21(6), 650–666. https://doi.org/10.1080/13603116.2016.1243738

Foley, K. R., Blackmore, A. M., Girdler, S. et al. (2012) To feel belonged: The voices of children and youth with disabilities on the meaning of wellbeing. *Child Indicators Research*, 5, 375–391. https://doi.org/10.1007/s12187-011-9134-2

Gasser, L., Malti, T. & Buholzer, A. (2014) Swiss children's moral and psychological judgments about inclusion and exclusion of children with disabilities. *Child Development*, 85(2), 532–548.

Gibb, K., Tunbridge, D., Chua, A. & Frederickson, N. (2007) Pathways to inclusion: Moving from special school to mainstream, *Educational Psychology in Practice*, 23(2), 109–127. https://doi.org/10.1080/02667360701320770

Hayden, H. & Prince, A. (2020) Disrupting ableism: Strengths-based representations of disability in children's picture books. *Journal of Early Childhood Literacy*. https://doi.org/10.1177/1468798420981751

Hintz, C. & Tribunella, E. (2019) *Reading children's literature* (2nd ed., pp. 174–176). Broadview Press.

Hodkinson, A., Ghajarieh, A. & Salami, A. (2016) An analysis of the cultural representation of disability in school textbooks in Iran and England. *Education* 3–13, 46(1), 27–36. https://doi.org/10.1080/03004279.2016.1168861

Jones, S., Ali, L., Bhuyan, M., Dalnoki, L., Kaliff, A., Muir, W., Uusitalo, K. & Uytman, C. (2020), Parents' responses to toys representing physical impairment, *Equality, Diversity and Inclusion*, 39(8), 949–966. https://doi.org/10.1108/EDI-08-2019-0213

Kim, S. J., Wee, S. J. & Lee, Y. M. (2016) Teaching kindergartners racial diversity through multicultural literature: A case study in a kindergarten classroom in Korea. *Early Education and Development*, 27(3), 402–420.

Kayama, M., Haight, W., Ku, M. L., Cho, M. & Lee, H. Y. (2016), Perspectives of elementary school educators in Japan, South Korea, Taiwan and the US on disability, stigmatization and children's developing self, *Children and Youth Services Review*, 70, 403–418.

Koller, D., Pouesard, M. L. & Rummens, J. A. (2018) Defining social inclusion for children with disabilities: A critical literature review. *The Children Society*, 32, 13. https://doi.org/10.1111/chso.12223

Koster, M., Jan Pijl, S., Nakken, H. & Van Houten, E. (2010) Social participation of pupils with special needs in regular primary education in the Netherlands. *International Journal of Disability, Development and Education*, 57, 59–75. https://doi.org/10.1080/10349120903537905

Kutnick, P., et al. (2007) The role and practice of interpersonal relationships in European early education settings: Sites for enhancing social inclusion, personal growth and learning? *European Early Childhood Education Research Journal*, 15(3), 379–406. https://doi.org/10.1080/13502930701679429

Le Boutillier, C. & Croucher, A. (2010) Social inclusion and mental health. *British Journal of Occupational Therapy*, 73(3), 136–139. https://doi.org/10.4276/030802210X12682330090578

Maciver, D., Hunter, C., Adamson, A., Grayson, Z., Forsyth, K. & McLeod, I. (2018) Supporting successful inclusive practices for learners with disabilities in high schools: A multisite, mixed method collective case study. *Disability and Rehabilitation*, 40(14), 1708–1717. https://doi.org/10.1080/09638288.2017.1306586

Mâsse, L. C., Miller, A. R., Shen, J., Schiariti, V. & Roxborough, L. (2012) Comparing participation in activities among children with disabilities. *Research in Developmental Disabilities*, 33(6), 2245–2254. https://doi.org/10.1016/j.ridd.2012.07.002

Meloni, F., Federici, S. & Dennis, J. L. (2015) Parents' education shapes, but does not originate, the disability representations of their children. *PLoS One*, 10(6), e0128876.

McConkey, R., Dowling, S., Hassan, D. & Menke, S. (2013) Promoting social inclusion through unified sports for youth with intellectual disabilities: A five-nation study. *Journal of Intellectual Disability Research*, 57(10), 923–935.

McCoy, S., Maître, B., Watson, D. & Banks, J. (2016) The role of parental expectations in understanding social and academic well-being among children with disabilities in Ireland. *European Journal of Special Needs Education*, 31(4), 535–552. https://doi.org/10.1080/08856257.2016.1199607

McNamara, B. (2019) *Barbie is now in a wheelchair and has a prosthetic leg* [Blog post]. Available at https://www.teenvogue.com/story/barbie-wheelchair-prosthetic-leg [Accessed 05/21/2021]

Monoyiou, E. & Symeonidou, S. (2015) The wonderful world of children's books? Negotiating diversity through children's literature. *International Journal of Inclusive Education*, 20(6), 588–603. https://doi.org/10.1080/13603116.2015.1102338

Mu, G. M., Hu, Y. & Wang, Y. (2017) Building resilience of pupils with disabilities in China: The role of inclusive education teachers. *Teaching and Teacher Education*, 67, 125–134.

Nota, L. Ginevra, M. C. & Soresi, S. (2018) School inclusion of children with intellectual disability: An intervention program. *Journal of Intellectual and Developmental Disability*, 44(4), 439–446. https://doi.org/10.3109/13668250.2018.1428785

Nowicki, E. A. & Sandieson, R. (2010) A meta-analysis of school-age children's attitudes towards persons with physical or intellectual disabilities. *International Journal of Disability, Development and Education*, 49(3), 243–265.

Nowicki, E. A., Brown, J. & Stepien, M. (2014) Children's thoughts on the social exclusion of peers with intellectual or learning disabilities. *Journal of Intellectual Disability Research*, 58(4) 346–357.

Patel, D. & Brown, K. A. M. D. (2017) An overview of the conceptual framework and definitions of disability. *International Journal of Child Health and Human Development*, 10(3), 247–252.

Rheams, T. A. & Bain, S. K. (2005) Social interaction interventions in an inclusive era: Attitudes of teachers in early childhood self-contained and inclusive settings. *Psychology in the Schools*, 42, 53–63. https://doi.org/10.1002/pits.20029

Scottish Government. (2017) *Additional support for learning act* [online] Available at: <http://www.gov.scot/Topics/People/Young-People/legislation/proposed-bill> [Accessed 05/21/2021].

Selfe, L. (2021) Changing ideologies and the role of the educational psychologist. *The Psychologist*, 34, 44–47.

Shakespeare, T. (2013) *Disability rights and wrongs revisited*. New York: Routledge.

Shalev, R. A., Asmus, J. M., Carter, E. W. & Moss, C. K. (2016) Attitudes of high school pupils toward their classmates with severe disabilities. A pilot study. *Journal of Developmental and Physical Disabilities*, 28(4), 523–538.

Spencer-Cavaliere, N. & Watkinson, E. (2010) Inclusion understood from the perspectives of children with a disability. *Adapted Physical Activity Quarterly*, 27, 275–293.

Trepanier-Street, M., Hong, S., Silverman, K., Reynolds Keefer, L. & Morris, T. L. (2011) Young children with and without disabilities: Perceptions of peers with physical disabilities. *International Journal of Early Childhood Special Education*, 3(2), 117–127.

UNICEF. (2013) *The state of the World's children 2013*. Available at https://www.unicef.org/sowc2013/files/SWCR2013_ENG_Lo_res_24_Apr_2013.pdf [Accessed 05/21/2021]

Van der Veen, I., Smeets, E. & Derriks, M. (2010) Children with special educational needs in the Netherlands: Number, characteristics and school career. *Educational Research*, 52(1), 15–43. https://doi.org/10.1080/00131881003588147

Waldschmidt, A. (2018) Disability–culture–society: Strengths and weaknesses of a cultural model of dis/ability. *Alter: revue de phénoménologie*, 12(2), 65–78.

Wilkins, J., Howe, K., Seiloff, M., Rowan, S. & Lilly, E. (2016) Exploring elementary pupils' perceptions of disabilities using children's literature. *British Journal of Special Education*, 43(3), 233–249. https://doi.org/10.1111/1467–8578.12138

Bereavement: Impact on Learner Identity, Mental Health, and Wellbeing

Sukhbinder Hamilton

Synopsis

This chapter addresses the taboo subject of bereavement, and particularly the need for educators to have an understanding of the impact of grief and how they can enable children and young people to move through this process. It addresses the need for an understanding of the impact of bereavement on children and young people. It starts with an introduction to key terms that should be known and utilised by professionals. The discussion then moves onto contextualising the topic of death first through a historical overview, and then through understanding how death and bereavement are perceived within the context of a 21st-century Eurocentric lens that is applied to childhood within the context of a diverse and multicultural Britain. Following on from this, the chapter situates how bereavement impacts on a young person's mental health and wellbeing, specifically looking at the challenges and barriers that need to be considered. Next, suggestions are made with regard to how teachers can support young people in their charge through strategies that could be adopted on an individual, class, and whole setting approach. Finally, there is a snapshot of key takeaway points and some crucial reading to enhance one's understanding of this emotive topic.

Background

Death is a certainty in the lives of all humans and yet it is a topic that is rarely discussed and is especially avoided in conversations with children and young people. The Childhood Bereavement Network (2015) suggests that each classroom will have at least one child who has experienced bereavement, and figures from Child Bereavement UK note that the parent of a young person under the age of 18 dies every 22 minutes in the UK (2020), which means that about 111 children lose a parent every day. That equates to about 70% of UK schools having a pupil

DOI: 10.4324/9781003160526-15

who has been recently bereaved, on a rolling average (Childhood Bereavement Network, 2015).

One of the most stressful and emotionally difficult experiences for a young person is the death of a parent. With this death, there is a shift in the normal mechanics and functioning of their family unit. This new reality and how the surviving parent navigates it will undoubtedly impact on the young person. Parenting difficulties may arise for surviving parents if they are themselves unable to work through their own grief. Equally, it will affect the way in which the young people in that family unit work through their own understanding of death and grief. These difficulties may then ensue and lead to longstanding unresolved issues that could be with them into adulthood. Kirwin and Hamrin (2005) note that parental death can impact on a young person in a multiple of ways ranging from a change in economic circumstances to issues with health and self-concept. McCarthy and Jessop (2005) suggest that for children who are living disadvantaged lives, it is even more likely that the death of a key member of their circle will have stronger negative implications.

Although death is a taboo subject, it is not always as hidden as might be expected. Television programmes, films, computer games, and even cartoon openings display the demise of characters, but the portrayal is still removed from reality. Thus, problems arise from this because when death is experienced in a school community, the response tends to be a reactive one rather than a proactive measure that has been built into a robust curriculum. Whilst many teachers and other professionals working within the educational sector may feel that dealing with bereavement is not an issue for educational settings, it is widely accepted that the emotional, mental, and physical manifestations of grief impact on the learner's ability to fully comprehend and engage with learning. Moreover, young people spend a significant proportion of time within schools and yet teacher training generally does not encompass any support strategies for young people experiencing bereavement with approximately 90% of teachers acknowledging that they have had no training within this topic. This is worrying because 86% also report dealing with death in their school community and approximately three quarters acknowledging that they have taught a pupil who has experienced death of somebody significant (Child Bereavement UK, 2019).

Key terms

In order to be familiar and comfortable with this topic it is important to create an understanding of five key terms that are frequently, and often interchangeably used: loss, bereavement, mourning, grief, and complicated grief. Loss is often used interchangeably with bereavement and grief. *Loss* can be defined as a process of losing a person or an object. It is also often used to explain or understand the feelings of grief but in a softer way, such as when voicing condolences: 'I am sorry for your loss' as opposed to 'I understand your husband is dead'. *Bereavement* can be seen as a broad term that can be equally applied to both loss and death. Moreover, there has been discussion in academic circles for almost two decades about how to narrow this term down. For example, it could be defined as no longer having something, or someone that is of value in your life. A person might say 'I have felt bereaved ever since that coffee shop closed down', implying a sense of loss that might be felt. Equally, bereavement could also be applied to loss experienced after a change in status or through divorce. However, for the purposes of this chapter, which focuses on young people, it is important to understand and use the term to give a name to the intense sadness felt after someone dies.

Mourning is the expression of the sadness felt following a death and is often symbolised externally, perhaps through clothing worn. *Grief* is a natural personal response to bereavement. It is the way in which an individual may process both emotions and new realities that they are faced with after the death of someone they are connected to. Whilst grief is a normal response to bereavement, sometimes there can be complications whereby the person may have difficulty in working through the grief process. Complicated grief is when a person continues to struggle to work through grief by themselves and the grief is having a prolonged impact on them. This was previously known by a range of labels such as unresolved or prolonged grief, but the most accepted term now is 'complicated grief'. However, even the term 'complicated grief' is not straightforward because in order to be seen as being complicated, then 'normal' grief would need to follow a particular path or process, but sadly that is not the case as it is an individualised process. It is also important to recognise that a traumatic death of a loved one, such as through suicide or an accident can also be comorbid with factors, such as post-traumatic stress disorder, especially if the death is witnessed by the person who is bereaved.

Historical overview and 21st-century Eurocentric childhoods

Death has not always been a taboo subject. In fact in the UK, the Victorians had a keen interest in death and dying. They observed stringent rituals to do with death and mourning. An example is how clothing, specifically the wearing of dark sombre clothes, was used to externalise the grieving period that was being observed. The normal protocol for most people nowadays is to use a funeral parlour to house the deceased person and for all rituals to be undertaken there either by the family or the undertakers. However, historically, a dead body would remain in the house for people to pay their respects and until a burial could take place, and it was also during this period that it was not unusual for family portraits to be taken with the deceased in a coffin. Over time, cremation rather than burial has been the preferred choice of dealing with a body. More recently we have moved away from death being a normal part of life, and this is particularly true for children and young people. Until fairly recently, many family units were comprised of what are deemed extended family with three generations often living under the same roof. However, with the population moving around more and with the advent of the nuclear family, this scenario has changed. The repercussions of this for young people is that the death of an elderly relative within a care home is different, and somewhat removed from the death of a grandparent who may have lived under the same roof. For those interested in historical perspectives, see 'Death, Grief, and Poverty in Britain, 1870–1914' by Julie-Marie Strange (2005), 'Death in the Victorian Family' by Pat Jalland (1996), and 'Lawn Cemeteries: the Emergence of a New Landscape of Death' by Julie Rugg (2006) (details in the reference list).

Childhood is often seen through different lenses across the globe, but within the west, a child is protected in order to preserve a sense of 'innocence'. The sociologist Jane Pilcher (1995) argues that childhood is a stage that is different to adulthood and western societies have a created 'separateness' between the two. As a society, we no longer talk openly about death and dying, and this is applied to how the topic is very much seen as a taboo subject when conversing with children. This Eurocentric notion of childhood (Blundell, 2018) means that children in the UK are often deemed vulnerable and so the need to protect them from anything that might cause them distress is avoided. What this means is that conversations about death become a reactive response rather than a proactive measure. The conversations only happen when death is experienced, and even then, in a limited brief way. This taboo status means that children are unable to naturally process the information but instead have to do so whilst trying to understand what is happening to them after a bereavement. The trauma of bereavement is marked enough for an adult, but for a child, it can be majorly disruptive. Alongside the pain of losing that person, especially if it is a close family member, such as a parent, grandparent, or sibling, it has to be understood that the young person will also experience a change in their family dynamic and view the evidence of the grief of others within their remaining family unit.

Diverse and multicultural Britain

Twenty-first-century Britain has a rich tapestry of heritages and traditions from all across the globe. This can mean that British young peoples' experiences of bereavement can be vastly different for each one. For example, many Asian communities within the UK, such as Sikhs, have rituals that combine communal, as well as individual, grieving. Upon hearing news of death, members of the wider Sikh community visit the house of the deceased and pay their respects to both the dead person but also the family of that person. Whilst the body is not in the house at this point, it is a physical manifestation of bereavement because there is collective sharing of grief, stories, and weeping that takes place. Sikhs believe that this is cathartic for the immediate family who have experienced loss as they express their grief rather than bottle it up. Also, it is a way of remembering their own loved ones who may have died. On the day of cremation, it is customary for the deceased's body to be brought home so that the family can say a final goodbye. The body is then taken to a temple in order for the wider community to be able to see the face of the dead person one last time. Whilst these practices are common amongst first and second generations, it is less evident amid the younger generation. See Ahluwalia and Mohabir (2017) for more information on Sikh death customs.

If a child has been protected from death, and if this is their first experience of death, this situation can be both overwhelming and confusing. Yang (2012) suggests that cultural differences do impact on how death is experienced by communities but that the western framework invariably dominates, and differences are minimised. For those young people being brought up as second or third generation British, the Eurocentric 'protected' model is certainly becoming the norm and young people are only experiencing death as an immediate family occurrence rather than a community ritual. Moreover, this locating of childhood as a period of innocence means that young people from multiheritage communities and those from disadvantaged backgrounds are being doubly disadvantaged if schools do not engage with 'death work' proactively because data indicate that it tends to be middle class young people who are adept at accessing wider support services for bereavement.

As a teacher, it could be extremely daunting to have to be mindful of all the potential differences in how young people are exposed to death. Thus, whilst it is acknowledged that within 21st-century Britain, there are a range of cultural belief sets and rituals surrounding death, the practical suggestions in the next sections focus on broad elements which transcend cultural divides and therefore are easier for the class teacher to implement.

Wellbeing, challenges, and struggles

Historically, there has been a lack of consensus from clinicians and researchers regarding whether children have the ability to grieve and whether young people actually experience mourning. Many early theorists, including Wolfenstein in 1966, argued that it was not until adolescence that children experienced grieving but others, such as Bowlby, noted evidence of grief in children even under the age of one (Kirwin & Hamrin, 2005). Whilst there is much debate within professional circles about whether there are any long-term impacts of bereavement on children, there is agreement about the initial impact of the death of a loved one on a young person. It is also important to note that young people's response to the death of someone close will be varied and experienced differently dependent on developmental stages and age of the young person. Furthermore, young people do not grieve in the same way as adults. Numerous studies (Kennedy, Chen, Valdimarsdottir, Montgomery, Fang & Fall, 2018; Kirwin & Hamrin, 2005) note that adults who have not been given the space as children to move through the process of grief are more likely to develop depression and anxiety.

Understanding about bereavement, grief, and death has developed and moved on from Freud's 'Mourning and Melancholia' (1917), which was essentially about separating/breaking links to the deceased, and building new relationships. There is growing recognition of the fact that, if an individual, particularly a young person is given a supportive framework to navigate the grief process, they are more likely to emerge at the other end without longer-term detrimental implications. Although grief does not need pathologising, because it is a normal response to death, it is equally important to look out for signs of intense grief reactions which continue for an extremely long time as it may be an indicator of complicated grief which would require specialist input.

It is important to remember that, particularly for young people, grief is not linear. Equally of note is that not all young people will be adversely affected or indeed present any changes to display their grief. Moreover, it is complex to process and extremely tiring. Making sense of a new reality can be challenging for adults, hence for young people who are also having to deal with hormones and other adolescences issues, it can be doubly so. Society often attaches unrealistic time frames for individuals to process grief, mainly because of personal emotions tied to death and dying. Someone significant in your life dying is not just about the absence of the person, it is also about unfinished stories and hopes and futures. Bereavement and grief in young people can present in a number of ways dependent on the developmental stage and age and they range from emotional to physical and behavioural symptoms. Kirwin and Hamrin (2005) stress that life changes such as bereavement can impact on physical and emotional wellbeing. This change in persona can last for up to two years and in the case of complicated grief, significantly longer. Listed below are a range of emotional, physical, and behavioural responses that can be evidenced in children who have been bereaved.

Emotional responses

- Some regression, that is behaviours and tendencies that are not age appropriate, may be displayed. In young children, this can be evidenced by examples such as being clingy or needing more reassurance.

- Quick to anger or short fuse.

- Fatigue or apathy, whereby they seem overly tired or unable to muster any enthusiasm for anything.

- Swift transitions through many different emotional responses.

- Panic attacks.

- Stress.

- Blank mind.

Physical responses

- Struggling to sleep.

- Loss of appetite or eating excessively.

- Pain which can range from tummy aches to headaches to feeling nausea.

- Shortness of breath.

- Sweating.

- Heavy limbs.

- Going red in the face.

Behavioural responses

- Emotional outbursts

- Withdrawn.

- Poor concentration.

- Becoming an extrovert.

- Fighting and/or needing to lash out.

- Feeling overwhelmed.

- Being confrontational.

What can teachers do?

As a teacher, you are not expected to be a bereavement specialist, but you do know your pupils. Schools, and individual teachers in particular, have an opportunity to create a rich environment within which young people feel nurtured and able to grow. This is especially true for grief support because with scaffolding and time, young people can make sense of what they are experiencing. Young people should be given ownership of their grief work as well as a toolkit that includes language and the permission to use that language, to express what they want and need within this journey. With scaffolding and understanding through the grief work, teachers can help the young person develop resilience and demonstrate strong emotional wellbeing despite having to travel through difficult turbulent waters.

What to look out for

■ Anything, or any behaviour that is unusual for that young person (see the above lists).

■ A 'can't be bothered' attitude. This major event has changed this young person's reality and so they can feel a lack of control over what might happen in the future.

What to avoid

■ Do not shut down conversations. Remember, for many pupils, it takes a lot of courage to admit they are feeling vulnerable or confused or upset.

■ Do not overextend conversations that the young person may be unwilling to participate in about the bereavement.

■ Do not tell the young person to be strong or that everything will be alright.

Strategies to use

■ Let the young person know that you are present and willing to listen.

■ Let the young person know that all emotions they feel are valid. Work with them to understand that it is how we act on those emotions that can create difficulties. Put in support mechanisms to work through those emotions in as safe a way as possible.

■ Give them time and space to feel safe.

■ Keep the routines and boundaries as normal as possible.

■ Allow the young person as much control over what happens to them as is possible, for example, within routines and expectations.

■ Ask the young person what they think, want, need rather than assuming.

■ Consider using emotion logs and diaries for the young person to track/narrate what they are feeling and needing.

■ Allow the young person to work through their grief in their own way.

Whole school measures

Practice

■ Create an open culture that allows for organic conversations about death and dying.

- Enhance the curriculum to open discussions about death. For example, in history, questions such as "how did the family of a soldier who died in the first world feel when they got a letter to say he was missing/dead?" be posed.

- Use the curriculum to weave in more emotional literacy sessions which allow young people to give voice to what they are experiencing and/or feeling.

- Have a safe space that is accessible for the young person so that they can seek refuge if they need to.

- Devise support bubbles with peers/mentors who have either experienced bereavement or had some training in being a listening champion.

Policy

- Have a school policy that specifically deals with bereavement.

- Crucially ensure that the policy on bereavement is a working document and not another booklet on a shelf.

- Within the policy, ensure that there is a readily available list of current support portals for advice and guidance as well as resources and training materials.

Takeaway points

- Be proactive. Do not wait for a bereavement within your class to tackle the topic but instead build it into other areas covered.

- Do not access support from unsubstantiated sources on the internet as there is material that is considerably outdated and being presented as current thinking. Instead use websites from children's charities, such as Child Bereavement UK, Winston's Wish, or Cruse.

- Keep lines of communication open with the young person's family. This builds trust and openness and will give you an insight into where the family is in the grief process and which, in turn, will allow you to have a greater understanding of what is happening within the environment for the young person.

- Answer questions as honestly as possible and in line with the young person's understanding of death. Ask them for clarification of what they know before jumping in with what you believe. Avoid euphemisms or phrases such as 'fell asleep' or 'passed away' but instead use age-appropriate language to be as clear as you can be.

- Look out for any displays that are out of the ordinary for that young person such as panic attacks or bouts of sickness.

Further reading

Child Bereavement UK. (2018). *Summary Research Report: Improving Bereavement Support in Schools*. Retrieved https://www.childbereavementuk.org/research-reports.

Dyregrov, A. (2008). *Grief in Young Children: A Handbook for Adults* (2nd ed.). London: Jessica Kingsley.

McManus, E. & Paul, S. (2019). Addressing the Bereavement Needs of Children in School: An Evaluation of Bereavement Training for School Communities. *Improving Schools*, 22(1), 72–85.

Ribbens McCarthy, J., & Jessop, J. (2005). *The Impact of Bereavement and Loss on Young People*. Retrieved https://www.jrf.org.uk/report/impact-bereavement-and-loss-young-people

References

Ahluwalia, M.K. & Mohabir, R.K. (2017). Turning to Waheguru: Religious and Cultural Coping Mechanisms of Bereaved Sikhs. *OMEGA—Journal of Death and Dying*, 78(3), 302–313. https://doi.org/10.1177/0030222816688907

Blundell, D. (2018). Eurocentrism, Modern Childhood and Children's Globalised Lives. In: R. Race (Ed.), *Advancing Multicultural Dialogues in Education*. Pp15–31. Cham: Palgrave Macmillan.

Childhood Bereavement Network (2015) Key Statistics. http://www.childhoodbereavement-network.org.uk/research/key-statistics.aspx [accessed 27/08/21].

Child Bereavement UK. (2019). *Summary Research Report. Improving Bereavement Support in Schools*. Retrieved https://www.childbereavementuk.org/research-reports

Child Bereavement UK. (2020). *Statistics for the UK*. Retrieved from https://www.child-bereavementuk.org/death-bereavement-statistics#:~:text=A%20parent%20of%20children%20under,child%20in%20every%20average%20class.

Giorgio, G. (2009). Traumatic Truths and the Gift of Telling. *Qualitative Inquiry*, 15(1), 149–167.

Jalland, P. (1996). *Death in the Victorian Family*. Oxford: Oxford University Press.

Kennedy, B., Chen, R., Valdimarsdóttir, U, Montgomery, S., Fang, F., & Fall, K. (2018). Childhood Bereavement and Lower Stress Resilience in Late Adolescence. *Journal of Adolescent Health*, 63, 108–114.

Kirwin, K., & Hamrin, V. (2005). Decreasing the Risk of Complicated Bereavement and Future Psychiatric Disorders in Children. *Journal of Child and Adolescent Psychiatric Nursing*, 18(2), 62–78. doi: 10.1111/j.1744–6171.2005.00002.x

Pilcher, J. (1995). *Age and Generation in Modern Britain*. Oxford: Oxford University Press.

Ribbens McCarthy, J., & Jessop, J. (2005). *The Impact of Bereavement and Loss on Young People*. Retrieved https://www.jrf.org.uk/report/impact-bereavement-and-loss-young-people

Rugg, J. (2006). Lawn Cemeteries: The Emergence of a New Landscape of Death. *Urban History* 33(2), 213–233. https://www.jstor.org/stable/44614196

Strange, J.M. (2005). *Death, Grief and Poverty in Britain, 1870–1914*. Cambridge: Cambridge University Press.

Yang, S. (2012). An Autophotography of the Young Adult Children of Bereaved Families in Korea. *Journal of Loss and Trauma*, 17(1), 1–11. https://doi.org/10.1080/15325024.2011.575710

16 Conclusion: What Can We Do to Support the Mental Wellbeing of Pupils from Diverse Backgrounds?

Arif Mahmud and Liam Satchell

Synopsis

Here, we conclude the text by identifying the key concepts and practices recommended throughout the book. We summarise key themes in risks to pupils' mental wellbeing and re-occurring practical suggestions to address these concerns. By recognising common themes, we can also additionally consider how we might consider groups of pupils not yet discussed as well as better understand the need for an intersectional approach to working with young people's mental wellbeing.

Key issues in mental wellbeing for pupils from diverse backgrounds

In the introduction to this text, we broadly paraphrased the important social factors that affect young people's everyday mental wellbeing as (1) social inclusion from family, peers, and society; (2) a sense of control and agency in their own lives; and (3) space and time to explore and understand their developing identity. Throughout this book, we have seen a range of challenges to these key components of mental wellbeing.

Social inclusion

Social inclusion matters for wellbeing because it allows young people to share, reflect, and seek support from their peers. In almost all the chapters in this book, we have seen the damage bullying, prejudice, and societal disconnect can have on the mental wellbeing of a young person and we have seen these biases described

DOI: 10.4324/9781003160526-16

at the societal, institutional, and interpersonal level. Many of the young people we have discussed in this book experience overt, aggressive, discrimination, such as bullying or harassment, as part of their everyday life. These behaviours are motivated by erroneous prejudicial beliefs about someone's ethnicity or religious belief (Chapters 2–5, 12, and 13), gender and sexuality (Chapters 6–9), homelife circumstances (Chapters 10, 11, and 15), or physical or mental impairments (Chapter 14). Prejudicial biases and abusive behaviours discourage interaction with unfamiliar people. We know that engaging with a diversity of people is a productive way to break down barriers and address prejudicial biases. Unfortunately, one of the most problematic outcomes of social exclusion behaviours, such as bullying and abuse, is that they promote yet further social exclusion. These are behaviours that put more distance between one's 'in-group' and 'out-group', decreasing the chance for listening and understanding others. All levels of abuse and bias, on the societal, institutional, and interpersonal levels, serve to increase the social distance between people, and hinder opportunities for positive future interaction. Understanding the cyclical nature of how prejudicial behaviours and language creates further distance between people is important when trying to address mental wellbeing concerns and has been a re-occurring theme in this book.

For example, Chapter 4 described how Gypsy, Roma, and Traveller (GRT) communities experience discrimination due to widely held myths about their culture (for example, the assumption that all GRT communities are nomadic). This chapter described how these biased views of the community can lead to authorities and schools making decisions about retention and mental wellbeing based on false assumptions. Opportunities to follow up with missed attendance or welfare concerns might not be picked up because of these beliefs about GRT communities. In this situation, the outreach from the school to the family could break down, the social distance could grow, and the chance for social inclusion is further limited.

One way pupils might avoid the risk of social exclusion is by hiding elements of their identity and culture. Antisemitism is still widespread in school and society, and in Chapter 13, it was described how Jewish pupils try to avoid antisemitism by not wearing 'markers' of their identity, such as kippot, which would identify their religious and cultural background. Research summarised in Chapter 13 showed how schools are a place where many Jewish pupils experience antisemitism and abuse, which can lead to pupils changing school or attending Jewish secondary schools. Finding ways to encourage social inclusivity is an essential part of supporting pupils' mental wellbeing.

Other groups experience persistent abuse and racism in society. In this text, it has been highlighted how Black (Chapter 2), Bangladeshi (Chapter 3), and Muslim (Chapter 12) young people often experience prejudice at all levels and how this can have consequences, such as mental wellbeing issues and barriers to health services. These chapters also remind us that the mental wellbeing of young people can be bolstered by supportive members of one's own community. These chapters highlight the significant societal challenges with extra-cultural prejudice, but also the benefits of a strong and empowering intra-cultural community. In Chapter 2, this was referred to as community cultural wealth and the power of words and actions of a caring community for the development of resilience – a protective factor against mental wellbeing challenges. Chapter 3 adds further depth to understanding the role of community in young people's mental wellbeing. Research in the chapter suggests that large U.K. Bangladeshi communities can promote a strong sense of cultural identity, and this can lead to better mental wellbeing outcomes for pupils. Similarly, Chapter 12 highlights how important cultural identity is for Muslim young people, in particular in adolescence, as young people develop a sense of cultural membership. Having the support of a strong community identity can be protective against the impacts of prejudice, racism, and discrimination on mental wellbeing. However, there is also evidence in Chapter 3 that young Bangladeshi people who have 'integrated' social groups, containing young people from their own community and from their host community, have fewer wellbeing issues. This is in line with the importance of broader social inclusion for mental wellbeing, and how this social inclusion might come from more than one source. This is further described in Chapter 12, which also highlights the benefits of bicultural integration on mental wellbeing. Here, a young person might consider themselves to have identities associated with their heritage community and the larger society they live in. This broad base of community support can increase the variety and diversity of social-emotional support that a young person might need. These chapters offer vital insight to the role of social inclusion and exclusion. Where larger societal systems and processes drive prejudice, bias, and social exclusion, both a sense of one's own heritage and the opportunity to interact with other heritages can help promote social inclusion, helping young people have social support, from their peers, families, and wider communities.

Agency and control

Across the chapters, we also saw re-occurring themes of agency and control over one's own life being limited by social and structural pressures. In some examples, highlighted in the chapters on British Chinese (Chapter 5) and Jewish (Chapter 13) pupils, a young person's family could be a source of pressure to pursue particular types of career and high expectations for their academic outcomes. In Chapter 5, this was described as parents' beliefs that prestigious jobs lead to happy lives and that pupils can be expected to 'work tirelessly' to meet high educational standards, including attending afterschool tuition. In contrast, in the chapters on white working-class boys (Chapter 6) and pupils with physical or mental impairments (Chapter 14), there were themes of low expectations of academic performance coming from educational settings themselves. Here, pupils' behaviour in classrooms is pathologised and educational contexts might set (implicit) upper limits on their performance. In all of the above cases of high or low expectations, the young person's capabilities are being defined by external processes. Regardless of the intention of setting expectations, these pressures can take away from a young person's ability to identify and work towards their own goals and maintain a sense of control over their own life. Critically a feeling of lack of control over one's own life is associated with the development of anxiety and mental health conditions. It is important to encourage and empower young people, without defining them by the expectations of their family or school.

Sometimes significant lifestyle changes can happen to pupils over which they have no control. Pupils who are experiencing bereavement (Chapter 15), or who might be facing instability of schooling due to the complexities of being looked after (CLA, Chapter 10) or a refugee (Chapter 11) can experience a loss of agency over their life through no fault of their own. These pupils will be redefining what their life trajectory looks like in their changing home environments. As the chapter describes, bereaved young people will be navigating many expectations from adults in terms of how they should mourn and how their grief manifests. At the same time, they face the possibility of being 'protected' from the taboo elements of losing a parent to maintain their 'innocence' (Chapter 15). This may lead to adults, at home and at school, excluding a young person from important decisions about their lives. Similarly, CLA are likely to experience a number of moves in their schooling experience, both in terms of moving houses and moving schools, for guardianship reasons. This experience can be disruptive and can remove a sense of having control over one's life. This is also the experience of refugee pupils as well (see Chapter 11). These young people are likely to have experienced a range of traumatising experiences on leaving their homes and having travelled to a country they have likely not experienced before, where they may have precarious accommodation and could be required to move with little notice. This is a particularly difficult environment in which to develop a sense of what one's own life is and where you can feel in control. In all of these cases, it can be difficult for a young person to develop agency and recognition of a personal sense of control amongst these powerful external factors defining their lives.

Developing identity

Having the time and space to better understand who you are is vital for young people. The transition from childhood, through adolescence to adulthood is a process of working out who you are, what you want from the world, and who you will be. Conflicts arising between social expectations of identity, (lack of) opportunities to explore (sub)cultures, and a young person's own reflections and explorations of their identity can lead to challenges with mental health. This is particularly pronounced in the mental wellbeing issues well documented in the LGBTQ+ (Chapter 8) and Trans* (Chapter 9) pupil chapters. These pupils often face societal, peer, and familial pressures to define their identity by the expectations of others. This conflict between an emerging sense of self and the expectations of who that should be, is distressing. Related to the above themes of social exclusion and lack of agency, being prevented from resolving one's own identity with the expectations of how one should be is traumatising and can lead to mental wellbeing issues. This goes for all expectations of a young person's sexual and gender identity development, and, for example, Chapter 7 describes how girls' experiences of school are shaped by how they present themselves in classical heteronormative patriarchal structures (i.e. through school uniform policies). Black girls are also faced with contrasting external narratives of their identity, being defined by hypersexualised or asexualised perspectives on their identity development (Chapter 2). These expectations of how adults 'should' act also have a role in promoting specific types of 'masculinity' which we see boys try to emulate (Chapter 6).

Giving young people the opportunity to explore their identity is important and can help protect against mental wellbeing challenges. This is particularly important when that identity might be based on different communities (Chapters 3–5 and 11–13), subject to societal prejudice (Chapters 2, 7–9, and 14), or disrupted by external pressures (Chapters 10, 11, and 15).

Key practical advice for teachers to support the mental wellbeing of pupils

Drawing upon the commonalities and differences of the practical suggestions in all of the chapters, we propose three key cross-chapter assertions, which include understanding (a) pupils as agents of change and support, (b) the role of communities, parents, and carers around school, and (c) the importance of school culture and curriculum. These practical considerations were raised in each specific chapter, and taking them together can help us better understand pupils described in this book and beyond.

Pupils as agents in change

Identities are complex, and one person is many things. We call the recognition of the many dynamic identities a person holds 'intersectionality'. Understanding intersectionality means recognising that not all pupils in a group are the same, and often challenges that pupils experience can be overlapping – for example, a bereaved Black girl or a gay refugee boy with their own unique experiences, perhaps reflected in the ways described in the chapters, but also with the complexity of their intersecting social pressures. It is for this reason of intersectionality that it is important for teachers to recognise pupils as agents of change in getting them help and support for mental wellbeing. It can be difficult to predict the needs of a young person from the outside and, as many of the chapters have described (see Chapters 2, 3, 6–10, and 15), speaking to and empowering pupils is an effective way of understanding their needs. This could include things like giving pupils the chance to talk about their everyday, lived, discriminatory trauma, determining realistic performance goals by taking into consideration the child's social and cultural background, or making practical arrangements such as catch-up revision or adjustments for exams. Through this, children may benefit academically, but also most importantly, they will be safeguarded emotionally.

Chapter 2 phrased this as "centring the voice of the Black child" and suggested that asking questions about a pupil's personal story related to access to resources, relationships, identity, etc. are the most effective ways of understanding their needs better. Asking pupils questions and enabling and legitimising their perspectives is a good way to mitigate against one's biases and assumptions about a group's leading beliefs about the needs of a particular child. Creating a space for pupils' voices to come through is also particularly important when they might be facing identity challenges not salient to their peers or parents (see Chapter 9). Ultimately, a secure and trusting relationship between pupils and teachers enables opportunities for sharing mental wellbeing challenges. Chapter 6 brought attention to how boys perceive 'relationally effective teachers' as those who reach out, show advocacy, establish common ground, and manage opposition. These core listening and interpersonal skills equally apply across chapters.

In Chapter 10, it was highlighted how, CLA are a group of very different children and the best way to offer wellbeing support is through making yourself available for the pupil to talk to you. It was also emphasised that teachers should recognise that CLA pupils may not need to be treated differently to others in the class and understanding the needs of each pupil on a personal level may lead to *less* intervention in some cases. Either way, encouraging the pupil to share with the teacher best enables the teacher to direct the pupils to the best advice.

In Chapter 7, it was highlighted how creating opportunities for girls to have a role in school policy and politics is a good way for them to build agency, when they often feel like they do not. This includes creating spaces and opportunities as part of school life to be in a position to feed into decisions that impact pupils. This is similar to the suggestions in Chapter 8 around developing an LGBTQ+ pupils' group. These organisations should be pupil-led and staff-supported. Such groups should be inclusive and be spaces for all pupils to be welcome (i.e. in Chapter 8, it is recommended that non-LGBTQ+ pupils be allowed to join) to foster more of a sense of community. Creating groups for girls, LGTQ+ pupils, or any other group, to feel empowered, supported, and more, a force for change, will allow more strategies for resilience and mental wellbeing to develop within the pupil body. Not only is increased agency and presence important for mental wellbeing in and of itself, but this is also a pipeline to peer-to-peer support and a powerful vehicle for directing pupils to formal help, where needed.

In summary, teachers should look to find strategies which enable pupils to feel safe and ready to talk to them during school. Schools more broadly should look for ways to develop pupil groups which can become sustaining peer-to-peer support systems and also act as opportunities for pupils to have a say on school policy, practice, and environment.

The role of parents, carers, and communities around school

Addressing wellbeing concerns cannot be done in schools alone. All of the chapters have highlighted how important it is to involve parents, carers, and wider communities in discussions about mental wellbeing. Good work on empowering pupils to discuss their mental wellbeing can occur in school contexts but have limited overall impact on how they view themselves if these conversations are missing or opposed outside of the school.

In Chapter 5, a case study on British Chinese pupils highlights the benefits of communicating pupils' expectations and needs with parents, to ensure that pupils and their family recognise that their learning is on track. This helps ease tensions and risks to mental wellbeing that can emerge when expectations are high and unclear. Communicating expectations and progress to parents or carers is an effective way of managing and ensuring consistency in understanding stages of learning and pupils' reflection of their work and experiences. Communicating directly with parents can help develop a 'culture of possibility' (Chapter 2) and find ways to highlight opportunity with parents and pupils together. It can be the case that parents do not have experiences with wellbeing and support services and may be procedurally unaware of how to be more supportive (as discussed in Chapter 3) and so teachers can play an important facilitative role in identifying safe and relevant services.

This is also important when parents and carers might be adjusting to new environments too. In the case of refugee pupils, it can be the case that the whole family unit might be disconnected from their new home (see Chapter 11). Working with parents, carers, and the wider community around a new arrival can help mitigate some of the mental wellbeing issues that might occur. Schools can often be one of the few consistent points of contact for key information around the local area and being aware of general information about the local area can be a vital step in building trust and cohesion with teachers, pupils, and their families.

These links with communities apply for other groups too. Information on how teachers can support the mental wellbeing of their pupils through engagement with wider communities has been highlighted throughout the chapters. For example, in Chapter 12, the advice on supporting Muslim pupils is to consider ways to 'co-produce toolkits' for supporting pupils. This involves inviting parents, community, and religious leaders to advise schools about what can be used at the educational and community levels to support young people. Doing so allows those with more expertise and advice on specific challenges to offer insight, perhaps outside a teacher's cultural knowledge. Advice toolkits with clear practical steps can be produced for pupils from a variety of diverse backgrounds, and by involving wider community members in this development, there can be consistency of information and resources in and out of school.

School culture and curriculum

Most chapters in this book highlighted the need for teachers to continue to focus on inclusive pedagogy to support pupils' mental wellbeing. In the ever-increasing climate of awareness around the prevalence of mental wellbeing issues and a widening of diversity of learners across the UK, this requires continuous professional development and the recalibration of pedagogy. Greater attention should therefore be placed on raising the cultural, emotional, and mental wellbeing information given to teachers, in developing variation of teaching delivery, and support for pupils from diverse backgrounds. This includes reforming the nature and content of education, and finally more effective development training to ensure greater focus on mental health and equity.

In nearly all chapters, the primary advice for teachers is to work more proactively to tackle racist and prejudicial language in schools. Developing and enforcing clearly defined policies against racist and prejudicial language is an important part of avoiding biases against pupils from diverse backgrounds. This should be part of a wider school culture that works to counter deterministic language and beliefs about ability, wellbeing, and identity. This involves a school culture shift to avoid defining anyone by their initial stages and making classrooms inclusive for development of self, identity, and educational attainment.

The promotion of inclusive practices to help pupils feel involved and socially welcome should also include the celebration and recognition of diverse cultures. Chapter 3 recommends that the identification of popular celebrities or cultural figures from diverse backgrounds should be recognised and exemplified for pupils to recognise wider societal impacts of their culture. Moreover, schools can better recognise diverse cultural events, such as Eid, Hanukkah, or Pride, to show pupils wider cultural appreciation. These are practical ways in which pupils can see themselves as recognised in, and not alienated by, the school environment.

Further, the curriculum content itself can be more diverse. Chapter 14 reported on how teaching materials rarely featured pupils with impairments and when they did, the messages they communicated to pupils could be problematic. Part of a strategy for making pupils feel appreciated and having a sense of belonging involves using materials that represent the class. As well as teaching materials, Chapter 9 asks teachers to consider how visibly inclusive their classroom is for trans* pupils. Ensuring that classrooms have posters and materials to declare that the classroom is a supportive environment for pupils from a diverse range of backgrounds makes the classroom a more inclusive space and one where pupils might feel more comfortable talking to the teacher or their peers about their wellbeing. This includes raising the salience of less discussed topics, such as forced migration or bereavement. The school can have an important role in engaging students in considering these important life events through the current curriculum. For example, Chapter 15 highlights how classes may encourage pupils to consider the impact of bereavement on families, and this reflection may help pupils better understand the experience of bereavement and grief on a sympathetic level. In all these cases, the aim is to promote inclusive conversations and create more opportunities for pupils to talk and begin to understand the concerns of their peers.

All of this involves humanising the curriculum and the experience of taught topics. For example, Jewish (Chapter 13) and GRT (Chapter 4) pupils still face the denial of the Nazi holocaust and persistent antisemitism and racism in everyday life. Informing pupils about these events as well as recognising persistent preju-dices in society today from a human perspective is vital. Recognising that events in science, language, and culture are created by, and impact on, real people helps to develop frameworks for empathy and understanding.

What next?

This book contains a wealth of literature and advice for addressing the mental wellbeing needs of pupils from a range of backgrounds. But we have not had the space to cover all pupil groups, and even if we had, the experiences of pupils are intersectional and complex processes that interact between their identities and environments. We advise teachers to recognise the importance of social inclusion, a sense of control, and identity development for the mental wellbeing of pupils. They can consider how to best support this through empowering pupils to be participants in school culture and policy, the involvement of parents, carers, and communities, and through the development of a visibly diverse curriculum and classroom. Above all, creating a space for pupils to express their unique needs and concerns, and listening to these issues, is essential. Doing so will create more opportunities to support the mental wellbeing of pupils from diverse backgrounds.

Index